D0015631

^{THE}Madman Theory

THE Madman Theory

Trump Takes On the World

Jim Sciutto

HARPER

An Imprint of HarperCollins*Publishers*

THE MADMAN THEORY. Copyright © 2020 by Jim Sciutto. All rights reserved.
Printed in the United States of America. No part of this book may be used or
reproduced in any manner whatsoever without written permission except in the
case of brief quotations embodied in critical articles and reviews. For information,
address HarperCollins Publishers, 195 Broadway, New York, NY 10007.

HarperCollins books may be purchased for educational, business,
or sales promotional use. For information, please email the Special
Markets Department at SPsales@harpercollins.com.

FIRST EDITION

Designed by Nancy Singer

Library of Congress Cataloging-in-Publication Data has been applied for.

ISBN 978-0-06-300568-6

20 21 22 23 24   LSC   10 9 8 7 6 5 4 3 2 1

To Gloria, Tristan, Caden, and Sinclair

Contents

THE
Madman
Theory

The Madman Theory

There was a frightening and telling moment in the depths of the Vietnam War when the reeling President Richard Nixon delivered an astonishing order to his national security advisor, Henry Kissinger. Nixon told Kissinger to convey to his North Vietnamese counterparts that he, the president, "will stop at nothing" if the stalling negotiations between the two sides failed to make progress toward the "honorable" withdrawal Nixon was seeking. And by "stop at nothing," Nixon meant—bluntly—to attack North Vietnam with nuclear weapons.

"You can say, 'I cannot control him.' Put it that way," Nixon said.

"Yeah. And imply that you might use nuclear weapons," Kissinger replied.

"Yes, sir," the president answered, specifying even the words Kissinger should use: "He will. I just want you to know he is not going to cave."[1]

As matter-of-factly maniacal as this sounds, according to Nixon historian Tim Naftali, President Nixon believed he was acting very reasonably on the wisdom of one of his predecessors, Dwight D. Eisenhower.

"Nixon's idea wasn't actually his," Naftali explained. "It was based on an idea of how the Korean War ended, that Eisenhower hinting that he might use nuclear weapons [against North Korea] encouraged the Chinese to settle."

The trouble is, he added, that there is not much evidence that any such threat from Eisenhower actually helped end the Korean War. Regardless, in 1971, at the height of another war that had already killed tens of thousands of Americans and hundreds of thousands of Vietnamese, the sitting US president deliberately communicated to his adversary that he was just mad enough to launch nuclear weapons.

"Nixon and Kissinger decide we have to scare the hell out of the Vietnamese," said Naftali. "Nixon believes the North remembers what Eisenhower had done and so he and Kissinger think of this idiotic scare tactic."[2]

In the end, Kissinger did send President Nixon's desired warning to the North Vietnamese, but Hanoi did not back down. According to Naftali, seeing their scare tactic wasn't working, Nixon and Kissinger then backed off themselves, and the threat of looming nuclear conflict disappeared.

The theory behind it, however, did not disappear. In fact, in the months and years that followed, Nixon took ownership of what he himself described as the "Madman Theory." As Naftali has noted, Nixon's chief of staff, H. R. Haldeman, later summarized the theory in his memoir as "a threat of egregious military action by an unpredictable U.S. President."[3]

★ ★ ★

NEARLY FIFTY YEARS LATER, A NEW US PRESIDENT INTRODUCED and executed a "madman theory" of his own. Donald Trump hinted he just might be crazy enough to start a nuclear war, with his infamous "fire and fury" threat against North Korea and public battle with the North Korean leader over whose "nuclear button" is bigger. He repeatedly bragged in public of his ability to kill "millions of people" in Afghanistan. Those were serious moments, when some of his own most senior advisors worried that he might take the country to war, wittingly or unwittingly, despite the fact that he has no real appetite for military conflict; quite the opposite, those same advisors say.

However, Trump's "madman" is more prolific—the product of his uniquely capricious and unpredictable decision making across the entire spectrum of US foreign policy. This is sometimes by accident and sometimes deliberate. And unlike Nixon, he has unleashed his "madman" not only on our adversaries but also on our allies and often, according to several senior advisors interviewed for this book, on his own government.

"The general concept was discussed, not as a strategy we deliberately adopted, but rather as something we pointed out as a matter of fact," said Mick Mulroy, who served as deputy assistant secretary of defense for the Middle East under former defense secretary James Mattis.

"The thing is, it wasn't a ploy," he explained. "I think both allies and enemies realize that his decision process was unpredictable even to those advising him up to and including the secretary of defense and national security advisor."[4]

The portrayal of Trump as unpredictable—the "madman"—is something that permeated official US interactions with the leaders of countries across the globe—from Syria to North Korea to Canada and Mexico to NATO allies.

Joseph Yun, who served as President Trump's special representative for North Korea policy and was thus often the main contact between the Trump administration and both North and South Korean officials, said that in some of the most tense times on the Korean Peninsula, he would tell his counterparts—frankly—that he did not really know what the president would do next.

"We used to only think of Kim Jong Un as unpredictable. Now we had Trump as unpredictable," he told me. "And I would communicate that."

Trump's "madman" unnerved even the most senior US officials. Yun recalled that during the worsening standoff with North Korea in 2017, the Pentagon hesitated to give the president a broad range of military options, concerned that he might indeed order a major military attack on the North. "You had to be careful what options you gave him," he said. "We were being very cautious, because any options you put out there, he could use them."

That frustrated the White House. "The White House viewed it as 'Goddamnit! The president is looking for all options!'" Yun recalled.[5] But the Pentagon, under Defense Secretary James Mattis at least, didn't budge.

Trump's capriciousness left the advisors responsible for virtually every corner of the globe guessing. "I had many meetings where my counterparts would ask, 'Can we really believe what you're saying? On whose behalf are you speaking?'" said Fiona Hill, President Trump's former senior director for European and Russian affairs on the National Security Council and key witness during the impeachment investigation of the president in November 2019. "This makes the US a capricious partner for anyone who is interacting with us as a collective."[6]

Trump's unpredictability was not a national secret. US adversaries were keenly aware that his own advisors and the institutions and agencies they lead were often in the dark about the president's intentions and therefore sought to take advantage, said Susan Gordon, who served as principal deputy director of national intelligence, the United States' second-highest-ranking intelligence official. "Our partners, adversaries, and competitors know we don't know the next play."[7]

With any other president or any other administration, such deliberate unpredictability might be seen as a flaw, identifying it as a criticism. But in the view of Trump and his most devout supporters, his "madman" is a keen negotiator's strength to be lauded. "For him, the unpredictability is a card that he liked having," said Yun.[8]

Depending on whom you ask, Trump the "madman" is either a danger or a secret weapon, brilliant or incompetent, a "madman" by choice to gain advantage in negotiations, or a "madman" by accident who overestimates his own abilities and undermines the interests and safety of the nation.

President Trump, in the view of some of his closest advisors, simply knows better.

"Look, this foreign policy establishment in this town. They were so elitist," Peter Navarro, Trump's trade advisor, told me. "It's like they want to just pat the American citizen and the taxpayer on the head and say, 'Don't worry, we'll take care of it.' 'We know better,' they say. It's like, 'No, you don't. You failed on every foreign policy major initiative, in the last thirty years. On China, on NAFTA, on Iraq, on Afghanistan.'"[9]

And isn't he right? Who can make a convincing argument that the foreign policy establishment, to the extent there is a contiguous group of decision-makers, has gotten the biggest foreign policy decisions entirely or even mostly right in the last several decades—whether on China, on Russia, on the Iraq War, or on a workable Middle East peace plan?

Steve Bannon, who served as the president's chief strategist early in the administration, agreed that Trump is "totally unpredictable." However, he explained his unpredictability not as a disturbing quality but one that is reflective of a businessman who has acted on his gut and instincts with success.

He suggested a telling analogy—Trump's golf game: "His swing is not taught to you by a professional. More importantly, he never hits practice balls. He's not on the range pounding balls. He's what's called a field player. I would talk to him about getting ready for the debates. He would say, 'I'm a game-day player.' He's not a guy doing reps. He does no practice. Game is practice."[10]

In the online groups where some of his most ardent supporters commiserate and organize, "madman" has become a badge of honor. From the very first days after his election to the present, his supporters on Reddit have celebrated Trump moments with joyful references to the "madman" Trump, ranging from his election victory, to his attacks on the press, to his promises to build the wall on the US-Mexico border.

"HOLY F*CK, THE MADMAN DID IT. 304 ELECTORAL VOTES!" wrote one Reddit user the night of the election.

"MADMAN! He did it. CNN, The New York Times, Politico and Buzzfeed were not allowed to attend the Press Briefing," wrote another when Trump blocked several news outlets from a press gaggle.

"THE ABSOLUTE MADMAN!!!!!! CONSTRUCTION OF THE WALL HAS BEGUN!!!!!!" wrote another Reddit user as Trump claimed a win on his longtime campaign promise.

But the "madman" of his online base and his rallies is, one could say, trumped up. Trump is unpredictable in every way but his desire for a full-blown war, nuclear or otherwise.

"He's not a confrontational person, particularly on national security," Bannon told me. "And the last thing he wants is the troops anywhere."[11]

Of course, "madman" is not a badge of honor for most close observers of this president. I asked everyone I interviewed for this book if, based on their firsthand experience, they personally doubted his mental fitness. No one told me they believed the president was truly mad or senile, an attack the president's allies have leveled without hesitation or evidence against some of his political opponents, most prominently against former vice president Joe Biden. They described Trump's unpredictability, his favoring his gut over hard data, his deliberate and almost reflexive ignoring of advice and counsel as simply who he is and how he operates. For some, this may provide comfort. For others, it might heighten the alarm.

As with so much else about this president, he is what people want to believe about him.

$$\star \star \star$$

AN UNPREDICTABLE, UNSTUDIED PRESIDENT CREATES OTHER DANGERS, however. Under Trump, every decision big and small, every strategy, every military deployment, every commitment to every alliance and more has come to depend on the vagaries of a president who makes decisions on the fly, without a policy process, and without a strategy, or at least a strategy that he sticks to. Trump is the foreign policy and the foreign policy is Trump.

"What we have seen in the past year is the hyperpersonalization of the presidency. And that's something we haven't had before in such an acute form," said Fiona Hill, the president's most senior advisor for European and Russian affairs for more than two years. "It's similar to what happened in Russia at the peak of 'Putinism,' where everything of significance had to go through him, and—ironically—even Putin is pulling back now and delegating more authority to others in the system given the complexity of the issues Russia faces."[12]

The United States has had powerful presidents before, and presidents who hoard authority, but not one who has so diminished the vast government made up of dozens of agencies and tens of thousands of experts built over decades not only to inform the president but to keep the ship of state sailing safely.

The reality is that a president makes a tiny percentage of the decisions that drive that ship, in particular, around the world. Susan Gordon sought to make the point by asking me a question: "Of all the decisions that get made in national security, what percentage do you think the president makes?"

I took a shot in the dark: "Thirty-five percent." I wasn't even close.

"Point 001 percent," she corrected me. "He's one guy. Only a small number of decisions come to the president's attention. When you have a gap, how do those other 99.999 percent of those decisions get made? And how do you make sure that they are being linked to good effect? That's what worries me.

"The president's conversations are not the only decision conversations that need to happen," she said. "And if the gap widens so much the system isn't confident of what the president's decisions are, then [the system] becomes either invalid or ineffective."[13]

"Invalid or ineffective" or perhaps both. Trump's version of the madman has upended the very way the United States—perhaps the most powerful nation in history—makes and carries out decisions and actions of enormous consequence around the world.

"As a result of this hyperpersonalization there is no effective delegation of authority, no other deciders in the system, even at the cabinet level," said Hill. "Our biggest liability domestically and internationally is not knowing if anyone else in the government can make a lasting, independent decision about anything important."[14]

★ ★ ★

THE MADMAN THEORY IS A BOOK ABOUT WHAT HAPPENS WHEN A sitting president decides that every president before him, Republican or Democrat, has been wrong about the world and the United States' place in it. Through the accounts of some of his most senior advisors, I'll explore Trump's deeply disruptive ideas, where and how he put them into action, and how those ideas have changed the country and the world during his four years leading a superpower. What is the United States without allies? What are international relations when every relationship is transactional? What is US foreign policy when policy making is downgraded and dismissed—in effect, when the man himself is the policy?

From his very first days in office, President Trump put his madman theory into action—whether by accident or with intent—with adversaries and allies alike and sometimes with both at the same time. In 2019, as the president and his team were considering military options in response to escalating acts by Iran in the Persian Gulf, senior Pentagon officials made clear to US partners that they could not predict how and where Trump would respond, or if he would respond at all.

"We told allies that we did not know what the president would be willing to do against Iran," Mick Mulroy recalled. "It was possible he could make a decision that would lead to an escalation of the conflict, and that escalation could lead to war, so they needed to relay that to Iran so they realized not even his staff knew what would happen if they attacked another oil facility, for instance."[15]

President Trump's early threats against North Korea contained incendiary lines seemingly drawn straight from the madman playbook. In August 2017, he ad-libbed the most infamous of them, saying outside a meeting at his New Jersey golf club intended to be focused on the opioid crisis, "North Korea best not make any more threats to the United States. They will be met with fire and fury like the world has

never seen."[16] The next month, he took personal aim at the North Korean leader, Kim Jong Un. "Rocket Man is on a suicide mission for
himself," he told the UN General Assembly in a fiery speech.[17] To this
day, Trump and his allies are convinced it was those very threats and
that very unpredictability that later helped bring Pyongyang to the negotiating table. Trump's madman theory, in their view, worked.

China has been one of his most consistent targets. Two years after using his UN General Assembly speech to threaten North Korea, President Trump harangued Beijing as Chinese diplomats looked
on: "Not only has China declined to adopt promised reforms, it has
embraced an economic model dependent on massive market barriers, heavy state subsidies, currency manipulation, product dumping,
forced technology transfers and the theft of intellectual property and
also trade secrets on a grand scale."[18]

In unleashing his trade war, Trump spoke openly about not just
altering Chinese behavior but forcing China to abandon its economic
model. His threat was, in effect: give in, or we will force the entire
international supply chain out of China. And his advisors have continued to speak proudly of how they believe that is happening regardless
of what Beijing does. That such a change is an existential economic
threat to China is, in the view of Trump loyalists, all the better. All's
fair in a trade war.

Trump, however, has taken the madman theory in directions even
Nixon never ventured into. Whereas Nixon reserved his most om-
inous "madman" threat for a country the United States was then at
war with, Trump has often applied the theory to the United States'
closest allies. He has threatened to withdraw from the United States'
decades-long participation in NATO, describing the organization as
"obsolete" and refusing to confirm that he would come to the defense
of the United States' treaty allies. He threatened and delivered economic pain on the United States' neighbors, Canada and Mexico. His

target was the North American Free Trade Agreement. He tweeted early on in the negotiations, "We are in the NAFTA (worst trade deal ever made) renegotiation process with Mexico & Canada. Both being very difficult, may have to terminate?" The next year, he threatened to withdraw once again, saying, "I'll be terminating it within a relatively short period of time. We get rid of NAFTA. It's been a disaster for the United States."[19]

There are no apologies for the friendly fire. In fact, Trump and his allies—as with North Korea and "fire and fury"—say the threats worked.

In each case, Trump's "madman" has been intended for audiences abroad and at home. He wants to convince Americans as much as foreigners that he's tough. And that perceived toughness is, to him, an end itself, often in spite of damage his approach has done to alliances, or even to the stated goals of Trump's own foreign policy.

The most fundamental question is: Has Trump made the United States greater or weaker? Safer or less safe? Fact is, the answer may not be as simple as his fans or his critics believe.

★ ★ ★

THERE IS A DEEP IRONY TO TRUMP'S MADMAN PERSONA AND ITS ties—even if unintentional—to Nixon's attempt to harness the same "madman theory" to his advantage. Nixon deliberately communicated to Vietnam that he was just crazy enough to start a nuclear war. President Trump, despite his glib references to nuclear conflict in his own threats to North Korea and Kim Jong Un, has grand ambitions beyond threatening countries into submission. He actually sees himself as a leader uniquely committed to reducing the danger of a nuclear conflict.

At the root of his interest, say some advisors, is family. He has made frequent references to his late uncle John Trump, who was a physicist at MIT, and the conversations they had about the power of nuclear weapons.

"Nuclear is powerful, my uncle explained that to me many, many years ago," Trump said in a campaign speech in July 2016.[20]

Later, as president, he referenced his uncle again following his first summit with Kim Jong Un in Singapore, explaining his desire to address the nuclear threat: "I had an uncle who was a great professor for, I believe, 40 years at MIT. And I used to discuss nuclear with him all the time. . . . You're talking about a very complex subject."[21]

President Barack Obama warned Trump during the transition that North Korea's nuclear program would be his greatest and most immediate national security threat—and Trump believed it. With Pyongyang, he then launched an unprecedented series of face-to-face summits to address the threat and perhaps move closer to achieving his goal of a planet safer from nuclear war. With Iran, he withdrew from a deal that had restricted Iran's nuclear program, in part, because he wanted to negotiate an agreement to deny Iran from ever achieving a nuclear weapon.

When he went to Helsinki in July 2018 to meet with Russian president Vladimir Putin, he had bold visions of finishing what Presidents Ronald Reagan and Mikhail Gorbachev had begun three decades earlier, when the two sides discussed the lofty but ultimately failed goal of banning all ballistic missiles. Instead, Helsinki took another, deeply damaging turn for Trump and the United States. Trump's high hopes were shattered by another of his personal fixations: denying Russia's interference in the 2016 election, which he still cannot help but perceive as undermining his election victory.

The "madman" again interfered, this time to Trump's embarrassing detriment.

★ ★ ★

EVEN UNDER THE RULES OF HIS ZERO-SUM APPROACH TO GEOPOLI-tics, Trump's "madman" theory requires a trade-off. A leader—even of the most powerful country in the world—cannot be both a reliable partner and an unpredictable madman.

"The madman theory is basically shock-and-awe diplomacy," said Tim Naftali. "Bullying may work if it's a small item for another party but if it's their very existence, you are asking people to violate an essential proposition."[22]

As a result, some of Trump's most aggressive stands have so far failed. With North Korea, Trump's "maximum-pressure" campaign followed by his diplomatic charm offensive has not changed North Korea's belief that only nuclear weapons will ensure its survival. His demands that Mexico "pay for the wall" never had a shot of overcoming two successive Mexican presidents' refusals to be seen as the United States' toady. And his one-sided Middle East peace plan could not convince Palestinian leaders to give up yet more of their territory in exchange for aid, even under waning support from their Arab partners.

In many respects, neither adversaries nor allies want to deal with the "madman." Tim Naftali believes they want something very different. "They want a cage," he said.[23]

What does Trump's madman theory mean for the United States? Has it made us safer or less safe? Has the president accomplished his own goals? And at the root of it all, is there a strategy? This book will try to answer those questions, by asking some of the people Trump himself chose and appointed to put his "America First" policy into action.

1

The End of American Exceptionalism

AMERICA FIRST OR TRUMP FIRST?

Trump's madman theory is one facet of a broader Trump revolution in US foreign policy that carries with it a redefinition of the United States' role in the world. The circus of events may seem like chaos, but they fit a pattern: Over four years in office, he has deliberately dismantled the existing policy-planning and decision-making process. He has often made policy decisions on the fly and delivered them summarily and without consulting his seniormost officials and advisors. He has decided on and announced not one but two US withdrawals from Syria via tweets, each time surprising his staff and commanders on the ground. Whatever "process" followed rather than preceded the decision, with loyal aides having to then figure out how to deliver on Trump's newly stated desires.

There is a worldview that forms the basis of his policy, and it is a consistent one: Trump believes that the United States is powerful but not exceptional. He believes that the United States is a winner, that it can and should beat its competitors, including both allies and adversaries. He believes in a game with no rules that pays little or no attention to human rights, international law, or multilateral treaties. He asks, Why should we play by the rules when other nations do not?

Intertwined with this cold, practical, even Machiavellian view of the world is a question about Trump's own priorities. It's a question his own seniormost advisors have asked themselves at times throughout his administration: What is the Trump policy: America First or Trump First?

S usan Gordon, the former principal deputy director of national intelligence, suggested a simple phrase to summarize Trump's foreign policy: "'Don't be a patsy' is how I'd describe it." Wedded to that notion, she told me, is Trump's conviction that the United States has so much power that it is an "irresistible" force in the world. In his view, why not use that power?[1]

She witnessed that approach play out in virtually every international relationship and equally so with allies and adversaries. So the president would be just as comfortable imposing tariffs on China to force Beijing to make concessions on trade as he would be threatening to pull some US forces from South Korea to force Seoul to pay more to support those forces.

I asked several current and former senior administration officials and presidential advisors to define Trump's foreign policy similarly, in a word or phrase. What may surprise you is that their responses were significantly consistent, regardless of whether they are seen by the president's loyalists as critics or fans.

JOSEPH YUN: "TRANSACTIONAL"

"I think Trump supporters would like to believe Trump's foreign policy is a part of MAGA," Ambassador Joseph Yun, the former special representative for North Korea policy, told me. "For me, transactional is the word I would use to describe it."[2]

Ambassador Yun saw Trump's transactional approach play out firsthand in the context of perhaps Trump's defining foreign policy challenge: North Korea. North Korea's horrendous human rights record went by the wayside. Even the death of American student Otto Warmbier days after his release from North Korean custody did not derail Trump's personal relationship with Kim Jong Un. And America's decades-long alliance with South Korea became increasingly dependent on South Korea paying more to cover the costs of US forces deployed to defend America's treaty ally against the North. That Trump's transactional view of his country's relationship with its ally, South Korea, might weaken his position in his negotiations with its adversary, North Korea, did not alter the equation. What did Trump expect from North Korea in return? The promise of success where his predecessors had failed in achieving an elusive peace on the Korean Peninsula, and perhaps even the Nobel Peace Prize to prove it. For everyone—ally or adversary—zero-sum rules applied.

MICK MULROY: "WHAT ARE YOU DOING FOR ME?"

Mick Mulroy, the former deputy assistant secretary of defense for the Middle East, agreed with Yun, adding one important characteristic: "I would say transactional *and* not comprehensive."

By "not comprehensive," he means these engagements were not tied to the long-term strategic goals of what the United States wanted to achieve.

"There was a belief in the policy community that the president did not read the strategies developed in the interagency process and instead viewed all international relationships as solely one-on-one. It was leader to leader and either good or bad, based on their personal relationship."

Mulroy added that this approach is deeply personal, not only in the relationships Trump maintains with international leaders, but also in his motivations for the decisions he makes on international affairs.

"It is 'What are you doing for me?'" he said. "There's a lot of that. And that's blurred. So sometimes it's 'What are you doing for me as the president of the United States representing the people in the United States?' And then sometimes it's 'What are you doing for me, Trump?' So it's a personal relationship. It's transactional, just based on what the benefit is for him specifically or him as the president."[3] It is a re-markable guiding principle for a sitting US president in the realm of US international affairs. Presidents of both parties have sometimes allowed domestic politics to influence their foreign policy decisions. In 1972, President Nixon discussed delaying the US withdrawal from Vietnam until after the approaching presidential election given the political implications, according to taped conversations with his national security advisor, Henry Kissinger.[4] In 2012, President Obama was caught on camera telling then Russian president Dmitry Medvedev that he would have "more flexibility" on issues such as missile defense after the upcoming election. But it is the more complete merging of personal and national interests that sets Trump apart.

There have even been times, some of his own former advisors say, when they weren't certain Trump saw a difference between his personal and national interests.

STEVE BANNON AND PETER NAVARRO: ECONOMIC SECURITY = NATIONAL SECURITY

Trump advisor Steve Bannon argued that Trump's foreign policy is simply about the unambiguous and unapologetic exercise of US power for US interests, leveraging not only US military power but also US economic might.

"Trump looks at overall national security as having two fundamental component pieces: it is American military power and economics," said Bannon. "Really economic power and military power combined for national security."

Trump is waging what Bannon and other Trump advisors described as nothing short of "economic warfare" against a whole host of adversaries and even allies, or, more precisely, nations that previous administrations viewed as allies, including fellow NATO member Turkey.

"He did say, 'If I put sanctions on your economy, I will tear you down. You're done,'" Bannon said. "That's economic warfare. Think about it. Brutal sanctions against the Russians. Brutal sanctions against the Iranians. Could be brutal sanctions against Turkey. The tariffs are brutal sanctions against China."[5]

Peter Navarro, who serves as the president's director of trade and manufacturing policy, said economic power is rightly at the center of Trump's approach to the world. "Economic security is national security," he told me with the conviction of a true believer. "To me that's the integrative theme of the whole administration, because he's always thinking about how to create good jobs with good wages. He's always thinking about national security and border security, and the intersection lines of those two things are many."

A president's trade advisor wouldn't normally be an official you'd ask to distill his or her foreign policy or worldview. Except for this president. For Trump, trade is the best measure of the United States' position in the world: positive trade balance, good; negative trade balance, whether with an adversary or with an ally, bad. In fact, for Trump, there is no better measure of whether another country is really a friend or foe of the United States than its balance of trade with the United States.

"Previous presidents have generally siloed those compartments, and traded off economic security for national security," said Navarro. "And as the president has said, when you do that, you wind up losing both."

When I pressed him on other US national security interests, from restraining Russian aggression to limiting or ending North Korea's nuclear program to the broader goal of advancing liberal democracy, Navarro, like the president, drew no lines between any of those issues and a purely dollar-for-dollar measure of the United States' position in the world.

"Economic security to the exclusion of all else?" I asked him.

"It's 'Economic security *is* national security,'" he answered. "They're indistinguishable."[6]

"It is much simpler than people think," a former member of Trump's National Security Council told me. The point, this advisor explained, is that Trump has a worldview that he believes in and has, for the most part, stayed true to. In Trump's view, the United States has been taken advantage of by its allies and disrespected by its adversaries. There was a period, sometime after World War II—his sense of history is, by all accounts, fuzzy—when the United States was prospering and could afford to foot the bill for policing the world. That time is now gone. And Trump is righting the balance. Unlike Bannon and Navarro, this former member of the National Security Council disagrees with Trump's worldview but does not dispute the president's consistency.

Trump's crusade for fairness, as you might call it, in the United States' relations around the world is driven by his read of his domestic political base. He believes that by upending relationships with allies and adversaries and using every element of US military and economic power to get "better deals" with everyone from Iran to North Korea to Europe to Mexico and Canada, he is fighting for the people who elected him.

"This is about: Why is Trump president?" Bannon explained. "Trump is president because of the deplorables. We've been in managed decline now for thirty years by our elites. The industrial heartland of this country has been gutted while the kids, they were the cannon fodder in Iraq and Afghanistan."

The political calculation fueling Trump's foreign policy may be more transparent than that of most previous presidents, but it is one that makes sense to him and to his supporters. Among them are the working-class Americans who first bore the brunt of globalization as jobs disappeared overseas and are now shouldering the burden of US military commitments abroad.

"Can you define this postwar international order?" Bannon went on. "Here's what it is: It's a series of commercial relationships, capital markets, trade deals, and an American security guarantee underwritten by the United States taxpayer, but most importantly with the deplorables' kids serving.

"The kids on the thirty-eighth parallel, the kids on patrol in the South China Sea, the kids in the Hindu Kush, the kids on the border up in Ukraine are all the deplorables' kids."[7]

This is the driving force behind Trump's worldview, and it is deeply personal and emotional. In this view, the United States has been taken advantage of by friends and foes, and so average Americans—the "deplorables"—have also been taken advantage of. Trump has arrived to change that, to put the United States back on top where it deserves to be, and to put average working Americans back on top as well. He is the disrupter, the righter of past wrongs, the savior.

Even former advisors who clashed with the president on both the style and substance of his foreign policy point to successes. They grant that, on several issues, his instincts can be right.

"Look at the China policy, for example. That is actually a well-thought-through policy," said his former national security advisor H. R. McMaster. "Now, implementation is not always perfect. Like the steel and aluminum tariffs, I mean, that was something that was not helpful. But the overall shift to competition with China, that's going to stay. And it's bipartisan."[8]

His advisors give him credit for forcing NATO allies to increase their financial contributions to the alliance, something his predecessors had also complained about but hadn't managed to fix.

President George W. Bush pushed NATO partners at alliance summits in 2006 and 2008 to increase their contributions. In 2008, in Bucharest, Bush goaded the United States' allies one final time, saying, "At this summit, I will encourage our European partners to increase their defense investments to support both NATO and EU operations. America believes if Europeans invest in their own defense, they will also be stronger and more capable when we deploy together."[9]

Following Russia's invasion of Ukraine in 2014, which was seen by many as a direct challenge to NATO dominance in Europe, President Obama raised the level of rhetoric. "If we've got collective defense, it means that everybody's got to chip in," he said in Brussels in March 2014. "And I have had some concerns about a diminished level of defense spending among some of our partners in NATO. Not all, but many."[10]

President Trump elevated the demands and the attacks to a new level. Yet his effort has garnered rare praise for the president even in Europe, where Jens Stoltenberg, the secretary general of NATO, has repeatedly credited Trump for pressuring alliance members to pony up. "I'm saying that his message has been very clear and that his message is having an impact on defense spending," he said at the Munich Security Conference in February 2019. "And this is important because we need fairer burden sharing in the NATO alliance."[11]

SUSAN GORDON: "WE WERE SAFER"

Susan Gordon recalled other accomplishments during Trump's first year in office, noting that "Trump came in with ISIS operating in Iraq and Syria, with China taking what it wants, with multiple North Korean missile tests."

By 2018, she recounted, the United States and its coalition partners had nearly destroyed the ISIS caliphate, had put China on notice for its malign trade practices, and had forced a pause in North Korean long-range ballistic missile tests. "We were safer," she said.[12]

However, his fixation on certain problems and certain parts of the world blinded him to others. In fact, there were entire corners of the globe he ignored. His most glaring omission, identified by one former senior advisor, was a policy or approach for the entire Western Hemisphere.

Other than wanting to build a wall on the US-Mexico border, Trump failed to articulate a consistent or clear policy or core objectives for Latin America, including continuing hot spots such as Venezuela. He had a momentary interest in overturning the government of Nicolás Maduro. At the peak of his interest, in early 2019, President Trump publicly raised the specter of military intervention. "Certainly, it's something that's on the—it's an option," he told Margaret Brennan on CBS's *Face the Nation* in February 2019. He then added that he had declined a meeting with Maduro, claiming, "I've turned it down because we're very far along in the process. So, I think the process is playing out."[13]

That "process" included sanctions on Maduro's regime but also high hopes for Trump's champion on the ground, opposition leader Juan Guaidó. But the hope of Guaidó leading a revolution or takeover faded. And by the time Trump invited him as special guest to his 2020 State of the Union speech, Guaidó was less a serious political contender than a photo op for Trump.

★ ★ ★

WITH HIS NEW APPROACH TO THE WORLD, TRUMP IS REDEFINING not only how and to what end the United States conducts foreign policy, but how the nation sees its very mission in the world. Trump's most radical innovation may be the end of American exceptionalism.

This is not conjecture. The shift is in Trump's public statements. Trump's comments to Bill O'Reilly in a February 2017 interview, in which the Fox News host pressed the president on his respect for

Russian president Vladimir Putin, were an early and telling expression of Trump's view of his own country.

"But he's a killer," O'Reilly said to Trump of Putin.

Trump responded, "There are a lot of killers. You think our country's so innocent?"[14]

Less than one month into his presidency, Trump had equated the United States with authoritarian Russia. He was not misspeaking; he was speaking his mind. And his decisions—real decisions with real consequences—would reflect that. An unexceptional America is, in Trump's view, therefore just another power player on the world stage, albeit in his view the most powerful player. And his willing abandonment of a more principled US role and more idealistic US goals further reinforces his view of the world in zero-sum terms. Each international relationship—whether with adversary or ally—becomes a transactional tug-of-war.

For his most loyal supporters, however, Trump's minimalism is wisdom, not folly. "As Madison said, 'Men aren't angels,'" Peter Navarro told me. "'Countries aren't angels."[15]

By numerous accounts, President Trump as commander in chief is self-confident, impulsive, and skeptical of official advice. The "how" of his foreign policy reflects the man. But Trump has upended how the United States both develops and executes foreign policy and to what end. He has redefined what the United States is seeking in the world, rejecting a vision of the nation as anything other than a power player in a zero-sum game.

"He does not have a romantic view of geopolitics or alliances," said Susan Gordon. "And he's so completely focused on putting America first, and absolutely confident that it's an economic thing, and that he—he better than most—can see the way forward economically for the United States."

Once again, what emerges is a former businessman applying the lessons and rules of the New York real estate market to world affairs and in the process jettisoning a values basis for US foreign policy. "He's a leverage guy," said Gordon. "How much leverage can he have? How does he use the leverage he has? And then when he thinks he's gotten what he can get, he'll take that. My sense of him is as a pragmatist, and with no ideological view of good/bad, right/wrong."[16]

STEVE BANNON: "UNCLE SUGAR'S NOT GOING TO BE THERE ANYMORE"

Trump's approach has abandoned not only notions of American exceptionalism but also the allies the United States has cultivated to help deliver on those notions. His advisors unanimously describe Trump's deep personal skepticism of allies. To begin, he sees some of the United States' closest friends as freeloaders on US military might and financial support. Moreover, he consistently refuses to see the less tangible benefits of allies, from joint diplomatic efforts to cooperation in law enforcement and intelligence.

For the Trump loyalists I spoke with, his skepticism about, or even rejection of, allies is, again, wisdom rather than folly. This is a further iteration of Trump's conviction that the world—adversaries and allies alike—has been taking advantage of the United States, and, less forgivably, the United States has allowed itself to be taken advantage of.

"We have historically provided Europe with its security umbrella, yet it refuses to pay its fair share of that," Peter Navarro told me. "In part, because many of those governments are welfare-state governments, and they simply don't have the money to spend on guns, because they're spending too much on the welfare state.

"I think what the president understands better than anybody is that in today's world, unlike thirty years ago, the US can no longer afford to essentially pay for those other countries. Subsidize them, provide them with that security umbrella. So it's tough love. It's 'Look, you guys got to pull an oar on this,' and the result of that has been, in my judgment, a stronger NATO already. You've got countries competing to provide their fair share of government spending."[17]

It is true that NATO allies have contributed more financially to the alliance under pressure from Trump. However, Trump's skepticism of the United States' oldest allies doesn't end at the NATO budget's bottom line. Navarro, like the president, openly questions whether our European partners are allies at all. "The assumption that some countries are, quote, allies, unquote, I think is a misplaced assumption in a lot of ways," he said.

I asked for an example.

"So Germany," he answered.

"You don't think Germany is an ally?" I asked.

"Germany is the poster child of a country that, first of all, does not anywhere near carry its fair share of NATO. It is one of the worst bad actors in NATO," Navarro said. "But secondly, its economy is almost fifty percent dependent on exports."

There was the president's national security math again: if a country is exporting more than it is buying—especially if it is doing so to the United States—then the United States is losing and that country, whether ally or adversary in historical terms, is now something of an adversary, by definition. All other measures of friendship or shared vision are irrelevant.

"You don't think they're an ally?" I pressed Navarro. "What about their support of liberal democracy? Or standing up to Russia? They were in Afghanistan after 9/11."

"All of these countries that we were dealing with, in many ways, are economic competitors," he insisted. "And they have strategic goals which are often divergent from ours."

Germany, the United States' partner in NATO and beyond, is not the only ally turned adversary by this new viewpoint. Navarro described France as "imperialist," due largely to its pursuit of a digital tax on US tech companies.

South Korea, the United States' ally against North Korea's dictatorship and its nuclear program, is an unnecessary burden, he feels. "You go to somebody in Youngstown, Ohio, and say, 'You know what? Do you think we should have been spending all this money on the military in South Korea, and letting them take your job?' I think the answer is 'No.'"

And how about the United States' neighbor to the north? Partner in the longest peaceful border in the world, the other half of the largest trading relationship in the world, and loyal ally from the Normandy invasion to the Gulf War to Afghanistan?

"Let's take Canada. I mean, what's good about Canada?" Navarro asked. "They have some of the highest dairy barriers to entry of any country in the world. What's good about that? What's good about Canada being a transshipment point now for some of the Chinese stuff that we've got countervailing duties on? I mean, it's like this blue-eyed brother kind of thing. It's just Canada. It has its own national interests and self-interests."

And by the way, Ottawa is not on board with Trump's domestic economic policy. "Their ideology is really out of step with Trump world," Navarro told me. "They're much more kind of Bernie Sanders and Elizabeth Warren."

I reminded him how bravely Canadian forces have fought and continue to fight in Afghanistan. Canada provided forces without the restrictions on frontline operations other allies demanded—and they paid with their lives. On several embeds in Afghanistan, I could always spot the Canadian forces because they would build a wooden roller hockey rink to satisfy their ice hockey obsession. They paid their dues in blood.

"Were they doing us a favor, or were they bought into the idea that they needed to do that as part of the global effort against terrorists?" he answered. "I mean, if they were just doing us a favor, maybe their government should have been thrown out of office. I mean, every time that a Canadian shows up in a uniform, it's doing us a favor? How's that work?

"When we were rich, fat, dumb, and happy after World War II, we led on security umbrellas, paid the freight. Then the music stopped, right? And it's the game of musical chairs. We got left out, and we've been picked apart ever since."[18]

Similarly, Steve Bannon argued that the United States' partners in Europe and Asia are less allies than protectorates, with the United States providing them a free or largely free security umbrella, paid for by US taxpayers and manned by US soldiers, who, as he argued earlier, are often the children of the so-called deplorables who voted for Trump.

"We allowed the Europeans just to pay for their domestic programs. We've really had to pay for their common defense," he said. "And this is why we're in the situation we're in. It's not isolationist."

In Bannon's view, Trump is not looking to end allies, just to make the relationships with them fairer. "If you're going to be an ally, you have to be an ally. We're not looking for protectorates, we're looking for allies. So NATO's got to step up. The Gulf emirates have got to step up. Israel, UAE, Egypt, Saudi Arabia, and the nations around the South China Sea, particularly places like Australia, Vietnam, Philippines, and then most particularly South Korea and Japan, they have to step up.

"Trump looks at it as a landlord, like you're in arrears on your rent. Uncle Sugar's not going to be there anymore."[19]

But is it just about fairness? Just about righting the balance of burden sharing? Trump's view of allies seems to question not only their contributions but their very motivations. In other words, Trump and his loyalists seem to be asking if they are really allies at all.

THE "SPREADSHEETING OF ALLIANCES"

Some of Trump's former senior advisors see enormous dangers in the president's skepticism about US allies and alliances.

"This is the spreadsheeting of alliances," is how one of his former advisors described it to me. This advisor cited a surprising historical parallel: the Roman Empire. At its peak, this advisor explained, Rome treated allies as sources of tribute. In this sense, President Trump is actually willing for the United States to act as world policeman in certain circumstances, but only if allies pay the rent, in effect. In its most extreme terms, this is a vision of the United States as a private security firm. And we have seen evidence of Trump delivering on this vision when he bragged about Saudi Arabia paying for increased US troop deployments to the Gulf region—and in his efforts to squeeze US allies Japan and South Korea for enormous increases in their contributions to the costs of US troop deployments in Asia.

This former senior advisor explained a remarkable consequence of Trump's view of allies: With his focus on financial contribution over every other element of these relationships, from shared histories to shared democratic values, Trump sees allies in Europe and Asia as being in some ways *worse* than adversaries such as China, because the United States has bankrolled them. Therefore, they owe us in a way China and Russia do not.

Is Trump's departure from American exceptionalism as unique and unprecedented as it appears? In his paring down of US ambitions and military commitments abroad, Trump has surprising commonalities with Barack Obama. There are parallels between Trump's "America First" and Obama's "Don't do stupid sh*t."

Mr. Obama debuted the phrase, sometimes sterilized to the less salty "Don't do stupid stuff," in an off-the-record conversation with reporters in 2014. And although at first it sounded as though he had misspoken or underplayed his foreign policy vision, the phrase would quickly evolve into an officially sanctioned, even proud, mantra of Obama's guiding view for the United States' role in the world.

Over a few weeks in the middle of 2014, as Mike Allen of Politico chronicled at the time, the phrase had been repeated in articles in the *Los Angeles Times*, the *Chicago Tribune*, and the *New York Times*.[20] It also found its way into a Tom Friedman column on the *New York Times*' editorial page.[21] That was no accident. The White House had struck on both a bumper sticker and a guiding philosophy—one that would compare favorably, they believed, with the "dead or alive" style of his predecessor.

At the time, many commentators, including those who had lauded Obama's candidacy and early years in office, lamented the shrinking of not only the United States' place in the world but the ambitions of a politician who had ridden into office on far higher and more profound hopes.

"How far we have come from the audacity of hope," *Foreign Policy* editor David Rothkopf wrote; "yes, we can; the soaring expectations framed by the brilliant oratory of the president's Cairo speech on relations with the Muslim world; his Prague speech on eliminating nuclear weapons worldwide; and his Oslo speech when accepting the Nobel Peace Prize."

Rothkopf went on to describe "how disappointing it is for this president—who once was seen as a potentially transformational figure— to have embraced defensive minimalism."[22]

President Trump's shrinking of the United States' international

ambitions shares some of Obama's minimalism and bias toward disen-
gagement. However, Trump has accelerated the retreat and extended
it to encompass not only conflicts and commitments abroad but the
United States' very mission in the world.

THE MADMAN'S FIRST MOVE:
THE TAIWAN PHONE CALL

Observers who have been surprised by Donald Trump's unorthodox
and precedent-breaking foreign policy decisions over his four years in
office shouldn't be. He had telegraphed his worldview throughout the
presidential campaign and long before. And although it is true that
many previous presidential candidates staked out positions outside
the mainstream during the campaign, only to reverse or moderate
those positions once elected, President Trump made clear immediately after his election that there would be little to no daylight between
before and after. The brash, unpredictable, and unstudied candidate
would serve as a brash, unpredictable, and unstudied president.

Trump—the "madman"—made his debut with a phone call. On Fri-
day, December 2, 2016, less than a month after his election, President-
elect Trump took a phone call from Taiwan's president, Tsai Ing-wen.
The Trump transition team, still forming after the initial team had
been disbanded, quickly dismissed the conversation as one of many
congratulatory phone calls Mr. Trump received from around the world.

"During the discussion, they noted the close economic, political,
and security ties (existing) between Taiwan and the United States.
President-elect Trump also congratulated President Tsai on becoming
President of Taiwan earlier this year," read the transition document.[23]

President Trump himself assigned sole responsibility for the call
to his Taiwanese counterpart, tweeting, "The President of Taiwan

CALLED ME today to wish me congratulations on winning the Presidency. Thank you!"

In fact, the call was not at all routine. It was the first direct communication between the United States and Taiwanese leaders since the United States had normalized relations with the mainland People's Republic of China in 1979. Asia diplomatic veterans in both parties described the call as reckless and potentially explosive for US-China relations. In diplomatic terms, such official communications amount to official acts of recognition of leaders and their countries as sovereign states, a privilege the United States had denied Taiwan nearly four decades earlier. The United States now recognized the PRC and Beijing as the "one China."

Beijing's response was swift. Chinese foreign minister Wang Yi called the phone call "a shenanigan by the Taiwan side" and reasserted the immutability of the "one China" policy. "This will never change the one-China consensus reached in the international community. I also believe that this will never change the one-China policy recognised by the US over the past years," he told Hong Kong's Phoenix Television.[24]

I had met Wang in official meetings while serving as a diplomat in Beijing. He was a dour and serious Chinese official who—in person—delivered messages to his US counterparts in calm but unyielding tones. From his demeanor on camera, it was clear to me that he was not pleased.

China experts and diplomats in the United States were equally alarmed. Some wondered whether the call would upend the entire US-China relationship. They asked, did Trump intend to end the "one China" policy? Or did he simply not know there was a "one China" policy? That was not a gratuitous question. Some Trump defenders were already hinting that the president-elect, proudly a Washington outsider, simply wasn't aware of the policy or what it meant for official presidential communications. For any other president, the ignorance defense would be embarrassing. For Trump, it would become standard for unscripted comments or policy moves.

Soon, however, the incoming administration was owning the call. Trump administration officials claimed it had been long planned, a decision made weeks or even months before the election to signal a change in approach to Beijing.[25] One of his seniormost advisors and most aggressive public defenders, Kellyanne Conway, now said that Trump was very aware of what he had done.

"He either will disclose or not disclose the full contents of that conversation. But he's well aware of what U.S. policy has been," Conway told my colleague Anderson Cooper on *Anderson Cooper 360°*.[26]

As the questions grew, Trump himself only grew more defiant, tweeting in response to Beijing's protests: "Did China ask us if it was OK to devalue their currency (making it hard for our companies to compete), heavily tax our products going into their country (the U.S. doesn't tax them) or to build a massive military complex in the middle of the South China Sea? I don't think so!"

"Shock-and-awe" diplomacy had begun. The call would prove to be a harbinger of a consistently aggressive approach to China—the "one China" policy and free trade be damned. This was a new president with a new way of doing things, no matter how powerful the adversary or how deeply entrenched the previous policy. The call was no accident. It was the plan.

PLACATING RUSSIA

While President-elect Trump was laying the groundwork for what would become a defining principle of his foreign policy—standing up to China—he and his most senior advisors were making preparations for another defining position: what one of his most senior advisors would describe to me as an "inexplicable" deference to Russia.

Russia had just made its power and malign intentions well known with its systematic interference in the 2016 presidential election, which the US intelligence community would assess was personally ordered and directed by President Putin himself.

The intelligence community's report on Russian election interference had an unassuming title: "Assessing Russian Activities and Intentions in Recent US Elections." But its analysis and conclusions were scathing for Moscow and troubling for the newly elected US president. The report read:

> Russian efforts to influence the 2016 US presidential election represent the most recent expression of Moscow's longstanding desire to undermine the US-led liberal democratic order, but these activities demonstrated a significant escalation in directness, level of activity, and scope of effort compared to previous operations.
>
> We assess Russian President Vladimir Putin ordered an influence campaign in 2016 aimed at the US presidential election. Russia's goals were to undermine public faith in the US democratic process, denigrate Secretary Clinton, and harm her electability and potential presidency. We further assess Putin and the Russian Government developed a clear preference for President-elect Trump.[27]

That final sentence would become a festering wound for Donald Trump, twisting him into knots of insecurity and anger for the duration of his presidency. It may also have helped spark another unusual move by the incoming commander in chief.

As one of his final acts in office, President Obama had ordered a series of retaliatory measures against Russia for its election interference. Punishing the Kremlin for what the White House called "significant malicious cyber-enabled activities," President Obama issued executive orders sanctioning four Russian officials and five Russian entities. He also expelled thirty-five Russian diplomats, whom the United States believed were in reality intelligence officers operating under diplomatic cover, and closed two "diplomatic compounds," which the United States believed Russia used for spying and intelligence collection.[28]

"Russia's cyber activities were intended to influence the election, erode faith in U.S. democratic institutions, sow doubt about the integrity of our electoral process, and undermine confidence in the institutions of the U.S. government. These actions are unacceptable and will not be tolerated," read a White House statement.[29]

President Trump and his advisors had another approach in mind. In secret communications, Trump's then national security advisor Michael Flynn urged his Russian counterparts not to retaliate. The message seemed to be that the president-elect would be taking a softer approach to Russia and Russia should do the same.

Flynn later lied to the FBI about his communications with then Russian ambassador Sergey Kislyak. His lie, the second of two he told the FBI according to an FBI memo detailed in the Mueller Report, came in response to FBI agents asking him about the United States' expulsion of Russian diplomats and closure of Russian properties ordered by President Obama.

According to CNN reporting at the time, the agents asked him if he had encouraged Kislyak not to retaliate. "Flynn responded, 'Not really. I don't remember.' It wasn't, 'Don't do anything,'" the FBI memo said. But the FBI knew that Flynn had in fact asked Russia on that call not to escalate its response to the United States.[30]

It wasn't only the FBI that knew Flynn was lying. Former acting attorney general Sally Yates would later testify before a Senate Judiciary Subcommittee that she had alerted White House Counsel Don

McGahn on January 26—six days after Trump's inauguration—that Flynn had lied to Vice President Mike Pence about his conversations with Russians. That, she said, had created an enormous security risk for Flynn and the country, because the Russians would also know Flynn was lying, therefore opening the president's national security advisor to blackmail by a foreign power.

"We believed that Gen. Flynn was compromised with respect to the Russians," Yates told the subcommittee. ". . . We weren't the only ones that knew all of this, that the Russians also knew about what General Flynn had done and the Russians also knew that General Flynn had misled the vice president and others."[31]

President Trump, in predictable fashion, took no responsibility for Flynn's missteps, instead directing blame toward his predecessor, Barack Obama.

"General Flynn was given the highest security clearance by the Obama Administration—but the Fake News seldom likes talking about that," Trump tweeted on May 8, 2017. "Ask Sally Yates, under oath, if she knows how classified information got into the newspapers soon after she explained it to W.H. Counsel." Trump's tweets ignored the fact that in 2014, President Obama had fired Flynn as director of the Defense Intelligence Agency, and in November 2016, in an Oval Office meeting days after Trump's election victory, he had warned Trump specifically against hiring Flynn.[32]

On February 13, Flynn was gone, making the decorated army lieutenant general the shortest-serving national security advisor ever. However, President Trump's effort to delay or weaken sanctions on Russia would persist throughout his term, even in the face of rare bipartisan congressional action to force Trump's hand. With some exceptions, often driven by political realities even Trump was forced to acknowledge, his deference toward Russia would be as consistent and unwavering as his toughness toward China. And the outreach began even before his inauguration in those quiet communications between Kislyak and Flynn.

THE MUSLIM BAN

Just one week after his inauguration, President Trump turned another, seemingly unserious campaign threat into a new foreign policy reality with Executive Order 13769, titled "Executive Order Protecting the Nation from Foreign Terrorist Entry into the United States."

Trump had planted the seeds for the measure more than a year earlier, during a campaign stop in South Carolina in the wake of an ISIS-inspired terror attack in San Bernardino, California. In a deadly shooting and attempted bombing, a husband and wife had killed fourteen people inside a local government building during a Christmas party. The fear of ISIS and Islamist terror was peaking in the United States.

On December 7, 2015, first in an official campaign statement and then at a campaign rally, Trump proposed a radical step to respond to the terrorism threat: "Donald J. Trump is calling for a total and complete shutdown of Muslims entering the United States until our country's representatives can figure out what the hell is going on."

Such bigoted words by a major candidate had not been heard in a US presidential campaign since George Wallace. Yet his declaration sparked cheers and a standing ovation from the crowd.

"Where this hatred comes from and why we will have to determine," Trump said. "—we're going to have to figure it out; we're going to have to figure it out. We can't live like this. It's going to get worse and worse. You're going to have more World Trade Centers. It's going to get worse and worse, folks."[33]

Amy Davidson Sorkin noted in *The New Yorker* that many Republicans, including fellow contenders for the GOP nomination, were hesitant—though it was still eleven months to election day—to directly contradict Trump: "The Republican Party, apparently fearful of losing his voters, has not truly confronted Trump on any point but his buffoonery, which is not the main problem; the bigotry at the heart of the clown act is. Perhaps this will be the party's chance."[34] It wasn't quite.

After his election, President Trump made his Muslim ban the law. He claimed the initial ban was temporary, although a concurrent ban on refugees from Syria was permanent. Still, several court challenges followed, blocking the ban from taking immediate effect. Throughout, the president and his administration insisted the restrictions were driven purely by security needs, specifically, the administration's concern that the affected countries were not sufficiently screening travelers for terror ties or sympathies. The White House was forced to revise the measure twice, adding the non-Muslim-majority countries North Korea and Venezuela to the list of those affected.

Ultimately, in June 2018, the Supreme Court upheld the Trump administration's third revised ban in a divisive 5–4 decision. Chief Justice John Roberts, writing for the majority, wrote, "The proclamation is expressly premised on legitimate purposes: preventing entry of nationals who cannot be adequately vetted and inducing other nations to improve their practices. The text says nothing about religion."

Writing for the minority, Associate Justice Sonia Sotomayor sharply dissented, citing Trump's December 2015 comments as indicative of the true motivation of the ban: "Taking all the relevant evidence together, a reasonable observer would conclude that the Proclamation was driven primarily by anti-Muslim animus, rather than by the Government's asserted national-security justifications."[35]

In January 2017, Trump's longtime advisor and personal attorney, Rudy Giuliani, gave an answer in a Fox News interview that seemed to confirm Sotomayor's suspicions—that the subsequent revisions to the ban had been made primarily to overcome legal challenges.

"I'll tell you the whole history of it: When he first announced it, he said 'Muslim ban,'" Giuliani said. "He called me up, he said, 'Put a commission together, show me the right way to do it legally.'

"And what we did was we focused on, instead of religion, danger," he continued. "The areas of the world that create danger for us, which is a factual basis, not a religious basis. Perfectly legal, perfectly sensible."[36]

Over time, Trump and his allies came to own the ban. Once again, he had moved the outrageous to the mainstream—transformed a "madman" threat into official US policy. And more than three years later, Trump expanded the reach of his ban even further, extending the ban to six more countries: Nigeria, Eritrea, Sudan, Tanzania, Myanmar, and Kyrgyzstan.

"The ban should be ended, not expanded," the director of the ACLU's Immigrants' Rights Project, Omar Jadwat, told CNN. "President Trump is doubling down on his signature anti-Muslim policy—and using the ban as a way to put even more of his prejudices into practice by excluding more communities of color."[37]

ARGENTINA AND BRAZIL

As president, Trump sometimes defied his senior national security staff, seemingly for the sport of it. In April 2017, he was preparing to welcome one of his first visiting foreign leaders, Argentinian president Mauricio Macri. In his briefings in advance, his advisors warned him that Macri would push for Argentina's entry into the Organisation for Economic Co-operation and Development (OECD), a club of the world's most developed economies. To date, only two Latin American nations, Mexico and Chile, had gained membership. Joining was a prize for a long list of Latin American leaders. Argentina had been lobbying for membership for years, but its domestic economic instability made its entry a nonstarter for the time being. Trump's briefers reiterated this position and prepared the president to deflect Macri's request.

When Macri entered the Oval Office, however, Trump stunned his team when he began the meeting by immediately bringing up Argentina's desire to join the OECD. Trump told Macri that his staff was telling him he should deny Argentina membership, but he said, in effect, that he disagreed and would do everything he could to guarantee that Argentina got in. True to his word, after the meeting, Argentina was moved up to the top of the list, just as Trump demanded.

Nearly three years later, however, Trump abandoned Argentina at the altar. In January 2020, Trump removed Argentina from the top of the list of countries to be added to the OECD, replacing it with Brazil. The move was a favor to Brazilian president Jair Bolsonaro, with whom Trump shared an affinity for nationalist politics. Argentina, having recently elected a leftist president, was summarily moved down once again.[38]

THE JERUSALEM EMBASSY

In the final days of his first year in office, President Trump turned another controversial campaign promise into official US policy. Prior presidential candidates had promised to move the US Embassy in Israel from Tel Aviv to Jerusalem, before backing off in office fearful of damage to the peace process. A 1995 law passed by Congress called for the move but allowed presidents to issue a waiver every six months on grounds of national security. Presidents Bill Clinton, George W. Bush, and Barack Obama had repeatedly issued such waivers. Jerusalem was a shared capital city, and any remaining hope for a two-state solution was seen as dependent on leaving Jerusalem's final status to a final peace accord. Moving the US Embassy to Jerusalem unilaterally would indicate that the United States recognized Jerusalem as Israeli, rather than Israeli *and* Palestinian.

But as with the decades-long US policy toward Taiwan and China, President Trump discarded what had been a bipartisan policy toward Israel and Palestine.

"Today, we finally acknowledge the obvious: that Jerusalem is Israel's capital. This is nothing more, or less, than a recognition of reality. It is also the right thing to do," he announced from the White House Diplomatic Reception Room on December 6, 2017.

Moving quickly, he also announced plans to move the US Embassy there to make that recognition official. "After more than two decades of waivers, we are no closer to a lasting peace agreement between Israel and the Palestinians. It would be folly to assume that repeating the exact same formula would now produce a different or better result," he added.[39]

The reaction in the region was angry. Palestinian groups organized "days of rage" to protest the Trump administration's decision. US allies Jordan, Egypt, Saudi Arabia, and Qatar all urged the United States to reconsider. European allies warned of irreparable damage to the peace process.

French president Emmanuel Macron, who had cultivated perhaps the warmest relationship with Trump among the United States' skeptical European allies, cautioned the US president that the final status of Jerusalem must be negotiated between the two parties. The French Foreign Ministry reiterated France's support for "the establishment of two states, Israel and Palestine, living side by side in peace and security with Jerusalem as their capital."[40]

Trump moved the embassy. Nothing moved Mr. Trump. In May 2018, the United States made it official, opening the new US Embassy in Jerusalem at an event attended by, among others, the president's daughter Ivanka Trump and son-in-law, Jared Kushner. And in January 2020, Trump unveiled his long-delayed Middle East peace plan, which called for an Israeli capital encompassing virtually all of Jerusalem, including the Old City, and leaving small sections of the outskirts to make up a future Palestinian capital. The diplomatic die was cast.

★ ★ ★

TRUMP'S EARLY "MADMAN" MOVES SIGNALED THAT DISRUPTION was the order of the day under Trump. He disrupted the US-China relationship more than any president since Nixon, though pulling the two countries further apart rather than closer together, perhaps irreparably. He undermined a decades-old bipartisan consensus against Russian aggression, leading US allies in Europe to prepare for a future without the United States on their side. He engineered a restrictive and quota-driven US immigration policy, with limits on poverty-stricken and nonwhite nations not seen for decades. And he abandoned core principles of what had been a bipartisan approach to peace between Israel and the Palestinians. In short, the "madman" had become the status quo.

Those early moves did not, however, lead to immediate crises. "The 'free world' didn't end," Susan Gordon told me, discussing Trump's early foreign policy surprises.[41]

The reaction to Trump's decision to move the US Embassy in Israel was particularly instructive to him, some of his former advisors say. All the intelligence assessments had forecast mayhem after the move: sustained violent protests, terror attacks, the Arab world united against the United States. But the most dire predictions failed to materialize. The lesson Trump took from it was that he had been right all along, and his advisors and the intelligence wrong. The muted repercussions reinforced his own already formidable self-confidence.

So in his second year in office, as one former senior administration official told me, Trump began "thinking bigger." In his view, the world now wanted to get on his side and was seeing the United States as having new "red lines." This former official described Trump as entering a "Why can't I just" mood.

It is a mood that proved lasting, perhaps best exemplified, according to this official, by the July 2019 call with the Ukrainian president, which sparked the impeachment inquiry that threatened his presidency.

THE ANSWER

So: America First or Trump First? The best answer is likely a combination of both. Trump has made consequential foreign policy decisions based significantly on cold political calculus (the Jerusalem embassy move), personal pique (softening sanctions on Russia for 2016 election interference), and even at times just to needle his staff (Argentina and the OECD). But he has a consistent worldview in which he sees himself as righting an imbalance in the United States' relationships with its allies and adversaries.

Some of his most senior advisors, however, believe his effort to right that balance has in fact put US national security interests last, not first.

2

Commander
in Chief

DO TRUMP'S OWN ADVISORS TRUST HIM?

If his foreign policy is abandoning long-held American principles, what does that say about President Trump himself? What are his motivations in leading the nation abroad? This is a question of open public debate, often based more on speculation than on evidence. So how do the people who served him in senior roles describe Trump as commander in chief?

Do they trust him to do the job of president?

President Trump's decision making is better understood, say some of his former advisors, when you understand how he receives information—and how he does not. Early on in his administration, his national security staff realized that he was not reading his briefing notes. When they came into the Oval Office to discuss national security issues, some of which were of urgent concern, Trump would ask questions demonstrating that he was hearing the information for the first time. That would be a disturbing and demoralizing discovery for any national security team. They worried that if the president wasn't reading the briefing notes, he wasn't making informed decisions.

In response, his team, under the direction of then national security advisor H. R. McMaster, developed a new system to brief him. Instead of multipage documents, they would boil down the day's topics into three simple bullet points on a single note card. They knew the president needed the information to make informed decisions impacting US national security. They had to find a way through to him.

"We struggled to adjust to President Trump," said a former senior national security staffer. "We knew that it was our job to adapt to the president, not the president's job to adapt to us. But no matter how much we tried, we couldn't get him to read our briefing materials. Finally, after many failed attempts, we realized that note cards with three bullet points on them seemed to work. While troubling to those of us used to briefing prior presidents with three-page papers, it was a relief to figure out something that would get through to him."

For a time, his briefers found that the new three-bullet system worked—or appeared to—until they came to believe that Trump was reading only the first two of the three bullet points. Again, his questions indicated that he hadn't gotten to the end of the simple note card.

His national security team then devised yet another new strategy: they would concentrate the most salient information into the first two of the three bullet points, using the third bullet-point entry for something less important or not important.

"Eventually the president stopped reading the third bullet, so we had to really prioritize the top two critical points we needed to get across; that was all that we had," the former national security staffer said.

Over time, however, his staff came to believe that the president often wasn't reading the note cards at all. He didn't spend the time, or didn't have the interest, to do so.

In the simplest terms, they didn't trust him to read. But how he makes decisions is one thing; *why* he makes them is another.

One of the most difficult things for his advisors to explain, or attempt to explain, is why the president has such an affinity for Russia and its leader, Vladimir Putin. They have briefed him countless times on facts and intelligence that show growing Russian aggression against US interests from Ukraine to Syria to cyberspace to outer space. But Trump has remained unmoved.

Some of his former advisors have raised the possibility that Russia somehow holds sway over him. Those advisors don't claim to have evidence of Russian leverage, only the absence of any other explanation.

"How else do you explain how each of his positions—on Syria, on Afghanistan, on NATO—aligns perfectly with Russia's?" one former senior official asked me.

In the final analysis, Trump's deferential approach to Russia could just as easily be the result of selfish political calculation, a failure to recognize Russia's threat to US interests around the world, or some combination of the two. But the result was the same: when it came to Russia, he simply didn't listen.

For some in the US intelligence community, the concern regarding the president and Russia was not that he was colluding with the Kremlin but that he was being "recruited"—that is, that he was the target of an influence operation by one of his country's most dangerous adversaries.

The language intelligence officials use here is "unwitting," that is, that Russia was trying to influence him, in ways he didn't even realize. The attempt to influence targets unwittingly is, in fact, an essential part of Russian tradecraft. Intelligence officials with experience monitoring Russian intelligence note that Russian operatives often cloak their efforts in discussions of business or other subjects of apparently mutual interest in order to build a relationship over time.

To be clear, many of these officials emphasize that they never believed the president was willingly being influenced by Russia or, indeed, that he believed anyone was attempting to influence him. However, they did have concerns that Russia tried at times to influence Trump and he didn't see it.

In a broad sense, intelligence officials will emphasize that part of their job is to highlight threats that are hidden or somewhat hidden.

"We offer a view of things that were not intended to be seen or known," explained Susan Gordon. "It should provide wisdom and insight to couple with the events that you are seeing or what people are saying . . . to show you there are other interests at play. The risk is, if you don't believe intelligence, and if you don't take the time to understand its basis, you're missing half of the equation and are ignoring one of the great tools of decision advantage."[1]

Trump's willingness to ignore, contradict, and defy his seniormost advisors is a quality I heard from virtually everyone I have spoken with about him. He sees himself, several of his most senior advisors say, as simply knowing better than them. Some advisors who have dealt with him frequently face-to-face explain this in part by noting that he has an almost reflexive tendency to contradict, whether that be advice, which is subjective, or information, which is objective—or at least is objective outside Trump world.

According to the more generous interpretations I've heard from his team, this is Trump challenging his advisors to defend both their guidance and the sources of the information they are presenting. Such skepticism can serve a purpose. What troubles current and former administration officials is when Trump's skepticism persists even in the face of hard data and information. There are times, they say, when the president simply does not believe the information put before him. And so he not only believes his own advice over those of his advisors, he believes his own "facts."

Trump's dismissal of hard data manifested itself particularly clearly in the early weeks of the coronavirus pandemic. Even as health experts were warning him of the danger and the likely extent of the spread in the United States, the president expressed his conviction that those experts were overstating the risks. Trump repeatedly declared that covid-19 was no worse than the seasonal flu, even though the data showed that it carried a much higher death rate, and he claimed that the number of cases in the United States would go down when the data showed they were going up. Again, as so often with this president, he was convinced that he was right and the experts were wrong.

On Russia, Trump's inexplicable intransigence on the threat presented a particular challenge to his national security briefers, including those who delivered his President's Daily Brief, or PDB, a daily summary of the most recent and urgent intelligence and intelligence analysis on the nation's top national security threats.

Early in his term, Trump's briefers from the Office of the Director of National Intelligence (ODNI) discovered that when the PDB included intelligence related to Russian malign activities against the United States, including evidence of its interference in US politics, Trump would often blow up at them, demanding why they kept focusing on Russia. He doubted the intelligence itself as well.

That presented an enormous challenge to intelligence officials. Their job is to present the president with the broadest view of all the threats facing the United States. If the president was obsessed with just one threat, he wouldn't listen to intelligence on other threats, in which case a key line of communication between the intelligence agencies and the commander in chief would be damaged or lost.

In response, ODNI came up with a remarkable strategy, reducing the amount of Russian-related intelligence it included in the PDB. That was a difficult decision for senior US intelligence officials. Their logic was that if he bristled at or complained about all intelligence regarding Russia, they would have to pick and choose their moments. They could no longer casually include Russia-related intelligence in his briefings or devote time to second-tier threats or indicators; they would have to focus their efforts and his time on only the most essential intelligence. Their best option was to reserve their limited chances to include such intelligence only when it really mattered. The end result was that the president now heard less, not more, about the threat posed by one of our most dangerous adversaries.

That of course generated another problem: among his national security staff, it led to fears that the president was becoming less and less aware of the Russia threat, even as the intelligence confirming the country's misbehavior mounted.

"It became a self-fulfilling prophecy," one former national security staffer told me, explaining that when Trump later claimed in public that he hadn't seen evidence of Russian aggression, he was sometimes telling the truth. But the reason he hadn't seen it was that they hadn't shown it to him. Therefore, his own misinformed view of Russia became more, not less, entrenched.

Trump's refusal to hear information he doesn't want to hear infused his entire approach to a whole range of national security threats.

Again, he simply believes he knows better than his advisors and the agencies they run. That created yet one more danger for the United States. For experienced intelligence professionals, such self-belief as displayed by the president in the face of counsel and intelligence can be a weakness that foreign countries and their intelligence agencies exploit.

"Overconfidence is probably the biggest indicator of risk in these things because you don't believe that anyone could possibly influence you," Gordon told me. "Of course people are trying to influence you all the time. If you never imagine that they would do so for bad purpose, then you run the risk of being had."[2]

INSTITUTIONAL DISTRUST

It's a feature, not a bug, of the Trump presidency that some members of his own administration don't trust him. They don't trust him not only to tell the truth, but also to do the job of president. This will strike some readers as an editorial statement, but it's in the public record—from the sworn testimony of officials involved in his decision to withhold military aid to Ukraine to the resignation letter of Secretary of Defense James Mattis after Trump's first decision to withdraw from Syria to a public disagreement with his Navy secretary over the pardoning of a Navy SEAL convicted of a crime, and beyond. In each case, his own appointees cited not policy differences with the president but differences over the role and values of the United States in the world.

The list is remarkably long and the comments deeply critical. For Gary Cohn, Trump's then chief economic advisor, it was Trump's "both sides" comment on Charlottesville. "Citizens standing up for equality and freedom can never be equated with white supremacists, neo-Nazis, and the KKK," he told the *Financial Times* in August 2017.[3]

For Daniel Coats, Trump's then director of national intelligence, it was Trump's acceptance of Putin's denial of Russian election interference in Helsinki in July 2018. "We have been clear in our assessments of Russian meddling in the 2016 election and their ongoing, pervasive efforts to undermine our democracy," Coats said in a statement that CNN reported had not been cleared with the White House.[4] For Attorney General William Barr, it was Trump's tweeting about ongoing Justice Department legal proceedings, which, he told ABC News in February 2020, had made it "impossible" to do his job.[5] They were all serving officials of the Trump administration, appointed by the president, expressing deep opposition to comments made by that same president, knowing he could dismiss them at any time.

The Ukraine scandal, which sparked only the third presidential impeachment in US history, was indicative of the gaping chasm between the president and members of his own administration on a key national security issue. Soon after the whistle-blower's complaint was revealed, multiple officials, including officials appointed by the president to senior positions, both corroborated the core of the complaint and expanded on it in the House impeachment inquiry. As his one-time senior director for European and Russian affairs Fiona Hill testified under oath, the president had subjugated the needs of a crucial ally at war with the United States' only true existential adversary, Russia, for a "domestic political errand."

In her characteristically no-nonsense tone, Hill described the hijacking of US foreign policy in one of the most contested areas of the globe: "There was let's just say a different channel in operation in relations to Ukraine, one that was domestic and political in nature."[6]

Gordon Sondland, the president's ambassador to the European Union and one of the officials he entrusted with running his Ukraine policy, confirmed Trump's desired exchange in equally explicit terms. "I know that members of this Committee have frequently framed these complicated issues in the form of a simple question: Was there a 'quid pro quo?'" Sondland said in his sworn testimony. "As I testified previously, with regard to the requested White House call and White House meeting, the answer is yes."

He went on to say that the quid pro quo was not the objective of some rogue operation. It was the policy. "Everyone was in the loop. It was no secret."[7]

In the same month that the House impeachment inquiry was occupying Capitol Hill, the man Trump had appointed as secretary of the navy, Richard V. Spencer, was forced out of his post, explaining his departure this way: "I no longer share the same understanding with the Commander in Chief who appointed me, in regards to the key principle of good order and discipline. I cannot in good conscience obey an order that I believe violates the sacred oath I took."[8]

Their difference on "the key principle of good order and discipline" was the president's insistence on pardoning convicted war criminal and Navy SEAL Edward Gallagher and, later, Trump's further intervention to prevent the navy from taking away Gallagher's SEAL trident—a treasured decoration for the US Navy's revered special operations force.

From Ukraine to a military court-martial, those were no small disagreements over policy, as Republican lawmakers attempted to argue during the impeachment hearings; they were differences over the core values and functioning of the US military and government in the international arena. People who worked for him, many appointed by him, were saying the president was guilty of malfeasance.

Occasionally, these officials' alarm at the president's actions sparked serious discussion of intentionally undermining or blocking his agenda. Trump's former ambassador to the United Nations Nikki Haley recounted a particularly remarkable episode in her book *With All Due*

Respect. She claimed that she had been recruited by then chief of staff John Kelly and then secretary of state Rex Tillerson to deliberately stand in the way of some of the president's more damaging decisions.

"Kelly and Tillerson confided in me that when they resisted the President, they weren't being insubordinate, they were trying to save the country," she wrote. "It was *their* decisions, not the president's, that were in the best interests of America, they said. The president didn't know what he was doing."[9]

She went on to say that Tillerson had told her that "people would die" if they did not stand in Trump's way. In revealing that encounter, Haley's intention appeared to be to demonstrate her loyalty to the president by making clear that she had refused Kelly's and Tillerson's proposal to thwart Trump. But she also revealed a remarkable and disturbing reality: *Two senior members of the Trump administration believed the sitting US president was acting against the country's interests.*

The United States' core interests abroad are not normally the subject of a deep partisan divide, or, especially, a divide within the Republican Party. The United States supports its allies and challenges its adversaries. But at times, Trump has turned the tables—courting enemies while diminishing allies and undermining alliances that have served US interests for decades. And those who challenged such decisions, whether Republican or Democrat, were attacked as un-American.

Even officials outside Trump's loyalist camp reject the more alarming questions about his loyalties and inclinations. "I think he intends to serve America, like every other president, I really do," former principal deputy director of national intelligence Susan Gordon told me. "He is more than the caricature presented publicly."[10]

Where his advisors differ sharply is on how he makes decisions impacting US national security. To his supporters, his lack of a regimented policy-making process is a strength rather than a weakness.

"He's a strategic chess player, seeing all angles and moves," said Peter Navarro. "There's no preformed playbook. It's jazz versus classical music. He sees the chessboard and makes the appropriate moves."[11]

But to experienced national security professionals, this approach sets up Trump and the country for potential errors in judgment. "My larger concern is if the president continues to make decisions outside the system, that the system will atrophy and decisions will increasingly be unsupported," said Gordon.

By "unsupported" decisions, she meant decisions by the most powerful leader in the world unsupported by the best-resourced national security infrastructure in the world.

She went on to ask, "When these issues get more and more complex, when you're starting to see the second- and third-world effects, do you have the stable of experts assisting you to put things in front of you, so that you can have a better sight picture and make better and better decisions?"[12]

EXPERTS OR THE "DEEP STATE"?

Driving Trump's unconventional national security strategy is a self-belief that is often unmoved by even the best advice of his advisors and the best information and intelligence the US government can gather.

He is smart, advisors say, but not book smart. Several have told me they doubt he reads much of the briefing material he's given, as seen in the example of the note cards. And his grasp of basic facts of history can be incomplete or nonexistent. In discussions of the tensions on the Korean Peninsula, one former senior advisor noted with alarm that the president genuinely did not know how the United States had entered the Korean War. This is not an arcane fact of history but one relevant to understanding why US support for South Korea matters to this day. And given Trump's doubts about alliances, in that instance, knowledge matters a great deal and may have affected the policy.

His confidence without the facts appears to affect his view of US domestic history as well. In a May 2017 interview with *Washington Examiner* columnist Salena Zito, President Trump claimed that the Civil War could have been prevented. "People don't realize, the Civil War—you think about it, why?" he said. "People don't ask that question. But why was there a Civil War? Why could that one not have been worked out?"[13]

In the interview, he then implied that Andrew Jackson, whose election victory he had compared favorably to his own, could have prevented the war had he still been alive, though Jackson had died more than a decade before the war's outbreak. Moreover, did the president not know that slavery, and the extension of slavery to new states, was the primary cause of the conflict? And how did his lack of understanding of a crucial historical fact affect his view of present-day race relations and the South's view of the confederacy?

"He's very confident in how *he* sees the world, and how he understands economic issues and trade issues," says Gordon. "I think he extrapolates from his experience as a guy in real estate. And that's an interesting question, whether those international economic trends are the same thing as that."

For Gordon, who engaged with Trump repeatedly over two years on all of the most sensitive national security challenges, the most telling times were when Trump trusted his own judgment and knowledge over intelligence and analysis provided by the intelligence community.

"He is a confident decision maker," she said. "I've never met someone more convinced in his own rightness. And in my experience, though he listened to what the system put forward, he always goes with what he believes is right rather than what the bureau might generate. He seems to care little about strategic outcome or second- and third-order effects—which is what systems and bureaucracies care about the most, and provide the most value.

"I don't know whether to say that's overconfident or not. I think time will tell, right? I think we know this over time, that the effects of decisions, particularly on this scale, tend to play out over years, not over moments."[14]

A president has every right to question what he's told, Gordon acknowledges, and neither the intelligence itself nor the intelligence community's advice is always right. In fact, good intelligence professionals, such as Gordon, make it a habit to acknowledge what they know and what they don't know, as she said she did in her many direct encounters with Trump. Moreover, good presidents ask hard questions about what they're told.

"Intelligence is a craft that allows you to deal certainly with uncertain information," she said. "'Proof' is a hard standard with intelligence, but that doesn't mean that the data and assessments are invalid. I have no problem, ever, with questioning intelligence. And I believe that the intelligence community always has to be able to explain the basis for its assessments."[15]

The questions become disturbing when they persist even in the face of hard facts. When did he refuse to believe things his advisors knew for certain? I asked officials who dealt with the president face-to-face on a series of national security issues. Though they could not discuss individual instances in which they discussed classified information with the president, they did recount times when the president refused to listen even to hard data on issues as simple as trade deficits and allied contributions to US military deployments abroad. In these cases, the information the president believed was contradicted by what agencies of the US government knew based on the hard evidence before them. Their worry was that he was believing what he wanted to believe, not what was true to the best of the US government's knowledge.

Trump's initial dismissal of the seriousness of the coronavirus outbreak followed the same pattern. Even in the face of hard medical data and the experience of countries that had already witnessed the severity of the outbreak, he insisted that he knew better: the outbreak was less severe than the experts were warning.

★ ★ ★

ASK HIS DEFENDERS, HOWEVER, AND THEY WILL SAY THAT PRESIdent Trump has every reason to doubt the advice and information provided by the heads of US institutions and the institutions themselves.

"He's rightfully skeptical of some of the information he's given by some of the career bureaucrats that grace the presence of the Oval," Peter Navarro told me with biting sarcasm. "To the president's credit, he will challenge the so-called experts and sometimes reject their expertise. And rightly so, and I've seen it. I've seen it firsthand that not only would he reject that, but that they were wrong. Those experts were just flat-out wrong.

"So-called experts," he added with emphasis.

When I asked for an example of when his advisors had provided false or faulty information, Navarro said he could not cite specific instances for fear of touching on classified intelligence. However, he said the president viewed the establishment view of China with particular skepticism.

"There's a built-in bias among your career bureaucrats," he said. "They stay on the benefits of free trade and the globalist philosophy . . . and gloss over the obvious inequities to American manufacturers and workers and all these trade relationships."[16]

Multiple current and former advisors say the president expresses a reflexive doubt of what the "establishment" tells him. This applies both to advice, which is of course subjective by nature, and to hard data, which is not. This skepticism goes right to the core of the president's "America First" worldview. To Trump and his supporters, he is rightfully exposing the failures of the system. The system created and perpetuated the unfair world Americans are now living in. So why not ignore it now?

Even critics of his approach grant that his skepticism can challenge a system that isn't used to being challenged.

"My experience is, the answer 'Because we've always done it' is never sufficient with him," said Susan Gordon. "If the best the system can offer is 'This is the way we've done it,' he will say, 'Well, why? Why are we doing that? Why in the world is that to our advantage?'" she continued, describing some of the president's favorite questions. "And you will find the system struggling because we've been working issues and looking at situations for so long that some things have just become foundational beliefs."

The real trouble comes when their answers—those "foundational beliefs"—simply aren't enough for Trump.

"In the particular case of overseas presence, particularly military presence, the president would often ask, 'Why are we there?' and our best answer is that 'We have seen the consequence of not,'" Gordon explained. "Because over our organizational history, we've seen what happens when we allow a vacuum to exist."[17]

The vacuum created, say, if the United States were to abandon its NATO allies to Russian aggression in Europe or stop defending Japan and South Korea from Chinese and North Korean aggression in Asia. Sometimes, they say, the president just doesn't listen.

The question, then, is: If he's not listening to his advisors, senior officials, and the departments and agencies they run, who is he listening to? This can be a mystery at times, even to senior officials across his administration, though they saw patterns, with the president taking capricious turns after phone calls with people ranging from Fox News anchors to foreign leaders. His advisors often lived in fear of these conversations and how they might suddenly disrupt US policy.

One danger of having so many informal advisors "in his ear," as one former senior administration official described it to me, is that he gets advice from people filling no formal government role but pushing a whole host of interests, some of which are independent of US interests. And, often, his advisors say, the president listens to them.

Electoral politics are in Trump's ear as well. With "America First," as Steve Bannon explained earlier, Trump is reflecting not only his own inclinations but also those of the voters who elected him in the first place. This is where the politics of the "deplorables" at home has influenced US policy abroad. He was elected by a portion of the US population who felt simultaneously left behind by globalization and bearing the bulk of the responsibility for it. They lost their jobs to foreign countries and then had to send their sons and daughters to fight other foreign countries in the "endless wars" abroad. They believe, as Trump does, that they and their country have been taken advantage of by allies and adversaries. The president regularly has people "in his ear" venting those views.

World leaders have picked up on Trump's aversion to his advisors' counsel and sought to exploit it. Several of his advisors recount multiple instances in which a major policy shift followed a presidential phone call with a foreign leader, the new direction sometimes coming the moment Trump had hung up the phone.

"I'm not a psychologist, but I do think all these world leaders have certainly picked up on the fact that he likes to be flattered," said a former senior Department of Defense official. "And if you spend a lot of time talking about things he's done that are great, it actually has a significant effect.

"Most people, I think, would see through that and just realize that they're just trying to flatter you and it's not really genuine. But they do, they just overly flatter him, more so than you'd expect, I think. Whether they're playing him, I don't know. He likes it."[18]

Trump's vulnerability to those "people in his ear" has been particularly disturbing for his advisors when those people are the leaders of America's adversaries, that is, leaders committed to undermining America's best interests. One of Trump's sources for hostility to European leaders, say his former advisors, is Vladimir Putin. Trump's advisors suspect that Putin was also a source of Trump's understanding of the Second World War. More than once, Trump has alluded to Russia's enormous losses in World War II, a fact of history that Putin has emphasized as he has conducted revisionist history on Russia's role in the war.

In an interview with Fox News in March 2020, Trump cited those losses as he disparaged Germany's role in the war, seeming to forget not only the Molotov-Ribbentrop Pact, by which Russia and Germany had divvied up Poland, but the decades of history that followed, in which Germany became a loyal ally and Russia the enemy of the Cold War. "They [Russia] also fought World War Two," he said. "They lost fifty million people. They were our partner in World War Two. Germany was the enemy. And Germany's like this wonderful thing."[19]

Putin, several of Trump's advisors feared, was carrying out an influence operation of sorts on the US president.

In May 2019, President Trump welcomed to the White House another foreign leader who has worked his way into Trump's ear: Hungary's far-right president, Viktor Orbán. Trump showered Orbán with praise in an availability with the media in the Oval Office during the visit: "Viktor Orbán has done a tremendous job in so many different ways. Highly respected. Respected all over Europe. Probably like me, a little bit controversial, but that's O.K. That's O.K. You've done a good job, and you've kept your country safe."[20]

In private, he took his deference to Orbán to a new level. At a meeting of his senior advisors during the visit, according to a former senior administration official, he cut off a member of his own cabinet, shouting, "Orbán knows more than you do!" The exchange was jarring. This was the US president taking the word of a foreign leader—and a right-wing one at that—over a cabinet member whom Trump himself had appointed. After the meeting, the cabinet member took members of senior staff aside to express alarm.

More alarming, this former senior administration official told me, is that Trump's deference to Orbán in the May 2019 cabinet meeting was not an outlier, but part of a broader and consistent pattern for the president: He will often take the side, in public and private, of foreign leaders over members of his own administration and often on issues of deep importance to national security. Trump's Helsinki moment with Putin in 2018 was no aberration.

POLICY MAKING UNDER TRUMP

Trump's preference for making decisions without the help of his advisors and the agencies they lead has been coupled with a more lasting assault on the entire policy-making process. With President Trump, there has always been his foreign policy as written and articulated in formal speeches and formal documents, such as the Department of Defense's annual National Defense Strategy, and his policy as delivered over time in a collection of decisions, often unexpected and often outside any policy process. The two sides of his foreign policy sometimes match, sometimes don't, and frequently contradict each other.

His national security team, though fluid and featuring an unprecedented turnover rate, has comprised a large number of respected and experienced experts in their fields. At the senior level, H. R. McMaster, James Mattis, John Kelly, Mike Pompeo, Robert O'Brien, and others could easily headline a more conventional Republican administration. Behind them, those in supporting but still powerful roles, such as Fiona Hill on Russia, Matthew Pottinger on Asia and later as deputy national security advisor, and others, could easily do the same.

This national security team, backed by a National Security Council of hundreds of nonpartisan staffers, has churned out the expected position papers, defense strategies, and public speeches, which read like the documents of any other administration. Together, the human and intellectual capital qualifies and operates as "normal."

McMaster, who served as national security advisor from February 2017 to April 2018, summarized the Trump administration's official approach as an aggressive pursuit of the United States' vital interests. And to deliver on that approach, McMaster and the rest of the president's national security team developed and articulated strategies for each country and region to achieve the president's objectives.

"There were a series of what we called 'integrated strategies' that integrated all elements of national power and elements of like-minded partners to accomplish clearly articulated objectives," McMaster told me. "And these are on all the key issues you could imagine: China, Russia, North Korea, Syria and the Middle East, Iraq, Iran, Venezuela, Cuba. So we had a really effective process that delivered options to the president, he made decisions, and we assisted in the sensible implementation of those decisions."[21] That is what a normal process for a normal president looks and sounds like.

McMaster cited President Trump's September 2017 speech before the UN General Assembly as the clearest expression of the Trump administration's foreign policy, at least as formulated by his foreign policy team. At the time, the speech made headlines largely for the fiery rhetoric he directed at the North Korean leader, Kim Jong Un.

"Rocket Man is on a suicide mission for himself and for his regime," Trump declared in tweet-like fashion. "The United States is ready, willing and able, but hopefully this will not be necessary."

But elsewhere in his address, and more broadly, his speech reads more like a think tank–generated policy paper on the United States' role in the world.

Each day also brings news of growing dangers that threaten everything we cherish and value. Terrorists and extremists have gathered strength and spread to every region of the planet. Rogue regimes represented in this body not only support terrorists but threaten other nations and their own people with the most destructive weapons known to humanity.

Authority and authoritarian powers seek to collapse the values, the systems, and alliances that prevented conflict and tilted the world toward freedom since World War II.

International criminal networks traffic drugs, weapons, people; force dislocation and mass migration; threaten our borders; and new forms of aggression exploit technology to menace our citizens.

Then he established his vision for the United States' and the United Nations' role in the world:

We do not expect diverse countries to share the same cultures, traditions, or even systems of government. But we do expect all nations to uphold these two core sovereign duties: to respect the interests of their own people and the rights of every other sovereign nation. This is the beautiful vision of this institution, and this is foundation for cooperation and success.[22]

Here Trump sounded like a classic globalist, a label that qualifies as an insult among his most loyal supporters and often himself.

"We said that we believe in strong sovereign states that respect the sovereignty of other nations, and the sovereignty of their own people, which is what we're all about, right?" McMaster said.

But that speech turned out to be not what President Trump is all about. Repeatedly, Trump went on to make major foreign policy and national security decisions outside of his administration's stated strategies—and even counter to them.

"You see a tension between what he rolled out in his National Security Strategy and these impulses—whether you call it paleoconservatism or neo-isolationism or whatever it is," McMaster said. "That's one of the fundamental tensions."[23]

"What was our overall national security strategy?" asked former deputy secretary of defense Mick Mulroy. "People don't know until they speak directly to the president.

"The mechanism of policymaking is still pretty much intact at the lower levels, and it's essentially not much different between administrations," he continued. "So the official written strategy for a lot of countries looks the same or similar as it did under the Obama and Bush administrations. And the president didn't challenge the strategy. I don't even know if he read or was aware of it."[24]

Once again, this pattern is a feature, not a bug, of Trump's approach to foreign affairs. And the president sees advantages in it, by keeping his adversaries at home and abroad off guard and relying throughout on the wisdom he trusts the most: his own. So when he bypassed or even contradicted his administration's own stated policies and dismantled the policy-making process, he was doing so deliberately. This is Trump's "madman" theory in action.

"The National Security Council process is scattershot," Susan Gordon said. "There is a foreign policy but without much underlying support.

"Fiona Hill, in her testimony, had a really great line but I think almost passed unnoticed. And she said, 'You know, this national security business is really boring stuff.' That no president is really going to pay attention to. What I understood her to mean is that there are a thousand conversations and relationships you need to have to make sure that intention becomes reality—especially when those intentions require partnership."[25]

That was the heart of the Ukraine matter: that the president had set into motion a shadow foreign policy, managed by his personal attorney, that was outside his administration's formal foreign policy and outside the institutions designed to carry it out. In the case of Ukraine, the president's shadow foreign policy was so far outside the normal process that it ran contradictory to it—and that appeared to be the intention. The stated policy, as backed by appropriations by Congress, was to provide military assistance to Ukraine to defend itself against Russia. The actual policy was to risk or even sacrifice that aid for Trump's personal political benefit.

His aides and advisors say that Trump is willing and able to course correct when he realizes that an out-of-the-box decision will do more harm than good. "You can see many times where we see what he wants to do. He'll even announce that he's going to do it. And then you'll see it walked back," said Gordon.[26]

Trump reversed himself twice on his orders to withdraw all US forces from Syria, in each case reducing rather than eliminating the US deployment there. And he reversed himself more than once on his administration's response to the coronavirus outbreak: raising, then delaying, a relaxation of stay-at-home orders; raising, then dropping, a unilateral quarantine on New York, New Jersey, and parts of Connecticut; and entirely dismissing the outbreak as a threat before later granting that one hundred thousand Americans might die. But even with those course corrections, his decisions still had real consequences. The United States' partial withdrawal from Syria opened the door to a Turkish invasion—and Trump's delayed response to the covid-19 outbreak cost the United States valuable time in which to respond and save lives.

★ ★ ★

FOR A PRESIDENT WHO APPEARS UNUSUALLY FOCUSED ON HOW HE is perceived on the world stage as much as what he accomplishes there, President Trump has generated a series of moments and images that cause even his defenders to recoil.

In foreign policy, US presidents are often defined by singular moments. In a complicated world that feels farther away to most Americans than it actually is, such moments—memorable and symbolic—are ways for people to measure a president's advancement or retreat of US interests around the globe.

They can be iconic, such as Ronald Reagan's demand that the Soviet Union "tear down this wall," signaling the United States' resolve in the Cold War and later foreshadowing its victory.

They can be consequential, such as Richard Nixon's trip to China, which transformed the relationship between a superpower and a rising power for decades to come.

They can be tragic, such as Jimmy Carter's failed operation to rescue US hostages in Iran in 1979, which still overshadows his earlier foreign policy success as president at the Camp David peace talks.

And they can be deeply contradictory. George W. Bush's resolve after 9/11 was undermined by his subsequent decision to take the country into a costly war in Iraq. Barack Obama's decision to order the raid that killed Osama bin Laden is balanced against his failure to defend his own "red line" in Syria when Syrian forces used chemical weapons.

Such moments are attached to presidential legacies like battle ribbons atop the flags of a military color guard. And although no single moment can easily define the success or failure of a president's foreign policy, they can reflect the character of the leader him- or herself and the character of the country he or she leaves behind.

Donald Trump's defining moments might snap a flagpole. As president, he stood next to Vladimir Putin in Helsinki and took his word over that of the entire US national security community. He excused the brutal murder of Jamal Khashoggi by Saudi agents. Saying he "fell in love" with the North Korean dictator, he turned a blind eye to North Korean aggression at home and abroad. He pressured Ukraine to investigate Joe Biden, withholding crucial military aid needed to fight the ongoing Russian invasion. He vowed to remove the president of Venezuela, before losing out and losing interest. He abandoned the United States' Kurdish allies in the fight against ISIS to deadly assault by Turkish forces.

He is the same president, however, who walked across the border into North Korea, a moment few would have imagined years or months before. He ordered the operation to kill the most feared man in Iran, Qasem Soleimani, a decision his predecessors had considered but balked at. And it was during his term that US forces killed the leader of ISIS, Abu Bakr al-Baghdadi, a terrorist leader not as feared or elusive as Osama bin Laden but a remarkable success regardless.

Which will be the defining images and decisions for Trump as commander in chief? The times he stood up to dictators or embraced them? The times he ordered dangerous military operations or pulled

them back? The times he threatened to abandon NATO or successfully pressured members to contribute more to the alliance?

Or the times he diminished his own country as a positive actor on
the world stage?

THE ANSWER

Do the president's own advisors trust him to do the
job of president? Do they trust his motivations and his
competence? For some of them, the answer is no. He often
didn't read his briefing papers, even the abbreviated ones
his staff created for him. His decisions often contradicted
his administration's own defense strategies. He dismissed
intelligence, data, and his advisors' counsel. He sometimes
took the word of foreign leaders over the word of US
officials. More enduringly, he shrank the policy-making
process created over decades to inform every sitting
president's decisions.

Where does that leave the country? Measured by the
standards of any previous president, whose focus might
be on the long-term historical legacy and position of
the United States in the world, the answer might be an
easy one. But measured by the president's less ambitious
standards, with a focus on transactional calculations and
short-term wins, a conclusion is more difficult.

The best way to reach an answer is to assess his success
country by country: what he inherited and what he is
leaving behind at the end of four years.

3

Strong Man Good: Russia

WHY DOES TRUMP FAVOR RUSSIA?

From the very beginning of his administration, President Trump has made a series of statements, decisions, and policy moves that align with Russia's interests and outlook over those of the United States. Why? This is a defining question of Trump's foreign policy. He has portrayed "America First" as restoring respect for the United States around the world by upending relationships—with allies and adversaries—that he sees as fundamentally skewed in their favor.

His approach to Moscow has seemed to follow the opposite track. Over the course of Trump's time in office, Russia has expanded, not reduced, its territorial aggression in Syria and Ukraine, to the detriment of US allies and US interests. Russia continued its interference in US politics via massive trolling operations and probing attacks of US election systems. The Kremlin also ordered more aggressive covert operations in Europe against Western targets, such as the attempted assassination with a powerful nerve agent of a former Russian spy and his daughter in the United Kingdom. If "America First" was intended to intimidate, not embolden, adversaries, it didn't appear to be doing so with Russia—and Trump's deference to Russia contrasts sharply with his more aggressive approach to China.

How can the United States truly be stronger if one of its most dangerous adversaries is stronger as well?

One of the starkest differences between the president and the national security community is over Russia. In public, he has taken the side of Vladimir Putin over US intelligence agencies on Russia's interference in the 2016 election. He has attacked not only the intelligence agencies' assessments but the agencies and their leaders themselves—and even pressured the Department of Justice to investigate them. Equally disturbing for many intelligence officials is something more lasting in their view: Trump's handling of the United States' gathering of intelligence on Russia.

A SPY IS COMPROMISED

In the early summer of 2019, I got into contact with former Trump administration officials who had an alarming story to tell. I'll go to great lengths here to conceal any identifying information about these people, as I did when first reporting this story for CNN in the fall of 2019. Contrary to the impression I have gotten from acquaintances and critics, sources very rarely come forward eagerly. In fact, most do not "come forward" at all but rather share information only reluctantly, conscious of the enormous costs they may bear if exposed. Those people expressed deep concerns about the potential consequences. That fear, however, was outweighed by their fears for their country.

In a series of conversations, those former officials told me that in the early months of Trump's term, the United States had rescued its highest-level spy inside the Kremlin in a daring and secret overseas operation. The very existence of the spy was remarkable in its own right. The CIA had cultivated the asset, a Russian national, inside one of the most hostile intelligence environments in the world and managed to maintain the source for more than a decade. During that time, that Russian official had risen to the highest levels of the Russian government's national security infrastructure, with direct access to Russian president Putin, including the remarkable ability to take photographs of presidential documents.

To the best of the CIA's knowledge, the Kremlin did not suspect that the spy was working for the United States. Even within the US government, intelligence officials went to enormous lengths to protect the asset's existence and identity. Intelligence the asset provided was restricted to the president, the CIA director, and a few other senior officials. Though the United States had other spies inside the Russian government, there was, one of my sources told me, "no equal alternative" to this one.

The spy had enabled a direct line into the thinking and planning of the Russian president. Such intelligence is some of the most difficult to obtain from any adversary, but particularly from one with a closed system such as Russia's, run by someone who happens to be a former spy himself. Intelligence provided by this spy had helped lead to the intelligence community's assessment that it was Putin who had directed Russia's interference in the 2016 US presidential election, with the intention of weakening Hillary Clinton and helping Donald Trump.

"We assess Russian President Vladimir Putin ordered an influence campaign in 2016 aimed at the US presidential election. Russia's goals were to undermine public faith in the US democratic process, denigrate Secretary Clinton, and harm her electability and potential presidency. We further assess Putin and the Russian Government developed a clear preference for President-elect Trump," read the 2017 Intelligence Community Assessment.[1]

The decision to pull the asset out of Russia was the culmination of months of mounting fear within the intelligence community. At the end of the Obama administration, US intelligence officials had already expressed concerns about the safety of the spy, given the length of the asset's cooperation with the United States.

Those concerns grew in early 2017 after the US intelligence community released its public report on Russian meddling, which had been based in part on intelligence the spy had provided. The intelligence community shared a classified version of the report with the incoming Trump administration, which included highly protected details on the sources behind the intelligence. Senior US intelligence officials considered extracting the Russian asset at the time but did not do so.

I was told that the final decision to extract the spy came soon after a May 2017 meeting in the Oval Office in which Trump discussed highly classified intelligence with Russian foreign minister Sergey Lavrov and then Russian ambassador to the United States Sergey Kislyak. Though the intelligence he shared had concerned ISIS in Syria and had been provided by Israel, the president's disclosure of such vital secrets to the Russians raised new concerns among some US officials about his overall handling of intelligence: Was the spy now at greater risk of potential exposure?

There was already wide concern in the intelligence community about mishandling of intelligence by Trump and his administration. Ultimately, intelligence officials decided to launch the difficult operation to remove an asset who had been working for the United States for years.

That was an enormous loss to the US intelligence community and one that was therefore enormously damaging to US national security. The secret removal of the high-level Russian asset left the United States without one of its best sources on the inner workings of the Kremlin and the thinking of the Russian president at a time when tensions between the two nations were growing. The fact is, the United States needed such a source now more than at any other time since the Cold War. Developing a comparable replacement would be extremely difficult, and close to impossible in the near to medium term.

"The impact would be huge because it is so hard to develop sources like that in any denied area, particularly Russia, because the surveillance and security there is so stringent," a former senior intelligence official told me. "You can't reacquire a capability like that overnight."

President Trump, however, views such spies and spying very differently. And this is one of the most remarkable instances of Trump's deferential approach to Russia. In his view, foreign spies do more harm than good, in particular to his personal relationships with foreign leaders such as Vladimir Putin.

The president "believes we shouldn't be doing that to each other," one former Trump administration official told me. In private conversations, President Trump has repeatedly expressed opposition to the use of foreign intelligence from covert sources, including overseas spies who provide the US government with crucial information about hostile countries.

In addition to his fear that such sources will damage his personal relationships, Trump has expressed doubts about the credibility of the information they provide. Trump "believes they're people who are selling out their country," another former administration official told me.

In June 2019, President Trump categorically disavowed the use of foreign spies against another adversary, North Korea. After the *Wall Street Journal* reported that North Korean leader Kim Jong Un's half brother Kim Jong Nam had been a CIA source, Trump said that he would not allow the use of CIA informants against Kim ever again.

"I saw the information about the CIA, with respect to his brother, or half-brother," Trump said when the news reports came out in June about Kim Jong Nam. "And I would tell [Kim Jong Un] that would not happen under my auspices, that's for sure. I wouldn't let that happen under my auspices."[2]

Trump's skeptical view of foreign spies undermines one of the most essential ways that US intelligence agencies gather information on foreign threats. In the intelligence community, this information is referred to as "HUMINT," short for "human intelligence," as distinguished from so-called SIGINT, or signals intelligence, which includes intercepted emails, telephone calls, and text messages. Intelligence assessments typically rely on a combination of HUMINT, SIGINT, and other sources. This includes assessments on everything from North Korea's nuclear program to terror plots by al-Qaeda and ISIS to election interference by Russia. By dismissing the value of HUMINT, the president was jettisoning a crucial and necessary component of intelligence.

President Trump's meeting with Lavrov and Kislyak would prove to be just one in a series of nervous moments for the intelligence community. Weeks after the Oval Office encounter and subsequent to the decision to extract the Russian spy, Trump met privately with Russian president Putin at the G20 summit in Hamburg in July. There he took the unusual step of confiscating his own interpreter's notes and demanding that the interpreter not discuss or share details of his conversation with anyone else. That was an enormous breach of protocol. Note takers are present at such meetings by design. First, a clear and accurate record ensures that the United States will be able to prevent the other country or its leaders from portraying the conversation inaccurately or otherwise to their advantage. Beyond that, an official US record allows senior US officials not present at such meetings to be aware of what transpired and offer analysis and interpretation.

President Trump was taking extraordinary measures to keep his discussions with the Russian leader to himself. When senior administration officials appointed by the president to oversee US-Russia policy asked to view notes and details of the meeting, they were denied.[3] More disturbing, two months after Trump's revelations to Lavrov and Kislyak in the Oval Office, intelligence officials expressed concern that the president might have again improperly discussed classified intelligence with Russia. And no one had the notes.

It's become an increasingly meaningless parlor game to imagine what would have happened had any other president taken the notes of a conversation with a foreign leader. In this case, we know that President Trump's unprecedented demand raised alarm among intelligence professionals. And it's likely they would have reacted similarly if another president, Republican or Democrat, had done the same. What the episode didn't do was spark bipartisan criticism or even questions. As with so many events of the Trump presidency, even long-standing, established good practices are run through the partisan mill. One of the few formal responses was a lawsuit by two progressive nonprofit watchdogs, American Oversight and Democracy Forward, which sued the administration "for failing to preserve the notes as required by the Federal Records Act."[4] As of early 2020, the lawsuit was still working its way through the courts.

PLACATING PUTIN

President Trump is fond of saying that no one has been tougher on Russia than he. And the evidence he and his supporters often cite to back up the claim is his administration's decision to provide *lethal* military aid to Ukraine, a step the Obama administration had resisted. These weapons were crucial to Ukraine's ability to defend itself against occupying Russian forces. It is true that the Trump administration provided Javelin antitank missiles to the Ukrainian military. It is also true that President Obama had rejected the measure, concerned that it would inflame the military conflict on the ground. However, the details of President Trump's support are more complicated.

More than a year before President Trump withheld nearly $400 million in military assistance to Ukraine—the decision that sparked the impeachment inquiry—the White House attempted to delay another form of assistance: those same Javelin missiles.

During the impeachment inquiry, Catherine Croft, the special advisor for Ukraine negotiations, revealed that previously unknown story to the House Intelligence Committee. She testified that the president's acting chief of staff, Mick Mulvaney, had told the Office of Management and Budget in late 2017 to put a hold on the sale of Javelin anti-tank missiles to Ukraine.

Croft said that the order from the White House had surprised her and her colleagues. "I can broadly say that all of the policy agencies were in support." Asked by committee members if she meant in support of providing the Javelin missiles, she responded, "Correct.

"The lone objector . . . on the Javelin decision was OMB," she told lawmakers before noting the obvious: that blocking the missile sale to Ukraine would be in Russia's interest.[5]

The attempt to block or delay the Javelin sale—again, the principal example cited by Trump supporters of his toughness on Russia—barely made a blip in the impeachment inquiry, overshadowed by the administration's 2019 delay of aid to Ukraine. (I deal with the Ukraine decision in depth in the next chapter.) Even when the attempted delay was revealed, Republican lawmakers and administration officials continued to cite the Javelin sale to counter claims that Trump's later decision to delay Ukraine military assistance signaled weakness on Russia.

In October 2019, when I pressed Congressman Michael Waltz on the delay of Ukraine military assistance, he referred immediately to the Javelins: "This administration, Jim, unlike the Obama administration, has sold lethal aid to the Ukrainians with the Javelin sale last year."[6] When I reminded him that the Trump administration had attempted to withhold that assistance as well, he stuck to the talking point.

And what had led to Mulvaney's hold on the Javelins in 2017? In Croft's words, Mulvaney was concerned "that Russia would react negatively to the provision of the Javelins to Ukraine."

"In a briefing with Mr. Mulvaney," she said, "the question centered around the Russian reaction."[7]

Mulvaney's push to delay the Javelin sale played out in private. In July 2018, the world would get a public demonstration of Trump's deferential approach to Putin's Russia. The setting was a summit between the US and Russian presidents in Helsinki, Finland. At their joint press conference televised live, Trump stood next to Putin and eagerly accepted the Russian leader's denial that his government had interfered in the 2016 US presidential election.

In fact, he would do so more than once from the podium that day.

Let's start from the beginning of his comments, because the president would later make a bizarre attempt to deny he had said what the world had heard him say.

The questions to the president from the AP's Jonathan Lemire were clear: "President Trump, you first. Just now, President Putin denied having anything to do with the election interference in 2016. Every U.S. intelligence agency has concluded that Russia did. My first question for you, sir, is who do you believe? My second question is would you now, with the whole world watching, tell President Putin, would you denounce what happened in 2016 and would you warn him to never do it again?"

Given the chance to back the assessment of US intelligence agencies and to warn Putin against interfering again, Trump chose to do neither. He began his answer by bringing up one of his favorite conspiracy theories, casting doubt on Russia's responsibility by asking why the FBI, in investigating the interference, did not take physical possession of one of the targets of Russian hacking: the DNC server.

"Why didn't they take the server?" he asked. "Why was the FBI told to leave the office of the Democratic National Committee? I've been wondering that, I've been asking that for months and months and I've been tweeting it out and calling it out on social media. Where is the server? I want to know where is the server and what is the server saying?"[8]

Trump's obsession with the DNC server denies the facts of the investigation. In reality, physical possession of the server was irrelevant to the intelligence community's assessment. US intel agencies had reams of digital fingerprints tracing the hacking of the DNC, as well as the hacking of Clinton campaign manager John Podesta's emails, to two Russian hacking groups tied to Russian military intelligence. Those same groups had infiltrated the State Department's email system in 2014–2015. And as a former deputy director of the National Security Agency, Richard Ledgett, described to me during the research for my book *The Shadow War*, by the time of the 2016 attack, those Russian hackers weren't even bothering to cover their tracks anymore. They didn't care if they were caught.

After citing the server, President Trump then credulously cited Putin's denial of Russian involvement. "I have President Putin. He just said it's not Russia. I will say this. I don't see any reason why it would be, but I really do want to see the server."

Moments later, he cited Putin's denial again: "I will tell you that President Putin was extremely strong and powerful in his denial today."

He then took his confidence in the Russian president a step further, praising a new offer from Putin for Russia to help investigate the election interference, to get to the bottom of who was really responsible: "What he did is an incredible offer. He offered to have the people working on the case come and work with their investigators. . . . I think that's an incredible offer."

Before he finished, he would double down on the server conspiracy theory and another favorite topic of his: Hillary Clinton's emails. "Where are those servers? They are missing. Where are they? What happened to Hillary Clinton's emails? 33,000 emails gone, just gone.

I think in Russia they wouldn't be gone so easily. I think it's a disgrace that we can't get Hillary Clinton's 33,000 emails."[9]

Throughout, he expressed no confidence in US intelligence agencies' conclusions and, more pointedly, delivered no warning to Putin never to do it again.

Days later, facing outrage from Democrats and Republicans alike, Trump attempted to gaslight his way out of the mess by blaming the transcript. In a meeting with reporters in the White House on July 17, the president said that "it should have been obvious" when he was asked if Russia had interfered in the 2016 election that he intended to say yes. All the confusion, he claimed, had been due to a missing word in the transcript. "In a key sentence in my remarks I said the word 'would' instead of 'wouldn't.' The sentence should have been 'I don't see any reason why I wouldn't' or 'why it wouldn't be Russia.' So just to repeat it, I said the word 'would' instead of 'wouldn't,' and the sentence should have been, and I thought I would be maybe a little bit unclear on the transcript or unclear on the actual video."

He continued, "The sentence should have been 'I don't see any reason why it wouldn't be Russia,' sort of a double negative. So you can put that in and I think that probably clarifies things pretty good by itself."[10]

Blaming one missing word from the transcript was ludicrous, given his comments before and after, not just from the podium in Helsinki but in numerous tweets and public comments throughout his presidency. Gaslighting was not a new tactic for Trump, as candidate or president. He had denied statements repeatedly before, even when those statements had been captured on video for the world to see. And he would continue to deploy his gaslighting in the months and years that followed, on everything from his tariffs on China—claiming that Chinese, not US, businesses pay the costs—to the path of Hurricane Dorian—apparently using a sharpie to retroactively back up his claim the storm was at some point headed to Alabama. To base such an easily controvertible claim on a stenographer's mistake as he did post-Helsinki was egregiously bold, however.

For anyone but his most devout loyalists, Trump's gaslighting his Helsinki moment failed. And the end result was an enormous disappointment for the president: he had gone to Helsinki with ambitions of making his mark on the world stage but had left with an indelible image of fealty to Moscow.

★ ★ ★

THE IMPEACHMENT INQUIRY OVER UKRAINE WOULD REVEAL OTHER instances in which the US president blocked, delayed, or questioned US policy and strategy intended to counter Russian aggression. One of the most egregious involved the US military's response to acts of aggression by Russian military aircraft and warships.

Christopher Anderson, a State Department official with responsibility for Ukraine, testified about one episode involving Trump himself. He recounted that in early 2019, President Trump had called then national security advisor John Bolton at home to complain about a story on CNN that described a planned US naval operation in the Black Sea as intended to challenge Russian aggression in the area. "Ambassador Bolton relayed that he was called at home by the president, who complained about this news report," he told lawmakers.[11]

The US Navy had taken the routine step of notifying NATO ally and Black Sea neighbor Turkey of a so-called freedom of navigation operation in the Black Sea, a routine maneuver in which US warships sail through international waters to demonstrate that the area is open for navigation by all parties. When CNN portrayed the operation as intended to respond to Russia, the White House had told the navy to cancel the operation.

"We met with Ambassador Bolton and discussed this, and he made it clear that the president had called him to complain about that news report. And that may have just been that he was surprised," Anderson said. "We don't—I can't speculate as to why, but that, that operation was canceled, but then we were able to get a second one for later in February. And we had an Arleigh-class destroyer arrive in Odessa on the fifth anniversary of the Crimea invasion."[12]

Once again, at the direction of the White House, the United States had delayed a move designed to challenge Russian aggression, and it appeared to have done so expressly to avoid delivering such a message to Moscow.

From Hamburg to Helsinki, from the Black Sea to Ukraine, one consistent feature of President Trump's foreign policy is decisions that align with Russian interests. This tendency has played out beyond direct US-Russia interactions.

President Trump's sudden decisions to withdraw US troops from Syria in December 2018 and October 2019 (which I deal with in depth in a later chapter) not only abandoned the United States' Kurdish allies to a brutal Turkish assault but also ceded large swaths of northern Syria to Russia and its ally Iran. In fact, within hours of the US troops' departure in October 2019 from a forward operating base in Manbij, Syria, Russian soldiers were already inside, shooting selfies as they explored the base and the equipment and supplies left behind.

The central allegation of the Ukraine scandal, which led to only the third impeachment of a sitting US president, was a gift to Russia. That allegation—that the Trump administration withheld military aid to Ukraine in order to pressure the new Ukrainian president to investigate Joe Biden—delivered an important and impactful favor to Russia: that is, delaying military assistance that would have helped Ukrainian forces to defend themselves against Russian-backed forces in eastern Ukraine.

SO WHY RUSSIA? THREE EXPLANATIONS

So why does Trump favor Russia? This is the question several of his senior advisors had the most difficulty answering with clarity. Susan Gordon, who worked for twenty-five years as an intelligence analyst and had numerous face-to-face interactions with Trump on the Russia threat, declined to speculate. "I have no knowledge or experience that allows me to answer that question from a data perspective," she said with an intelligence professional's stoic precision.[13]

The question is more than a parlor game. President Trump's decisions regarding Russia have frequently defied the advice of his seniormost advisors and his own administration's stated policy toward Moscow. At the worst times, his decisions have measurably undermined US national security.

Explanation 1: Trump the Transactionalist

One explanation for Trump's yielding to Russia is that the great dealmaker is simply laying the groundwork for a great "deal" with Russia. His deference, in this view, is mostly set up. He will butter up Moscow, build a relationship with Putin, and then, over time, coax, cajole, and pressure Russia into some sort of realignment that better suits both American and Russian interests and at the same time saves the world or at least makes the world safer.

Taking an intelligence analyst's approach, Susan Gordon attempted to see Russia from Trump's perspective. "If I were to take my experience and offer conjecture, it would be practical," she said of Trump's view. "I need Russia."

What does he believe he needs Russia for? I asked.

"To not be an adversary. To not drive up my need to respond militarily. To not force me to spend money in places I don't want to. To not have someone who I won't deal with. To not create another front where I have to engage militarily," she answered. "They are so powerful that to have them as an enemy is not in his best interest of what he's trying to achieve globally, and from a US perspective."

In this sense, Gordon sees Trump's approach to Russia as fitting into his broader desire to be able to deal with any country or any foreign leader on his own terms.

"Back to my pragmatist view," she said, describing her sense of Trump's mind-set, "I want to be able to kind of deal with anybody to be able to get anything. So I don't want any enemies. Because I want to be able to use everybody.

"To me, it makes sense in a way," she continued. "Because to him, it is important that he can pick up the phone and call anybody."

What is confounding to many of his advisors is that Trump's confidence he can get Russia right endured a series of setbacks, including Russia's continuing aggression in Ukraine and its expanding interference in US electoral politics. Both Presidents Bush and Obama eventually curtailed their Russian outreach. President Trump has not. More broadly, if Trump's "deal with anybody" approach explains his Russia policy, he pursued the opposite approach to China. "I think he saw China as much more important than Russia," said Gordon.[14]

Identifying China as a greater threat to the United States than Russia is not an outlier position in the US national security community. It is the prevailing view. But treating the two entirely differently raises questions about Trump's fundamental strategy.

Explanation 2: Trump the Contrarian

In doubting the threat from Russia, Trump is on an island. His advisors recount numerous episodes in which he simply would not believe the intelligence corroborating Russia's malign activities and intent.

This alarming disconnect happened most often when intelligence officials and advisors discussed the evidence establishing Russia's interference in the 2016 election. In private, as in public, Trump persistently expressed doubts that Russia was the principal bad actor.

"What we saw, documented in the Intelligence Community Assessment, was Russia. What the president believed is, yeah, there are a lot of people," recalled Gordon. "That was not the intelligence that we had at that time."

Note those words: "That was not the intelligence that we had at that time." Gordon told me she had briefed the president personally on the intelligence backing the intelligence agencies' assessment, but he remained unmoved. "It is an area of difference, not that Russia wasn't involved but rather that Russia was disproportionately responsible, where he tends to think differently," she said.

The president's intransigence extended beyond downplaying Russian interference in 2016. Defying a wealth of US intelligence on the broader Russian threat, the president refused to devote the necessary resources to defend against it—in effect, refusing to sufficiently protect the nation from a powerful foreign adversary.

"If Russia is an active adversary, you have to spend resources against it," warned Gordon. "And I'm not sure that this president wants to spend resources against it."[15]

Explanation 3: Putin Himself

The most alarming explanation for Trump's deference to Russia is that the Kremlin has compromising information on him. I tested this claim with several of his former advisors. Susan Gordon dismissed it outright. "I can't think of a single time where I had the sense that he had a disproportionate—I can't think of a better word than affection—for Russia," she said.[16]

So what if the accurate answer is less cloak-and-dagger than personal? Aides say Trump is simply envious of Putin's power and that his admiration for him is genuine. In fact, Trump, they told me, found numerous things to like about the Russian president.

He is a strong leader, as Trump envisions himself to be. Putin is a zero-sum player on the international stage, to which Trump sees similarities to his own "America First" approach. And Putin has an unromantic, nihilistic view of nations and their place in the world—a view Trump, unlike any US president in recent memory, appears to share in many respects.

When Bill O'Reilly challenged Trump's view of Putin less than a month into his administration, noting that "Putin is a killer," Trump's response—"You think we're so innocent?"—was therefore not an offhand remark or a case of his being imprecise with his language, as his defenders often claim; it was his honest view of the United States.

In this sense, his deference to Putin is not an outlier but part of a pattern, consistent with the admiration he has shown for other despots, from North Korea's Kim Jung Un to China's Xi Jinping to Turkey's Recep Tayyip Erdoğan. And he believes he can use his personal relationship with Putin to help not just himself but the country.

To be clear, Trump's desire to build a relationship with Putin is not entirely unprecedented. In fact, both of Trump's immediate predecessors also entered office with a confident belief that they could get Russia and Putin right, where others had failed.

In June 2001, after their summit in Slovenia, President George W. Bush said he had seen into Putin's "soul": "I looked the man in the eye. I found him to be very straightforward and trustworthy. We had a very good dialogue. I was able to get a sense of his soul; a man deeply committed to his country and the best interests of his country."[17]

Eight years later, and just months after Russia had invaded Georgia in an early sign of its territorial aggression beyond its borders, President Barack Obama dispatched his secretary of state, Hillary Clinton, to Geneva, where she gifted a "reset button" to her Russian counterpart, Sergey Lavrov.

"I would like to present you with a little gift that represents what President Obama and Vice President Biden and I have been saying and that is: 'We want to reset our relationship and so we will do it together,'" said Clinton, handing Lavrov a yellow box with an oversized red plastic button resembling an office desk toy.[18]

"[Trump] is the latest American leader to believe that he is going to get Putin to have a change of heart, which is utterly unrealistic when you look at Putin's background and the ideology that drives him," said H. R. McMaster.[19]

What confounds many of his advisors is why Trump's contrarian view of Russia and Putin has persisted in the face of clear setbacks. Over the course of his administration, Russia would disrupt and destabilize Ukraine more, not less. It would further violate the Intermediate-Range Nuclear Forces (INF) Treaty with the testing and deployment of new intermediate-range missiles, not maintain it. It would further expand its influence in Syria, not hold fast or retreat. Russian warships and military aircraft would challenge US forces around the world, more aggressively and more often, not less. Russia's approach was consistent: it was becoming more, not less, aggressive. Bush and Obama both eventually abandoned their outreach to Moscow. So why has President Trump done the opposite?

"Putin is Trump's honey trap," one of his former advisors told me, using an expression reserved for attractive spies who romance their marks into becoming double agents.

And Putin knows it. Some of the most experienced US intelligence officials have told me that Putin is aware of Trump's admiration for him and has sought to exploit it. Trump's motivations may be more innocent than some people fear, but the effects of his admiration can be similarly damaging.

Of all the misleading statements uttered by President Trump, his repeated claim that no one has been tougher on Russia than he has is one of the easiest to rebut. He has reversed or attempted to reverse his own weapons sales to Ukraine, which is fighting to defend itself against Russia. He has delayed and undermined sanctions against Russia passed by bipartisan majorities in Congress. And his outrageous claims about press conference transcripts aside, he has parroted Russian propaganda on its 2016 election interference.

His own former advisors say his frequent refusal to confront Russian acts of aggression risks undermining US national security and the security of US allies. That is a remarkable judgment to hear from officials who served in Trump's administration.

What's behind his approach? Is it Trump the transactional? Trump the contrarian? Or Trump the Putin admirer? It may be elements of all three. Trump believes that he, as no president before him, can get Russia right and can do so his way.

His public comments can be his most revealing. When he tweeted in January 2019 that "I have been FAR tougher on Russia than Obama, Bush or Clinton. Maybe tougher than any other President," he added this: "At the same time, & as I have often said, getting along with Russia is a good thing, not a bad thing. I fully expect that someday we will have good relations with Russia again!"

Improving relations with Russia is a sincere ambition— and one he hopes to follow through on in grand style with an arms control treaty to rival that of Reagan and Gorbachev.

But short of such a grand achievement, his lasting legacy is more likely to be one of giving Russia a pass, with deep consequences for US national security.

4

"L'État, C'est Moi": Ukraine

WOULD TRUMP SACRIFICE AN ALLY FOR HIMSELF?

Several Trump administration officials have told me of times they had worried that the president was placing his own personal interests above those of the nation. Those suspicions percolated through crucial periods in the Trump administration's dealings with Russia, Turkey, Syria, North Korea, and China. Sometimes the officials suspected that his personal motivations were political, short-term calculations intended to score political points at home. At other times, they wondered if his motivations were financial. Did his business interests in Moscow and Istanbul, for instance, factor into his making accommodations with Putin and Erdoğan?

Most of the time, these suspicions remained just suspicions. The officials had no way of knowing what was inside Trump's head. And Trump and his loyalists could always provide alternative arguments and explanations for his decisions, even if those arguments and explanations seemed thin.

Questioning Trump's motivations for his handling of Ukraine requires less imagination. His own senior advisors confirmed that he had conditioned military aid to an ally at war on that same ally's investigating his political opponent. Even some Republican lawmakers eventually admitted as much.

The details of how it happened, and the alarm bells it set off inside his own administration, document the personalization of US foreign policy under Trump.

The summer of 2019 was full of confusion across the sweeping web of US agencies responsible for US national security in Europe. From the Pentagon to the National Security Council, the State Department, and the relevant committees on Capitol Hill, one question loomed: Why was the White House delaying crucial military aid to Ukraine and a highly valued meeting between President Trump and the newly elected president of Ukraine? Ukraine was at war with Russia—a David-versus-Goliath conflict pitting the newly independent Ukraine, eager for closer ties with the United States and the West, against a revanchist Russia redrawing the post-USSR map of Europe under force of arms. Ukraine depended on the United States for military aid as well as economic and diplomatic support. With such help, Ukraine was merely overmatched. Without it, it appeared fated to defeat.

At the Pentagon, where US military officials were acutely aware of how much the aid affected the delicate balance of power on the ground, there was fear that the United States was hobbling an ally. There was also the pragmatic realization that if the delay persisted, the Pentagon and Ukraine would lose the money entirely. The Department of Defense is steeped in the cold reality that if it does not spend funds appropriated by Congress in the specified time frame, that money is gone. Now the DOD's comptroller was in the unusual position of facing what's known as an "antideficiency situation," but not for exceeding the amount of money appropriated by Congress—the action antideficiency laws were designed to prevent—but for failing to spend the money at all.

At the State Department, diplomats overseeing the United States' relationship with Ukraine began to see a pattern. In their view, there was a clear connection between the aid and the presidential meeting and Ukraine delivering an investigation that served the president's personal political interests.

As Deputy Assistant Secretary of State for European and Eurasian Affairs George Kent testified before the House Intelligence Committee during the impeachment inquiry, "In mid-August, it became clear to me that Giuliani's efforts to gin up politically motivated investigations were now infecting U.S. engagement with Ukraine, leveraging President Zelensky's desire for a White House meeting."[1]

Five thousand miles away, in Ukraine, there was growing alarm. Ukraine was fighting for its sovereignty against a far more powerful enemy. Since the Russians had first invaded in 2014, some 13,000 Ukrainians—civilians and soldiers—had been killed, according to UN estimates. Ukrainian and Russian forces were fighting pitched battles unlike any Europe had seen since World War II. One US diplomat compared the tank battles he had witnessed to scenes from the Hollywood film *Fury*. On a war footing and with losses both on the battlefield and off nearly every day, Ukrainian leaders expressed a combination of confusion and fear.

"Imagine you fight for your freedom against an enemy whose capabilities exceed yours by far," a senior Ukrainian official told me. "You got stronger over the years, but you still rely on support of your one true partner. And then this one true partner puts his support on hold. And rumor has it, it's because he wants something from you that has nothing to do with this war. Let's call it a 'favor.' So you have your just cause, your freedom, on the one hand and some 'deal' on the other."

The Ukrainian government struggled with how to respond to US pressure. The country needed US military aid to defend itself and perhaps to survive as an independent state, but the government did not want to get involved in domestic US politics. President Volodymyr Zelensky, the comedian turned politician, needed to show he could stand up for his country, but he did not want to risk getting on the wrong side of Trump. His country needed the United States and its aid.

Ukrainians were also acutely aware of how Russia would read the situation—and, crucially, how it would attempt to take advantage. Ukraine was only five years removed from popular protests that had removed a corrupt, pro-Russian president. Hundreds of Ukrainian protesters had died, many at the hands of Russian snipers. They knew the violence Russia was capable of.

In the starkest terms, Ukrainian officials worried the delay in aid could cost Ukrainian lives. To understand this requires a look at the assistance the United States was providing to Ukrainian forces. In June 2019, the Department of Defense detailed what was included in the Ukraine Security Assistance Initiative's 2019 allocation of $250 million:

> provide equipment to support ongoing training programs and operational needs, including capabilities to enhance: maritime situational awareness and operations as part of ongoing U.S. efforts to increase support for Ukraine's Navy and Naval Infantry; the defensive capacity and survivability of Ukraine's Land and Special Operations Forces through the provision of sniper rifles, rocket-propelled grenade launchers, and counterartillery radars; command and control; electronic warfare detection and secure communications; military mobility; night vision; and, military medical treatment.[2]

Counterartillery radars helped protect civilian and military targets from Russian artillery barrages. Losing such aid could allow more deadly Russian shelling. Night-vision goggles helped Ukrainian forces spot and track Russian snipers. Losing such assistance could free the hands of Russian snipers. And US battlefield medicine helped save the lives of wounded Ukrainian soldiers.

Crucially, that aid also included lethal weapons, including Javelin portable antitank missiles, as well as launchers, equipment, and training.[3] Tanks were one of Russia's most potent weapons on the battlefield. Delaying the Javelins put Ukrainian forces in more deadly danger. Again, withholding this military aid weakened a US ally in the midst of a bloody war.

Ukrainians communicated their fears directly to their US counterparts. The first questions came in July. Laura Cooper, the deputy assistant secretary of defense for Russia, Ukraine, and Eurasia, testified during the impeachment inquiry that a Ukrainian official had emailed a Pentagon staffer, asking, "What is going on with Ukrainian security assistance?"

Defense Department officials did not have a clear answer, though suspicions were building in the Pentagon. Moreover, the email—first revealed during the impeachment hearings—demonstrated that the Republicans' argument that Ukraine hadn't even noticed the aid delay was false. The Ukrainians were aware, and they were worried.

This point was lost to many Americans in the deluge of information and testimony during the impeachment hearings. Ukrainian officials were aware that the United States was delaying crucial military assistance. They were pressing their US contacts for information about how and why. Soon, the US officials they were pressing—which would come to include GOP lawmakers—began pressing the White House themselves. As Gordon Sondland would testify, the pressure on Ukraine was no secret; it was policy.

Nevertheless, the "Ukrainians weren't aware" defense has survived among many Trump loyalists even to this day.

THE FIRST PHONE CALL

President Trump had his first conversation with Volodymyr Zelensky in April 2019, just after Zelensky's surprise victory in Ukraine's presidential election. In a political twist worthy of a novel, Zelensky, a comedian made famous for imitating a billionaire president on television, had defeated Ukraine's billionaire president to become president himself.

During the call, Zelensky made it clear that his country was relying on US military and diplomatic support. The newly elected president asked Trump to send a senior official to his inauguration to demonstrate the strength of the US-Ukraine partnership to Ukraine's rattled domestic population and to Russia.

According to a rough transcript later released by the White House, President Trump assured Zelensky that he would grant his request and more. He said he would even consider attending the inauguration himself, adding that "at a minimum" he would send a "very, very high-level" official. He then promised to invite Zelensky to the White House for an official visit as well.

"When you're settled in and ready, I'd like to invite you to the White House. We'll have a lot of things to talk about, but we're with you all the way," Trump said.

He was effusive in his praise of the Ukrainian leader, referencing good things he'd heard from his "many friends" in Ukraine. "I think you will do a great job. I have many friends in Ukraine who know you and like you. I have many friends from Ukraine and they think—frankly—expected you to win. And it's really an amazing thing that you've done."[4]

During the impeachment hearings, Republicans, defending Trump's move to freeze the aid, claimed he was skeptical of the new Ukrainian president. The president needed time to verify that Zelensky's administration was not corrupt.

"When it came time to check out this new guy, President Trump said, 'Let's just see, let's just see if he's legit.' So for 55 days, we checked him out," Representative Jim Jordan, a top Republican defender of Trump, said in November 2019.[5]

The transcript of the call, however, recorded a warm conversation full of glowing praise. The president is at his most charming and comfortable, bringing up some of his favorite topics, including the strength of the US economy and the Miss Universe pageant.

"When I owned Miss Universe, they always had great people. Ukraine was always very well represented," Trump said, apparently referencing female contestants from Ukraine.[6]

Trump did not mention corruption at all. This contradicts the White House readout of the call, released the same weekend, which stated that the president "expressed his commitment to work together with President-elect Zelensky and the Ukrainian people to implement reforms that strengthen democracy, increase prosperity, and root out corruption."[7] More broadly, the president's omission undermines Trump's later claim that his general concerns about corruption in Ukraine, and specific questions about Zelensky's commitment to fighting it, were the sole reason he had delayed the aid.

In fact, within weeks of the call, the Pentagon conducted a review of the aid and determined that Ukraine had taken "substantial" action to fight corruption. In May, the Pentagon sent a letter to Congress confirming the review and its conclusion that Ukraine had met US standards in regard to corruption.

"On behalf of the Secretary of Defense, and in coordination with the Secretary of State, I have certified that the Government of Ukraine has taken substantial actions to make defense institutional reforms for the purposes of decreasing corruption, increasing accountability, and sustaining improvements of combat capability enabled by U.S. assistance," John Rood, the undersecretary of defense for policy, wrote. ". . . The United States has effectively helped Ukraine advance institutional reforms through a number of substantial actions to align Ukraine's defense enterprise more closely with NATO standards and principles."[8]

After Trump's first call with Zelensky, in keeping with his word, the White House scheduled Vice President Mike Pence to attend Zelensky's inauguration. Soon after, however, the vice president's visit was scrapped. Instead, Secretary of Energy Rick Perry and Ambassador to the European Union Gordon Sondland would attend. The complaint of an intelligence community whistle-blower, which first revealed the alleged quid pro quo, referenced this decision on the Pence trip as the first of several decisions the whistle-blower suspected were intended to pressure Ukraine to deliver on Trump's demand for an investigation into the Bidens. The whistle-blower's complaint read:

> I learned from U.S. officials that, on or around 14 May, the President instructed Vice President Pence to cancel his planned travel to Ukraine to attend President Zelensky's inauguration on 20 May. . . . According to these officials, it was also "made clear" to them that the President did not want to meet with Mr. Zelensky until he saw how Zelensky "chose to act" in office. I do not know how this guidance was communicated, or by whom. I also do not know whether this action was connected with the broader understanding, described in the unclassified letter, that a meeting or phone call between the President and President Zelensky would depend on whether Zelensky showed willingness to "play ball" on the issues that had been publicly aired by Mr. Lutsenko and Mr. Giuliani.[9]

In the weeks that followed, word began to spread among US national security officials of more alarming changes in US policy toward Ukraine. The White House, they were learning, had halted key US military aid to Ukraine.

On July 10, several senior officials responsible for Ukraine, including Special Envoy to Ukraine Kurt Volker, the NSC's senior director for European and Russian affairs, Fiona Hill, and NSC staff member Lieutenant Colonel Alexander Vindman, met with their Ukrainian counterparts at the White House. All would later testify that they remembered Ambassador to the European Union Gordon Sondland explicitly tying Ukraine's continuing desire for a Trump-Zelensky meeting to Ukraine investigating the Bidens.

"Ambassador Sondland, in front of the Ukrainians, as I came in, was talking about how he had an agreement with Chief of Staff Mulvaney for a meeting with the Ukrainians if they were going to go forward with investigations," Hill would testify.

According to her testimony before Congress, Sondland's comment sparked an immediate reaction from National Security Advisor John Bolton, who, she said, "immediately stiffened" and then closed the meeting.

Lieutenant Colonel Vindman testified that, in his view, it was clear what Ambassador Sondland was demanding of the Ukrainians. There was "no ambiguity," he said. The White House had, in the parlance of government officials steeped in state meetings, a "deliverable" in mind: the favor it wanted in return.

"On the 10th of July . . . it became completely apparent what the deliverable would be in order to get a White House meeting. That deliverable was reinforced by the President," Vindman told lawmakers in his closed-door deposition. "The demand was, in order to get the White House meeting, they had to deliver an investigation. That became clear as time progressed from how this thing unfolded through the 10th all the way through the conclusion."[10]

The July 10 meeting was a remarkable and disturbing one. It was not a private discussion among Trump administration officials but a meeting between US officials and their Ukrainian counterparts. The Trump administration was communicating a demand to its ally. The aid hold—and the quid pro quo—was now official US policy. Senior aides were laying the groundwork for the exchange before Trump did so himself to President Zelensky.

For Ukraine specialists across government, President Trump's second phone call with President Zelensky on July 25 removed any doubt as to what Trump wanted from the United States' ally. Once again, the machinery of government was set into motion to deliver on the president's unusual demand.

Earlier that day, special envoy Kurt Volker had texted Ukrainian negotiator Andriy Yermak to lay out the details of the quid pro quo: that is, President Trump would agree to meet President Zelensky once Ukraine had committed to launching investigations of the Bidens.

> [7/25/19, 8:36:45 AM] Kurt Volker: "Good lunch - thanks. Heard from White House—assuming President Z convinces trump he will investigate / "get to the bottom of what happened" in 2016, we will nail down date for visit to Washington. Good luck! See you tomorrow- kurt."[11]

Just before sending the text message, Ambassador to the European Union Sondland had texted Volker to communicate the same understanding. Asked during the impeachment hearings who had directed him to communicate such an arrangement, Ambassador Sondland testified that it was "likely I would have received that from President Trump."[12]

Inside the White House, other administration officials were communicating about the aid hold as well, just as the phone call between Presidents Trump and Zelensky was getting under way.

According to emails released by the Office of Management and Budget under a Freedom of Information Act request by the watchdog group American Oversight, Michael Duffey, a senior OMB official, wrote to a colleague at 9:00 a.m., "Did GC send the footnote?," referring to the OMB's general counsel and a footnote related to a document that would formalize the aid hold.[13]

"Mike, here's the OGC-approved, revised footnote," replied Mark Sandy, another OMB official.[14]

The conversation on the line put the president into the very middle of the scheme. Trump began his entreaty to Zelensky by making clear how much the United States was doing for Ukraine, indicating—falsely—that the United States did more than European countries. "We spend a lot of effort and a lot of time," he said. "Much more than the European countries are doing and they should be helping you more than they are."

Next, he indicated that he did not believe Ukraine was giving the United States enough in return: "I wouldn't say that it's reciprocal necessarily because things are happening that are not good but the United States has been very very good to Ukraine."

Then, having set up Ukraine's obligation to the United States, he delivered the "ask": "I would like you to do us a favor though because our country has been through a lot and Ukraine knows a lot about it."

He then asked Zelensky to open up not one but two investigations: one focused on former vice president Joe Biden, his son Hunter, and the Ukrainian gas company Burisma, on whose board Hunter had served, and another focused on the unfounded conspiracy theory that Ukraine, not Russia, had carried out the hacking of DNC computers during the 2016 election.

"I would like you to find out what happened with this whole situation with Ukraine, they say Crowdstrike . . . I guess you have one of your wealthy people . . . The server, they say Ukraine has it," Trump told Zelensky, according to the official White House transcript. ". . . The other thing, there's a lot of talk about Biden's son, that Biden stopped the prosecution and a lot of people want to find out about that so whatever you can do with the Attorney General would be great. Biden went around bragging that he stopped the prosecution so if you can look into it . . . It sounds horrible to me."

Trump made clear whom he had entrusted to follow through on the investigations: not the many officials at the State Department, Pentagon, and National Security Council whose job it was to carry out official US policy toward Ukraine but his personal attorney, Rudy Giuliani. "I will have Mr. Giuliani give you a call and I am also going to have Attorney General Barr call and we will get to the bottom of it," he said. "I'm sure you will figure it out."[15]

The president had other topics on his mind as well, one of which was the sitting US ambassador to Ukraine, Marie Yovanovitch. Fueled by a whisper campaign led by Giuliani, Trump took the deeply unusual step of disparaging his country's own ambassador to the president of the country in which she served. His language seemed borrowed from a Mafia movie script: Trump said ominously of Yovanovitch that she would "go through some things."[16]

Ambassador Yovanovitch would later testify before the House, "I was shocked and devastated that I would feature in a phone call between two heads of state, in such a manner, where President Trump said that I was bad news to another world leader and that I would be going through some things. So it was . . . a terrible moment."

When Trump tweeted further criticism of her as she testified, Intelligence Committee chairman Adam Schiff asked Yovanovitch if she found his tweets intimidating. "Well, it's very intimidating," she responded. "I mean, I can't speak to what the President is trying to do, but I think the effect is to be intimidating."[17]

One topic Trump did not mention once on the call was Russia, the country Ukraine was at war with. He did not once reassure the United States' ally that the United States stood with Ukraine against invading Russian forces. He did not make any personal commitment to US military assistance to Ukraine. Notably, he also did not bring up any interest in fighting corruption in Ukraine, the justification he and his allies cited repeatedly as his goal in suspending the military aid.

All in the same day, the pathway of this shadow foreign policy was made clear: Trump had communicated the quid pro quo to Sondland, Sondland to Volker, Volker to Yermak, and then, during the call, Trump directly to Zelensky.

Soon after the call, the same OMB official who had discussed the aid freeze in an email earlier that morning, Michael Duffey, followed up with a new instruction. He directed the Pentagon to conceal the freeze, citing the "sensitive nature of the request," according to a message released by the Defense Department later in the year.[18] Now the cover-up was under way as well.

WHERE WAS THE AID?

It was impossible to cover up the freeze from the people most invested in it. Former deputy assistant secretary of defense for Russia, Ukraine, and Eurasia Laura Cooper would later testify that her Ukrainian counterparts had inquired about the status of the aid three separate times at the very same time as the presidential phone call.

One email from the State Department at 2:31 p.m. that day said, "Ukrainian embassy and House foreign affairs committee are asking about security assistance." A second two hours later, also from State, said, "The Hill knows about the FMF (foreign military financing) situation to an extent and so does the Ukrainian embassy." Cooper also testified that "a member of my staff got a question from a Ukraine embassy contact asking what was going on with Ukraine security assistance."[19]

Where was the president's attention focused? A phone call the next day—between Trump and Ambassador to the European Union Sondland—would give the answer.

David Holmes, the counselor for political affairs at the US Embassy in Ukraine, delivered a riveting account of that call before the House Intelligence Committee on November 21, 2019. "He was quite loud when the president came on, quite distinctive," Holmes recounted. ". . . When the President came on, he [Sondland] sort of winced and held the phone away from his ear like this. And he did that for the first couple of exchanges. I don't know if he then turned the volume down, if he got used to it, if the President moderated his volume, I don't know. But that's how I was able to hear it."

The setting of the call itself was cause for concern. For the US president to call a sitting US ambassador on an unsecured mobile line in a public restaurant in a city crawling with Russian spies was an alarming security breach.

"This was an extremely distinctive experience in my—" Holmes said. "I've never seen anything like this in my Foreign Service career, someone at a lunch in a restaurant, making a call on a cell phone to the president of the United States, being able to hear his voice. He has a very distinctive personality, as we've all seen on television, very colorful language was used."

What Holmes heard on the call was a clear description of what the president desired from Ukraine—and what his priorities were in that crucial national security relationship.

Holmes testified that he heard Sondland tell Trump that Ukrainian president Volodymyr Zelensky "loves your ass" and that Ukraine was going to move forward with the investigations Trump had requested. Sondland went on to tell Trump that the Ukrainian president would do "anything you want" and confirmed that the Ukrainians were going to "do the investigation."

What Sondland relayed to Holmes after the call went to the core of the Ukraine scandal. According to Holmes, Sondland told him that Trump "doesn't give a shit about Ukraine," and that his primary focus was on "big stuff that matters to him, his personal interest like the Biden investigation that Giuliani wants." Holmes recounted that he had reminded Sondland that other "big stuff" was happening in Ukraine, namely, its ongoing war with Russia. But the president's focus was clear.[20]

Later, Ambassador Sondland and Special Envoy Volker would check in with each other on the status of the president's demand for Ukraine to announce an investigation into the Bidens. In text messages dated August 9, Sondland referred to that announcement once again as a "deliverable":

> [8/9/19, 5:35:53 PM] Gordon Sondland: Morrison
> ready to get dates as soon as Yermak confirms.

> [8/9/19, 5:46:21 PM] Kurt Volker: Excellent!!
> How did you sway him?:)

> [8/9/19, 5:47:34 PM] Gordon Sondland: Not sure i
> did. I think potus really wants the deliverable[21]

EVEN REPUBLICANS PROTEST

As with his orders to withdraw US forces from Syria, President Trump's decision to withhold military aid from Ukraine was getting him into trouble with even some of his most loyal GOP allies on Capitol Hill. According to emails released by the Office of Management and Budget in response to American Oversight's FOIA request, a staffer of Republican senator Rob Portman wrote to OMB official Michael Duffey on August 23, to say that Portman "is very interested in ensuring Ukraine has the military capabilities it needs to defend itself against Russian aggression." The aide continued, "I would appreciate if you could lay out for me the reason behind the O.M.B. hold and what the process is for getting the funding released."[22]

According to other OMB emails and records, Republican senator Jim Inhofe and Republican congressman Mac Thornberry also reached out to the administration with questions about the aid, but the White House did not respond.[23]

President Trump and his allies would later argue that the president had legitimate concerns about corruption in Ukraine and that an investigation involving Burisma—Ukraine's state gas company, on the board of which Hunter Biden served—did not amount to a politically motivated probe of Joe Biden. However, numerous officials involved saw a clear connection.

Former US special envoy to Ukraine Kurt Volker was one of the few to claim he did not make such a link. However, by the time he testified before the House on November 19, he confessed that that had been a mistake. "In hindsight, I now understand that others say the idea of investigating possible corruption involving the Ukrainian company, 'Burisma,' as equivalent to investigating former Vice President Biden," he testified. "I saw them as very different. The former being appropriate and unremarkable, the latter being unacceptable. In retrospect, I should have seen that connection differently, and had I done so, I would have raised my own objections."[24]

The essential allegation of the Ukraine scandal and the impeachment inquiry that followed was that the president had leveraged crucial military aid to an ally and the promise of a presidential meeting to extort a political favor. In sworn testimony, several Trump administration officials—including several appointed by the president—described the interaction as exactly that. As I noted earlier in this book, Gordon Sondland, the president's appointee as ambassador to the European Union and a $1 million donor to his inauguration committee, was one of them.

For emphasis, here are his comments again: "I know that members of this Committee have frequently framed these complicated issues in the form of a simple question: Was there a 'quid pro quo?'" Sondland said in his opening statement. "As I testified previously, with regard to the requested White House call and White House meeting, the answer is yes."[25]

In an apparent shot at other senior Trump administration officials, including Secretary of State Mike Pompeo, who had claimed ignorance, Sondland stated repeatedly that the exchange had been no secret. "Everyone was in the loop," he said, adding, "It was no secret."[26]

Some US officials were more withering in their criticism. Fiona Hill coined a phrase that would make headlines the day of her testimony describing how US policy toward a crucial ally had been hijacked for a "domestic political errand." As Hill explained, Ambassador Sondland, Rudy Giuliani, and others outside the official policy-making channels let presidential politics trump US national security. "When . . . [Sondland] said 'that these are the people who need to know,' he was absolutely right," she said. "Because he was being involved in a domestic political errand. And we were being involved in national security foreign policy. And those two things had just diverged."[27]

Lieutenant Colonel Alexander Vindman stated in equally clear terms what had transpired: "It is improper for the President of the United States to demand a foreign government investigate a US citizen and a political opponent."[28]

Faced with damaging testimony, some Trump allies reverted to personal attacks. During the president's months-long pressure campaign on Ukraine, he and his allies had already brought down the US ambassador to Ukraine, Marie Yovanovitch. During the impeachment hearings, they attacked more members of his own administration.

Vindman, a foreign area officer seconded from the US Army to

serve as Ukraine expert on the National Security Council, was a favorite target. Some Republicans and right-wing media drew attention
to his Ukrainian birth to question his loyalty to the United States.
President Trump referred to him, without basis, as a "Never Trumper."
Vindman's Purple Heart—and the shrapnel he still carries in his body
from an IED in Iraq—got less attention.

Asked by Congressman Jim Himes if he was indeed a "Never
Trumper," Vindman responded, "Representative, I'd call myself a never
partisan."[29]

Asked by Congressman Sean Patrick Maloney why he had told
his father not to be concerned about the consequences of his testifying
in public, he answered, "Congressman, because this is America. This is
the country I have served and defended, that all of my brothers have
served, and, here, right matters."[30]

It was a heartwarming moment, but it did not pierce the highly
partisan atmosphere. Republican congressman Chris Stewart took a
subtle dig at the army officer by noting that he was wearing his uniform to testify, though he wore civilian clothes to work. Stewart's questioning was not an accident. In the days prior to his public testimony,
conservative media had intimated that Vindman was somehow hiding behind his uniform or perhaps showing off his military service by
wearing his uniform.

In fact, military policy requires that active military wear their uniform when testifying before Congress. A US Army spokesperson told
my colleague Ryan Browne that "a Soldier performing duties in an official capacity will normally be in uniform," adding, "In cases where a
Soldier is detailed to an agency outside of DoD, the individual would
follow the policies of that agency."[31] It was not lost on several more
experienced reporters that another army lieutenant colonel, Oliver
North, had also worn his uniform when testifying during the Iran-
contra hearings in the 1980s.

For Vindman, the attacks struck a personal chord. When Representative Stewart asked Vindman why he had also asked to be addressed by his rank during earlier questioning by fellow Republican representative Devin Nunes, Vindman replied, "I'm in uniform wearing my military rank. I thought it was appropriate to stick with that. The attacks that I've had in the press and Twitter have marginalized me as a military officer."[32]

The president himself leveled yet one more attack on Ambassador Marie Yovanovitch as she was testifying. He tweeted to his tens of millions of followers, "Everywhere Marie Yovanovitch went turned bad. She started off in Somalia, how did that go? Then fast forward to Ukraine, where the new Ukrainian President spoke unfavorably about her in my second phone call with him. It is a U.S. President's absolute right to appoint ambassadors."

He continued, "They call it 'serving at the pleasure of the President.' The U.S. now has a very strong and powerful foreign policy, much different than proceeding [sic] administrations. It is called, quite simply, America First! With all of that, however, I have done FAR more for Ukraine than O."

THE "MISSING SERVER" CONSPIRACY DEBUNKED

Republicans did the president's dirty work in a more alarming way. Throughout the Trump administration's pressure campaign, the president had pressed Ukraine to investigate the debunked conspiracy theory that Ukraine, not Russia, had hacked DNC servers in 2016. Trump had mentioned that explicitly in his July 25 call with Zelensky. And he repeated the myth in public comments and on social media.

The allegation is false. The US intelligence community assessed with confidence that Russia alone had carried out the interference, stating in its 2017 Intelligence Community Assessment that "Russian President Vladimir Putin ordered an influence campaign in 2016 aimed at the US presidential election" and that the Russian interference "demonstrated a significant escalation in directness, level of activity, and scope of effort compared to previous operations."[33]

The Senate Intelligence Committee, chaired by a Republican and with a majority of Republican members, found the same, stating in its report released in July 2019, "the Committee found that IRA [Russia's Internet Research Agency] social media activity was overtly and almost invariably supportive of then-candidate Trump, and to the detriment of Secretary Clinton's campaign."[34]

The DNC server sits to this day in the basement of the DNC headquarters in Washington. Russia never had to take possession of it, because it hacked it and dozens of DNC servers electronically. The FBI didn't need to take possession of it, because it had, as normal with such investigations, taken a digital image of it. Moreover, the intelligence community had vast digital evidence tracing the hacking to two hacking groups (known as Cozy Bear and Fancy Bear) working for Russian military intelligence. The hackers were well known to US intelligence since it had determined the same groups had infiltrated the US State Department email system in 2014–2015.

However, the sitting president of the United States harnessed the machinery of the US government to pursue a lie. During the impeachment probe, GOP lawmakers were willing to help him do so. And the lie was not just a lie, it was also Russian propaganda—part of a Kremlin-led campaign to seed doubts about its interference in 2016. And now numerous US politicians were helping Russia do so.

Fiona Hill delivered a searing rebuke of Republican lawmakers, accusing them, in effect, of aiding and abetting a Russian misinformation campaign: "Based on the questions and statements I have heard, some of you on this committee appear to believe that Russia and its security services did not conduct a campaign against our country—and that perhaps, somehow, for some reason, Ukraine did. This is a fictional narrative that has been perpetrated and propagated by the Russian security services themselves."[35]

Some GOP lawmakers would still persist in amplifying and justifying the misinformation. Louisiana Republican senator John Kennedy would become one of the most ardent propagators. He equated critical commentary on Trump by Ukrainian officials during the campaign to Russia's systematic interference in the election.

"I think both Russia and Ukraine meddled in the 2016 election," Senator Kennedy said in an interview with Chuck Todd on NBC's *Meet the Press*. "I think it's been well documented in the *Financial Times* and Politico and *The Economist* and the *Washington Examiner*, even on CBS that the prime minister of Ukraine, the interior minister, the Ukrainian Ambassador to the United States, the head of the Ukrainian anti-corruption league, all meddled in the election on social media and otherwise."[36]

Misdirection, a classic Russian propaganda tactic, had enlisted— unwittingly or not—US cooperation.

There were other lies that persisted through the impeachment inquiry. One was that Trump had withheld the aid not only to ensure that Ukraine was tackling corruption but also to make sure that the United States' European allies were sharing the burden of providing aid to Ukraine. Trump would claim repeatedly that the United States paid far more than Europe.

On September 24, outside the United Nations in New York, Trump told reporters, "My complaint has always been—and I'd withhold again, and I'll continue to withhold until such time as Europe and other nations contribute to Ukraine. Because they're not doing it. Just the United States. We're putting up the bulk of the money. And I'm asking, why is that."[37]

David Holmes would contradict that claim under oath as well. When GOP counsel Stephen Castor pressed Holmes about a review of aid provided by European allies, Holmes noted that the review had happened after—emphasizing the word "after"—the administration had held up the aid. He then added that the results of the review had been "illuminating." "The United States has provided combined civilian and military assistance to Ukraine since 2014 of about $3 billion plus . . . three $1 billion loan guarantees—those get paid back, largely," he testified. "So just over $3 billion. The Europeans, at the level of the European Union plus the member states combined since 2014, my understanding have provided a combined $12 billion to Ukraine."[38]

So European nations together actually provided four times the aid provided by the United States. But for many of the president's defenders, the lie that the United States put up "the bulk of the money," as the president claimed, survived.

The United States did eventually release the aid, under pressure from Congress and the Pentagon, but the release did not relieve all the pressure. The essential imbalance of the US-Ukraine relationship had not changed. And if an ally had extorted an ally once, it could do so again.

At the impeachment inquiry, Holmes articulated his worry that Kiev would still feel pressure from Trump: "Although the hold on the security assistance may have been lifted, there were still things they wanted that they weren't getting, including a meeting with the president in the Oval Office. Whether the hold, the security assistance hold, continued or not, Ukrainians understood that that's something the president wanted, and they still wanted important things from the president.

"I think that continues to this day," he continued. "I think they're being very careful. They still need us now going forward."[39]

THE VIEW FROM UKRAINE

Ukrainian officials confirmed this fear to me in the weeks and months after the US finally delivered. They knew that the US president himself had not changed. They had observed him repeatedly reverse decisions on crucial national security issues, not only in Ukraine but in Syria, Turkey, North Korea, China, and beyond. With the 2020 election fast approaching, they knew that domestic US politics could again "infect" the relationship. In other words, they knew the president could take the aid away again.

Ukrainians still had a war to fight at home. I asked my Ukrainian contact if he and his colleagues believe that the aid delay had cost Ukrainian lives. We know Russia was likely aware of the distance between Ukraine and the United States. Given the ubiquity of Russian spying in Ukraine—via human spies and electronic surveillance—it had almost certainly heard the story in detail on that unsecured phone call between President Trump and Ambassador to the EU Sondland on the terrace of a Kiev restaurant.

"I don't know whether this situation cost us human lives. We lose them every day," the Ukrainian government official told me. "But I know for sure that at a very critical point of the peace negotiations, this whole situation made Russia feel more confident and less interested in peace."

Russia and Ukraine had been negotiating a peaceful end to Russia's armed occupation of large parts of the Donbass region of eastern Ukraine, a military presence Russia had maintained for five years. They were the first substantive talks in three years. In the midst of the talks, however, shelling from the Russian-controlled territory increased. On August 6, four Ukrainian soldiers were killed.

"The whole Ukraine was shaken. Voices got real loud to pull out of the peace process altogether," the official told me.

The Russian escalation surprised Ukrainian negotiators. Russia had not been hesitant to use deadly force, but to raise the temperature in the midst of talks President Putin himself had endorsed didn't make sense to them.

"Many were asking themselves: What made Putin cocky enough to jeopardize the dialogue with Zelensky like that?" the official said. "Well, maybe he wouldn't have been so brazen if it was a different kind of atmosphere."

Two months later, President Zelensky would make an unexpected concession: agreeing to allow special elections in the parts of the Donbass region controlled by pro-Russian separatists.

"The election should not be held at gunpoint but in accordance with Ukrainian law, with access for candidates from Ukrainian political forces, Ukrainian media and international observers," he said on Ukrainian television.[40]

Such elections—though conditioned on the withdrawal of Russian forces—could lead to special status for Donbass. That would not be outright annexation, as Russia had carried out in Crimea, but it would cede effective control of Ukrainian territory to Russia.

The Kremlin quickly welcomed the news. Many Ukrainians did not. Protesters numbering in the thousands gathered in Kiev's Maidan Square—the site of the protests that had brought down the previous pro-Russian government—chanting "No capitulation!" and "Shame!"[41]

Partisans continue to claim that Ukraine had never been aware of any delay in US military aid and therefore how could there have been a delay at all? In fact, Ukrainians were very aware of the hold and deeply afraid of the consequences for their country.

Was Trump willing to sacrifice Ukraine for himself? This is one of the easiest questions to answer in this book: Yes. His own aides testified under oath to that effect. Multiple emails corroborate that the direction to withhold the aid came from the White House. And even in voting to acquit the president of abusing his power in doing so, several GOP senators granted the substance of the allegation and rejected the president's defense that he had withheld the aid to Ukraine simply to fight corruption.

Ukrainian president Volodymyr Zelensky made his own revealing comment on the sequence of events. In an interview in December 2019 with *Time* magazine, *Le Monde*, *Der Spiegel*, and *Gazeta Wyborcza*, Zelensky denied having spoken with President Trump "from a position of quid pro quo." That was a comment the president's defenders would latch on to in arguing that there could be no quid pro quo if Zelensky himself denied it. But it's unlikely that they read the rest of the interview. Zelensky went on to explain that describing the interaction as a "quid pro quo" would make his country "look like beggars." Notably, he continued, "We're at war. If you're our strategic partner, then you can't go blocking anything for us. I think that's just about fairness." In other words, the president of Ukraine—a "strategic partner" of the United States, as he noted—said in clear terms that the United States had blocked aid it was depending on in a time of war. That was the essence of the Ukraine scandal.

Ukraine is the clearest illustration of the personalization of foreign policy under Trump. By withholding the aid to force an investigation of the Bidens, Trump had substituted his own interests for US interests. And contrary to the claim of some GOP senators that his impeachment would "teach him a lesson," the president followed his acquittal by immediately firing or transferring witnesses who had testified under oath as to the truth of his policy.

Would he do the same or similar again, and, if so, where?

5

Strong Man Bad: China

IN DEMONIZING CHINA, WHO WINS?

Confronting China is arguably the signature feature of Trump's foreign policy and the one most likely to elicit equal praise from loyalists and critics. The decades-old bipartisan consensus on China had held that engagement was the best way to achieve a mutually beneficial relationship, while coaxing Beijing over time into becoming, as former deputy secretary of state Robert Zoellick first put it, a "responsible stakeholder" on the world stage.

Trump rejected this. He did so first with a trade war that rocked the relationship between the world's two largest economies and, along with it, the entire world economy. By the measure of bilateral trade, the old, post-normalization approach had worked. Since President Richard Nixon had "opened" China with his landmark visit in 1972, bilateral trade had grown from less than $100 million a year to $1 billon a *day*—a nearly 4,000-fold increase. China had brought hundreds of millions of its people out of poverty. For Americans, trade with China had earned US companies hundreds of billions of dollars in profits and provided American consumers with cheaper versions of everything from washing machines to household furniture to the iPhones in their pockets.

However, there was a dirty underbelly to the US-China relationship that US political and business leaders failed repeatedly to address. As US manufacturers moved their supply chains to China, millions of American workers lost their jobs. And as China became an economic power, it became expert at cheating as well: stealing US commercial and state secrets, violating multilateral trade and currency agreements, and restricting foreign firms from operating in its own market while Chinese firms entered the US market virtually unabated.

On the campaign trail, Trump had vowed to confront China. As president, he delivered, unleashing a trade war with global consequences. Chinese exports fell and foreign manufacturers fled the mainland for other Asian countries such as Vietnam. "I am a tariff man," Trump proclaimed in 2018. But there were costs to US companies and consumers as well. Contrary to Trump's claims, US importers and consumers, not Chinese exporters, paid the tariffs. China reduced and then stopped its purchases of US agricultural products, and US firms saw their Chinese business shrink dramatically.

Trump launched a new line of attack with the arrival of the coronavirus pandemic. The president took to calling it the "Chinese virus" to emphasize the outbreak's origins in China. And some of his supporters spread rumors that the outbreak was no accident, but the product of a Chinese bioterror lab.

Habitual US deference to China with the aim of guiding Beijing to better behavior was over. But, as with Russia, Trump had his own hopes of changing the relationship for the better. Would antagonizing China on the coronavirus pandemic help or hurt the global response? Would the "tariff man" succeed not just in punishing China but also in benefiting the United States?

More broadly, does Trump's China policy have an endgame?

As a diplomat in Beijing from 2011 to 2013, I saw the old US approach to Beijing play into virtually every encounter. It's not that the United States never stood up to Beijing. During my time there, Washington successfully pressured Beijing to reduce oil imports from Iran to help force Tehran to the negotiating table over its nuclear program. It was an approach strikingly similar to the Trump administration's own "maximum-pressure" campaign against Iran and North Korea.

But in other areas, US officials would habitually tread lightly around China's sensitivities, largely out of fear of sparking a diplomatic uproar. Over a few days in 2012, I witnessed the best and worst of US China policy: a bold attempt to stand up to Beijing, followed by a rush to limit the damage. For me, the story that follows here illustrates the core problem President Trump rightly identified in the old approach to Beijing, which he then tried to correct.[1]

HE LEFT IN HIS SANDALS

In late April 2012, the Chinese dissident Chen Guangcheng sought refuge in the US Embassy in Beijing. It was a desperate request from one of the boldest challengers to the Chinese government. In the span of a few years, Chen had risen from a small-town lawyer to an internationally renowned champion of rural citizens' rights, remarkable under any circumstances but even more so as Chen is blind.

Early on, the Chinese government had celebrated his work championing the rural poor. But in 2005, he took on the government's one-child policy and became a prime target. In his native Shandong Province, he exposed the draconian aspects of the policy, including, in many cases, forced labor and even forced abortions and sterilizations. He organized a landmark class-action lawsuit against the government, charging it with excessive enforcement.[1] And with his new cause, Chen was transformed from a "barefoot lawyer," praised by his own government, to a traitor, imprisoned by it.

Chen paid a heavy price. He was placed under house arrest in September 2005. In 2006, he was sentenced to four years and three months in prison for "damaging property and organizing a mob to disturb traffic."[2] After he was released in 2010, he remained a prisoner in his own home.

That changed in the early hours of a late April morning in 2012. The blind dissident scaled a wall behind his house, injuring his ankle when he fell on the other side, and ran across fields through a police security cordon to the waiting car of a friend, who drove him through the night to Beijing. In Beijing, nursing a broken bone and fearing the Chinese secret police, he made a call to a diplomat at the US Embassy, asking for help. He needed immediate medical care, he said, and a safe place to stay.

It was a bold request that presented a major dilemma for the US government. With US ambassador Gary Locke out of the country, Deputy Chief of Mission Robert Wang called Washington for guidance. Remarkably, he was given permission, with the approval of Secretary of State Hillary Clinton, to take Chen in. On his arrival, Chen took up residence in a spare bedroom in the US Marines barracks in the embassy compound. Visiting him there, I found a small, slight man afraid for his cause and his family but determined to maintain his fight for basic rights for Chinese citizens.

His refuge in the embassy was a proud moment for me and other diplomats in Beijing. As we huddled in a series of meetings to discuss next steps, I remember the State Department's legal advisor, Harold Koh, telling a story from the Cold War era. Koh recounted the escape of a Soviet sailor who had jumped ship in Baltimore Harbor during the Gerald Ford administration. In one contentious cabinet meeting, as Koh recalled Henry Kissinger telling it at Ford's funeral, President

Ford had asked each of his advisors whether he should return the sailor to Moscow. All of them had answered yes. But Ford had overruled them, saying, in effect, "This is America." Nearly four decades later, we found ourselves witnessing the United States once again choosing a dissident over a superpower.

In the days after that bold decision, however, Washington's priorities changed. Now that the United States had let Chen in, the clear emphasis had shifted to getting him out. Assistant Secretary of State for East Asian and Pacific Affairs Kurt Campbell flew to Beijing from Washington with the task of negotiating Chen's departure from the embassy, with some guarantees for his safety and fair treatment. That was a tall order. China viewed Chen as a threat to Beijing's authority. The United States in turn had to view any Chinese promises with skepticism. But the priority remained clear: get Chen out.

Over several days of sometimes angry meetings, US and Chinese diplomats came to agreement: Chen would be transferred to a Beijing hospital for treatment and, later, be allowed to continue his legal studies at a Chinese university. Some of my diplomatic colleagues and I were skeptical of the agreement, and so was Chen. In his last hours inside the embassy, I watched him make several nervous phone calls to his wife. Would he really be able to continue his work? Would he and his family be safe? His wife knew that any advice she offered would be overheard by the Chinese government, which was certain to be monitoring the call.

Inside the ambassador's office, I watched Chen struggle with whether to stay or to go. The truth was, the decision wasn't his alone; his welcome in the embassy was fading. As he eventually walked to the door, he hesitated one last time, saying he didn't have his shoes. He was wearing only white socks and plastic sandals. "We'll get them to you," someone told him. And Chen was shuffled out the door of the US Embassy in his sandals.

Chen's next several days were extremely stressful. As he arrived at Beijing's Chaoyang Hospital, where he would continue his recovery, he began to panic, fearing that Beijing would renege on its promises. He was particularly concerned that the authorities would punish his family. US officials became increasingly aware of something that they could have predicted: that plans for him to continue his advocacy work inside China were subject to the whims of Chinese leaders who viewed him as a disloyal and dangerous dissident. In conjunction with New York University, US officials and NYU leaders, led by NYU professor of law Jerome Cohen, suggested an alternate plan for Chen: that he take up an academic fellowship in New York. It was a face-saving measure for the Chinese government but also something of a relief for it. Beijing has often preferred to export its most troublesome dissidents, rather than tolerate them at home.

Days later, Chen was on his way to New York and to safety. He left NYU in 2013, accusing the university of having forced him out to placate Beijing, a charge the university denied. He subsequently moved to Washington, DC, and accepted positions with the Witherspoon Institute and the Catholic University of America. By 2020, he still had not returned to China.

I have a picture in my office of Chen on the steps of the embassy as he exited, with me visible just over his shoulder. The look on my face captures what I remember feeling at the time: Why did he have to go? Why hadn't we, like Ford, stuck with the dissident over the superpower? Chen's demeaning departure from the embassy, right before my eyes, showed me that China seemed to be setting the rules once again.

OBAMA'S ASIA "PIVOT"

President Obama had attempted to change the rules. Virtually as soon as he entered office, all the talk among his foreign policy advisors was of a "pivot" to Asia. Obama's view, not unlike Trump's, was that the United States had spent too much blood and treasure in the wars in the Middle East and needed to pivot its resources and attention to Asia—the part of the globe he believed would define the twenty-first century.

Today, President Trump's former chief strategist Steve Bannon gives Obama credit for seeing the need for such a pivot early.

"Obama understood intuitively he had to get out of CENTCOM," he said, using the US military's "Central Command" designation for the countries of the Middle East and North Africa. "He had to change the center of gravity."

I spent my two years at the US Embassy in Beijing during the peak of the "pivot." And while the administration would change its preferred language from "pivot" to "rebalance"—in a clumsy effort not to disparage the United States' commitment to the Middle East—the shift remained a central part of Obama's foreign policy. Its implementation, however, was hampered by an unforeseen event, namely the rise of ISIS in Iraq and Syria, that exposed one element of the pivot—the untimely US withdrawal from Iraq—as having been disastrously premature.

By the end of the Obama administration, the United States was back in Iraq and now on the ground in Syria. The only significant new deployment to Asia was a small contingent of marines in Darwin, Australia.

Bannon believes that Obama underestimated the scope of China's ambitions and therefore underdelivered on the pivot to Asia. "The fundamental strategic mistake of Obama is they think [China] is just trying to become a western Pacific power, a hegemon to force us out of the western Pacific," he said. "That's not it at all. They look at this as the first step. All the Obama guys said, 'Well, they're not territorially expansionist.' I say, 'Have you lost your minds?'

"You know what at the end of the day he did?" he asked. "One marine brigade."[3]

THE TRUMP APPROACH

Enter Donald Trump. As with so many of President Trump's most aggressive positions, his approach to China was never a secret. He had harangued China's trade practices and the US-China trade imbalance for years. And as the GOP nominee, he laid out in clear terms what he would do as president to upend the relationship.

Trump's June 2016 speech at a campaign event in Pennsylvania would prove to be a manifesto for his China policy as president. Rejecting decades of Republican Party trade and economic orthodoxy, he argued that "the financial elite" had left "millions of our workers with nothing but poverty and heartache."[4]

"Hillary Clinton unleashed a trade war against the American worker," he said. ". . . A Trump administration will end that war by getting a fair deal for the American people and the American worker. The era of economic surrender will finally be over."[5]

One by one, he laid out aggressive steps that he would later take as president. First, he said, he would withdraw from the Obama administration's proposed Trans-Pacific Partnership (TPP), a trade deal among eleven Asian nations and the United States, describing it in a speech later the same day as the "rape of our country." He would renegotiate the North American Free Trade Agreement (NAFTA). As for China, he vowed to launch a new trade war. "You already have a trade war, and we're losing badly," he said.[6]

Today, Trump's trade advisor, Peter Navarro, points to that 2016 speech as the mission statement for Trump's new approach to China. "It's a jobs-plan speech," he said. "We're going to stand up against China's unfair trade practices. And if they don't clean up their act, we're going to basically do what we did. I mean, this idea that we don't have strategies . . . is just wrong."[7]

At the core of Trump's approach was his belief that, of the two countries with the world's largest economies, only the United States was playing by the rules.

"The problem is, there's no rules for China," said Bannon. "You got the elites looking the other way. China doesn't play by any rules. China doesn't agree to this. China has used the rules-based international order."[8]

Bannon, Navarro, and other Trump advisors argue that institutions such as the World Trade Organization (WTO) reinforced rather than policed China's rule breaking by letting China use the international trade regime to its advantage. For instance, since the WTO categorized China as a developing nation, Beijing was not subjected to the same standards as the United States on tariffs and other market protections, even as it gained enormous wealth following its accession in 2001. In the simplest terms, China could enter the US market virtually freely, while denying US and other Western firms equal access to its own market.

"We're not saying you don't need institutions," said Bannon. "The institutions have so lost their purposes; they don't stand for anything anymore."[9]

In Trump's view, China had allies in the United States. The "financial elite," as he called them, were aiding and abetting China's rise because it was in their interest. Wall Street, in effect, was part of the resistance.

"It's Wall Street. It's the corporations. It's the one percent that made so much off of China. That's why Trump's biggest opponents on the trade deal are Wall Street," Bannon argued.[10]

Trump's promise to his supporters was that his trade war wouldn't just punish China but also reward US workers by bringing back their jobs. Both as candidate and as president, Trump framed the solution in zero-sum terms: more Chinese jobs meant fewer American jobs, and so the reverse would hold true as well.

Trump's focus on jobs permeated every economic decision, including decisions about the defense budget.

"I mean, this was a learning experience for me," Navarro told me. "How does this all work? And so if you're going to do a defense budget and you're going to spend $700 billion on the defense budget, okay, that's a macro policy. Where are you going to spend that?"

Navarro said the administration would focus on directing even defense spending to particular contractors in particular states to add a measurable number of jobs. "So that assessment, the defense-industrial-base assessment I worked on with the president . . . gave us a kind of road map to go into Lima, Ohio, New York, Pennsylvania, Marinette, Wisconsin. So that's what we do."[11]

However, it would prove far easier to penalize China than to resurrect US jobs. For the location of his 2016 speech, Trump had chosen Monessen, Pennsylvania, a struggling steel town that had seen production and jobs flee overseas, including to China. Four years later, those jobs still hadn't come back. And the new mayor of Monessen would end up endorsing one of Trump's 2020 Democratic challengers, Peter Buttigieg.

TRUMP AND TARIFFS

To press China, Trump reintroduced a weapon long derided by presidents and economists of both parties: tariffs. Few phrases better encapsulate his China policy than his boast "I am a tariff man."

To do so, Trump employed decades-old legislation—the Trade Act of 1974—to apply unilateral tariffs on China through a Section 301 action. A driving force behind the successive tranches of tariffs on China was US trade representative Robert Lighthizer. A veteran of the Reagan administration and longtime critic of US free-trade policies, Lighthizer was a strong believer in the use of tariffs to protect US industry. As early as 2010, he advocated for the use of a Section 301 action to combat China's unfair economic practices.[12] Still, the breadth of the initial tranche of tariffs in March 2018 took the US business community by surprise.

Under that authority, Trump ultimately applied tariffs on hundreds of billions of dollars of Chinese exports to the United States, all the while falsely claiming that China, not US importers and consumers, would be paying them.

Don't tell that to Trump or some of his advisors who continued to propagate the falsehood that China paid the tariffs. Regardless, his trade advisor Navarro argued, the tariffs were working. "I'm a heretic I guess in the economics profession, but if you read the textbooks carefully, it is true that an economy will grow stronger if its trade deficit goes down. That's what's happening," he said. "The tariffs continued to do what they're intended to do, which is defend the US from the Chinese aggression with the collateral effect of really slowing down the Chinese economy without hurting us a bit."[13]

"Without hurting us a bit." That's a statement that's easily disproven. The US Chamber of Commerce, in another time a GOP stalwart and an organization made up of US firms that are in reality paying the cost of Trump's tariffs, constantly issues position papers stating the facts.

"American businesses and consumers are bearing the brunt of the global trade war," the Chamber stated. "By now, it's plain to see that tariffs are inflicting harm on the American economy and will continue to do so unless the administration changes course."[14]

The Chamber of Commerce publishes a state-by-state accounting of the impact of tariffs. Notably, it characterized the costs to Pennsylvania, the site of Trump's 2016 trade speech, as "extremely significant," totaling $2.7 billion, $2.4 billion of that due to the tariffs on Chinese goods.[15]

Beyond the cost to US businesses is the cost to Chinese firms. Of course, it's not up to the US president to protect Chinese exporters, which have inordinately benefited from state subsidies and preferential treatment in their own market. But Trump's advisors do not hesitate to advertise that the intent of Trump's trade war is to shrink the Chinese economy. In repeated conversations, Navarro and other Trump advisors bragged to me about how much China was suffering from the trade war. They also boasted of a more lasting change: how US and other foreign firms were moving their entire supply chains out of China and for good.

"Whether the supply chain leaves China or not depends on how China responds to the deal," Navarro told me.[16]

To China, this is a threat to its economic well-being. In effect, President Trump is demanding that China fundamentally change its economic model, or the United States will force the world to abandon it.

The upending of the US-China relationship is the element of Trump's foreign policy least likely to change when he leaves office. Despite all their differences, China may be the one issue that Republicans and Democrats have come to agree on. It is hard to find a politician of either party today who defends the old way of dealing with Beijing.

"You had an interesting merger of the Pelosi human rights democracy crowd with the economic nationalists coming together to say, 'Hey, these guys in China are a major problem,'" Bannon said.[17]

There is a confidence at the core of Trump's antagonistic approach to China. Despite the president's doom-and-gloom proclamations about the "rape" of the United States at the hands of Beijing, some Trump loyalists are actually contrarians on another aspect of the old approach to Beijing: China's seemingly unstoppable rise.

"China is a house of cards. The pandemic shows that it's a total house of cards," argues Bannon. "We're not a declining power."[18]

In the Trump administration's view, there are those in China who see it Trump's way: that China must change its economic model to survive.

"There [are] reformers like Liu He in China," said Navarro, citing China's lead trade negotiator and economic czar, "who understand that the Chinese model is likely to lead to an economic collapse at some point or at least stagnant growth and that China really needs to move to the next level.

"What they need to do is move to a more consumption-oriented economy and stop doing all this mercantilist stuff," he added. "They will be strong that way. So there's the reformers, but then there's also the hogs. The hogs—the mercantilist hogs—are those who believe the only way China succeeds is on the backs of everybody else. So that [internal] battle is going to fight itself out. And I think it bubbled to the surface last May."[19]

It was in May 2019 that President Trump and his advisors thought they had a deal. US negotiators, led by US trade representative Lighthizer and Treasury Secretary Steven Mnuchin, and Chinese negotiators, led by Vice Premier Liu He, had articulated the outlines of their agreement in a multipage document. But at the eleventh hour, China backed out. In the view of the US side, President Xi Jinping had balked, believing the deal forced the biggest concessions on China and undermined core Chinese interests.

According to Bannon, some Chinese leaders saw echoes of nineteenth-century colonialism in the agreement, harking all the way back to the deal Beijing had signed in 1842 ceding Hong Kong to Great Britain. This sense of historical victimization permeates Chinese leaders' view of their country's relations with the United States and the West. In their view, China's rise is simply restoring it to its

rightful place as world leader, a position the West usurped with a series of so-called unequal treaties and predatory conflicts.

"[Chinese leaders] sat there with Liu He and said, 'This is a port
treaty. This is Hong Kong. We're not doing this. In fact, we're not doing any of it. You got to go back and get something else. We will never
kowtow to the West again,'" Bannon said.[20]

What followed China's eleventh-hour rejection was months of
negotiations that showed little progress—in addition to continued
exchanges of tit-for-tat tariffs. President Trump gradually ratcheted
up tariffs on Beijing, while China continued to reduce purchases from
the United States. Trump, fearful of imposing further economic costs
on farmers in key swing states, pushed Congress to pass a series of
aid packages for affected farmers after China halted purchases of US
agricultural products in August.[21] But the election was getting closer
and the economic costs higher.

Inside the Trump administration, a fierce battle was taking place
between trade hawks, such as Navarro and Lighthizer, and more moderate administration officials, such as Steven Mnuchin, who were willing to accept a smaller deal now in order to avoid greater economic and
political damage. According to Bannon and other Trump administration officials involved, it was no friendly disagreement.

"The nastiest knife fights from the beginning have been on China
and trade and the economic war," said Bannon.[22]

In January 2020, that knife fight would claim a winner. The United
States and China reached a trade agreement, but one far short of the
comprehensive deal Trump had promised. Many of the most divisive
issues, including massive Chinese state subsidies to Chinese companies, remained off the table. China agreed to purchase some $200
billion worth of agricultural and other products, but trade experts
wondered what guarantee there was that Beijing would make those
purchases. Moreover, those promised purchases for the most part

simply replaced purchases China would have made regardless of any trade war.

More than one Trump advisor described the so-called phase one deal to me as a "capitulation." Beyond China's flimsy commitment to buy US farm products, some Trump advisors saw a more damaging dynamic. Far from righting the imbalance in US-China economic relations, the agreement, with its emphasis on agricultural purchases by Beijing, made the United States in effect a service economy, providing products and raw materials to China to fuel its own economic growth. The United States had effectively reaffirmed itself, one Trump advisor told me, as a "tributary nation" to the People's Republic of China.

China trade hawks saw other dangers in the deal. In the fine print were new provisions allowing US pension funds to purchase Chinese distressed debt. That was good for China, which has generated an enormous burden of non-performing loans, and for US financial institutions, which stood to profit from a business valued in the tens or even hundreds of billions of dollars. However, in the process, US banks would be taking the pension money of working Americans and investing it back into China. As one Trump advisor remarked to me, "It's an awful deal. The deplorables—they always get fucked."

Peter Navarro disputes that he and other China trade hawks lost out. "The enforcement mechanism itself is, as Bannon calls it, 'the judge, jury and executioner,'" he told me, referring to provisions cracking down on the sale by China of counterfeit US products. The agreement called for enhanced searches of shipments from China at US ports and better oversight of sales on e-commerce platforms such as Amazon.

"There's never been anything like this in a trade deal where we, America, have the ability to determine after ninety days whether the remedy is appropriate," he explained. "If it's not, we are allowed to take proportionate measures without China retaliating. Their only recourse is they leave the deal. If we can, in phase one, make a big dent on this [intellectual property] theft stuff, that's huge."

To make that "big dent," he said, Trump signed an executive order giving powers to Customs and Border Protection to conduct the searches of shipments from China.[23] Domestically, China took superficial steps to strengthen intellectual property protections and liberalize its investment regime in the ensuing months.[24]

"Out of that effort we've been able to develop a monitoring system with CBP," Navarro told me. "Once a month, we opened thousands of extra packages from China and Hong Kong. Look under the hood." Those new inspections, he said, have led to double-digit increases in the interception of counterfeit products as well as opioids and fentanyl, another priority of the president. "We've got a monitoring system in place now and if they don't reduce that over time, in a timely way, we're going to be able to take appropriate measures to deal with one of the worst things China does to us."

That is far from the kind of comprehensive agreement Navarro himself had called for, but in his view, it was valuable progress. "We're perfectly hedged," he pointed out. "If China honors the deal, we're in good shape. If they don't honor the deal, we got tariffs, which we've proven to be, certainly in the case of China, to be an optimal strategy."[25]

PHASE TWO?

In four years, Trump's "optimal strategy" had failed by Trump's own standards. The jobs he promised so grandiosely in 2016 to return to Pennsylvania had not returned. Average US economic growth, though strong, had not significantly exceeded the growth rate under President Obama. And the trade war had exacted a continuing price on US firms and consumers without delivering the comprehensive trade deal Trump had sought.

Trump's trade warriors continued to herald the president's ambitious vision of change—and his ability to deliver on that vision.

"I call on my profession to really rise to the occasion and get . . . into the twenty-first-century Trump model," Navarro told me[26]—the "Trump model" as a solution not just to the deficiencies of the US-China trading relationship but to all of the United States' trading relationships around the world.

Some current and former Trump administration officials are more skeptical. "The CCP [Chinese Communist Party] is never going to do phase two," Bannon said. "Liu He is a reformer. Liu He wanted this. At one time, he had guidance from Xi to try to put this together. He understands they can't keep the financial house of cards that they have, because they're going to collapse."[27]

The advent of the coronavirus may have permanently derailed the trade war as Trump's revolution in the US-China relationship. By the spring of 2020, the outbreak had pushed both US and Chinese economic growth into negative territory. US firms that could have withstood the costs of tariffs in good economic times were now breaking under the burden. Goldman Sachs was predicting zero or negative earnings growth for the biggest US companies. The stock market, Trump's favorite bellwether of his success, was in free fall. Quietly, some current and former Trump administration officials were conceding that tariffs, at least in the near term, may have to go.

Few foreign countries follow US politics more closely than does China. And in an election year, with a president who stakes his political fortunes on the strength of the US economy and stock market gains, Chinese officials sensed weakness. Trump was a weakened adversary in the trade war. A phase two deal became a nonstarter.

China's confidence, even as it grappled with a US assault on its entire economic model, is part of a decades-long growth in its own ambitions and self-belief. Just as Trump's approach to Beijing is based on his confidence in the United States, so is Beijing's approach to the United States. The fact is, Beijing sees Trump not as arresting the United States' decline but as accelerating it.

"What's striking is that if you look at what Xi Jinping has done and a lot of the sort of official commentary and so on, their vision for the timeline for when they might hit this status as a great power, superpower, however you want to put it, keeps coming closer, right?" former CIA senior China analyst Chris Johnson told Michael Morell on his *Intelligence Matters* podcast in November 2019. "So, we used to talk a lot about 2050 or even beyond that. Now, we talk about 2035, maybe even 2025. You see a lot more of that type of discussion.

". . . The global financial crisis, of course, the rise of Donald Trump, the withdrawal from alliance and these sorts of things, you know, they see that all as self-affirmatory of the judgment that they have already made."[28]

This is one irony of US-China relations under Trump: what Trump sees as strengthening the United States, China sees as weakening it. Trump's attacks on US elections as illegitimate and US institutions as corrupt amplify Chinese government attacks on the US political system. This serves one of Beijing's primary objectives: to prove to its people that the Chinese system of government is superior to that of the United States and therefore to discourage Chinese citizens from dreaming of replacing China's authoritarian system with American-style democracy.

Outside of domestic politics, Trump's assault on alliances, including NATO but particularly its partnerships with Japan and South Korea, strengthened China's hand in the region. A South Korea or a Japan without unwavering US support is a weaker adversary for China. Trump's abandonment of the TPP trade agreement—one of his first acts as president—was a gift to Beijing, breaking up a formidable coalition of Asia's most prosperous economies along with the United States—a union that would have proven particularly useful in shaping the rules of the road in terms of regional trade and confronting China's unfair trade practices.

★ ★ ★

THE CORONAVIRUS OUTBREAK THREATENED TO DISRUPT THE BEST-laid plans of both Xi and Trump. However, given widespread Democratic support, it's difficult to see a Democratic president reversing Trump's confronting of China. In fact, the fundamental change in the relationship Trump unleashed may be his most lasting foreign policy legacy.

Some of his advisors fear the consequences will extend beyond the two countries' economic relationship, worrying in the extreme that "decoupling" between the United States and China will accelerate an eventual military confrontation. Casual students of history are familiar with the "Thucydides Trap," a phrase coined by the Harvard historian Graham Allison to describe what happens when a rising power sizes up against an existing power. It is based on the Greek historian Thucydides' telling of the conflict between Athens and Sparta. Thucydides' line remains meaningful today: "What made war inevitable was the growth of Athenian power and the fear which this caused in Sparta." Substitute an increasingly powerful China for Athens and a fearful US for Sparta and the message is clear.

"Within five years, we'll be in a shooting war," warned Bannon.[29]

This is not an outlier prediction among some of the more aggressive China hawks around Trump: that the natural evolution of the two nations' competition leads to war. But this is a place where the president and those advisors starkly differ. As Bannon and others have noted, Trump is, in fact, deeply averse to war. From demonizing Beijing on trade to placing sole blame on China for the coronavirus, Trump unleashed dangers of historic proportions.

THE ANSWER

President Trump successfully and perhaps irreversibly upended the relationship between the world's two largest economies, and he dispensed with naive hopes that time and encouragement would alter China's behavior. In doing so, he promised that these changes would both punish China and benefit the United States. The second half of that equation has proven harder to deliver on. The minimalist agreement Trump branded a "phase one" trade deal featured commitments without enforcement. And the coronavirus pandemic has further sapped the US economy's ability to withstand a continuing trade war. Four years of confronting China have left the United States with uneven economic benefits and growing dangers of a broader conflict.

As with other national security priorities, Trump undertook an aggressive strategy without having first developed a clear endgame.

6

"Fire and Fury":
North Korea,
Part One

COULD THE "MADMAN" MOVE KIM?

Confronting and containing North Korea has been a national security white whale for successive US presidents of both parties. They have tried economic sanctions, military pressure, and multilateral negotiations. Each has made agreements or taken steps toward agreements with the North Korean regime, claimed progress, and yet ultimately ended up deceived and disappointed.

When President Trump was elected, Barack Obama advised him that North Korea would be his most pressing national security challenge. US intelligence had by then assessed that North Korea was close to achieving its goal of becoming a nuclear power. Though it had not yet successfully tested an ICBM, senior US intelligence officials told me they believed the United States had to assume that

Pyongyang had that capability, meaning US leaders had to assume the US homeland was vulnerable to a North Korean nuclear strike. It was an alarming new reality—and one that those successive US presidents had all vowed never to allow.

Heeding Obama's warning, President Trump made North Korea an early focus of his foreign policy. He introduced a "maximum-pressure" campaign of economic sanctions intended to bring the North Korean regime to its knees and force it to the negotiating table. At the same time, he directed a withering array of rhetorical threats at North Korea and its leader, Kim Jong Un, including not-so-veiled references to the United States' nuclear superiority. The "madman" was raising the stakes.

Would "fire and fury" bring North Korea to the negotiating table? Or could it bring the two sides to the brink of war?

President Trump entered office faced with a North Korea that was steadily expanding its nuclear and ballistic missile capabilities. For decades, successive US presidents had vowed never to allow a nuclear North Korea. Now, that grave prospect had, for all intents and purposes, become a reality. Meanwhile, Washington and Pyongyang were locked in a diplomatic impasse.

Joseph Yun served as US special representative for North Korea policy from October 2016 to February 2018, making him one of the rare officials who served both Presidents Obama and Trump in a senior position and worked on an issue central to Trump's focus.

"The US and North Korea really had nothing to do with each other," he told me. "And by the time I came in, it was becoming obvious that the Obama administration was very worried about the nuclear situation."

I first met Yun during my service as chief of staff to the US ambassador to China from 2011 to 2013, when he was principal deputy assistant secretary for East Asian and Pacific affairs. That was in the midst of President Obama's "pivot" toward Asia, a policy intended to rebalance US resources and focus away from the wars in the Middle East to Asia, an approach that mirrored Donald Trump's on many levels.

When he began serving in that crucial role, "strategic patience" remained US policy toward North Korea. In theory, the United States would apply pressure over time to achieve concessions, including restrictions on North Korea's nuclear and weapons programs. In practice, there was no such progress and almost no engagement. In fact, during his first four months as special representative under President Obama, Yun did not meet with his North Korean counterparts once.

"We were in the middle of a number of missile launches, and nothing seemed to work," he continued. "We had close coordination with Japan, South Korea, and China, but really, they were at a loss, too. All things considered, you would have to say that Trump inherited a very poor account."[1]

"MAXIMUM PRESSURE"

President Trump made his approach to North Korea clear to his cabinet from the moment he arrived: the United States would ratchet up economic sanctions on the regime immediately and significantly with the eventual goal of forcing North Korean leaders to the negotiating table. Crucial to the policy was enlisting China's support in enforcing the sanctions. North Korea depends on China for food, fuel, and, when necessary, the ability to get around international sanctions. But this time, China was largely on board with expanding sanctions.

Trump's "maximum-pressure" campaign was remarkably similar to President Obama's aggressive sanctions on Iran in the years prior to the 2015 nuclear agreement. I was a diplomat based in China at the height of the campaign and observed concerted efforts by US diplomats to get China on board for the tightened sanctions. The effort was an almost daily struggle. China depends on oil imports and is extremely sensitive to any impediment to its economic growth. China's participation, by greatly reducing its purchases of Iranian oil, further diminished Iran's already shrunken international market for oil. That pressure had helped push Tehran to the negotiating table over its nuclear program. Trump's approach to North Korea followed a similar strategy.

"As soon as the Trump administration came in," Yun told me, "they did focus quite sharply on North Korea. We had a number of NSC sessions, a lot of road maps, a lot of what to do. It became obvious to me that [the president] really wanted, and the administration wanted, maximum pressure."[2]

The pressure didn't end there. Trump's expanded sanctions were accompanied by an aggressive public messaging campaign, often delivered on Trump's favorite messaging platform: Twitter. And whether on social media or when speaking to reporters, his public comments could be frightening.

On August 8, 2017, speaking to reporters at his golf resort in Bedminster, New Jersey, Trump said, "North Korea best not make any more threats to the United States." Then he delivered what would become a signature line: "They will be met with *fire and fury* like the world has never seen." (Author's italics.)[3]

That was Trump putting his own "madman theory" into action, though not channeled through his secretary of state in private but delivered directly from his own mouth in public.

Within hours, Pyongyang responded with a threat of its own, declaring that it was exploring an "operational plan" to launch missiles against the US territory of Guam, "to send a serious warning signal to the US."[4]

The next day, Trump repeated his "fire and fury" threat, adding, "If anything, maybe that statement wasn't tough enough."

On September 17, 2017, Trump coined another signature phrase, this one aimed at the North Korean leader himself, dubbing Kim Jong Un "Rocket Man." "I spoke with President Moon of South Korea last night," he tweeted. "Asked him how Rocket Man is doing. Long gas lines forming in North Korea. Too bad!"

Two days later, Trump took his rhetorical attacks to the world stage. At the UN General Assembly in New York, the president alarmed world leaders by repeating his "Rocket Man" attack line and seeming to say that military conflict would be fatal for Kim.

"Rocket Man is on a suicide mission for himself," he said in a fiery speech at UN Headquarters.[5]

SECRET DIPLOMACY

Behind the public threats, however, Trump was making a private push for diplomacy. He made clear to his advisors, including Yun, that he was aiming for something new and dramatic: a face-to-face meeting with the North Korean leader.

"He wanted to have a role. He was open, even then, from the beginning, to doing some deal, or meeting with Kim Jong Un," Yun recalled. "I think he felt he could move the dial."[6]

Sue Mi Terry, a veteran of both the Bush and Obama administrations, understood the Trump administration's interest in experimenting with an entirely new tack. "I'm sympathetic to the argument that, with North Korea, we had tried everything else," she told me. "Working-level bilateral agreements, multilateral agreements, six-party talks about everything from Clinton on. So I can understand the argument that 'Hey, why don't we try it at the highest level?'"[7]

In any other administration, attempting to execute such a precarious balance between threats and diplomacy would follow an intense policy-making process. This would normally take place through the National Security Council with the consultation of other relevant departments, including the State Department, the Pentagon, and US intelligence agencies, as well as coordination with US allies, especially the ones forever on the front lines of the North Korean conflict, Japan and South Korea. Each would assess the costs and benefits, North Korea's current posture and openness to dialogue, and the relative chances of success.

From early on, however, Trump's North Korea strategy was more of a gut enterprise. As with virtually all his national security priorities, the policy was Trump himself.

Ambassador Yun was the special representative for North Korea policy—by title and position the number one interlocutor between Washington and Pyongyang. However, he saw no communication or coordination between the State Department and the White House. "The coordination between [Secretary of State] Tillerson and the NSC was so poor that we could never even get together to even consider doing such a thing," he told me. "There was nobody coordinating."

Something else was becoming clear to his advisors: Trump wanted that face-to-face meeting with Kim but without preconditions. "People thought that was a crazy idea," Yun said.[8]

Unlike Nixon with China, Trump had no Kissinger as a voice in his ear. Over time, the president was losing confidence in his secretary of state. Tillerson, unlike many of Trump's senior advisors, was willing to question the president where and when others would not. And with this president, second-guessing him does not engender job security. That led Trump to rely more on then CIA director Mike Pompeo for leadership and advice on North Korea, a role diplomats say he accepted without hesitation.

Nearly seven thousand miles away, in Pyongyang, North Korea's leaders didn't see the idea of a Trump-Kim summit as crazy. Or at least they saw an opportunity. From the moment of Trump's election, US diplomats assigned to the North Korean issue began to notice a change in their North Korean counterparts. Ambassador Yun, who had become almost resigned to the end of dialogue with the North Koreans, discovered a newfound interest among them in talking again.

"They did not want to talk to me at all while I was in the Obama administration, but as soon as the election was over, they wanted to talk to me," he told me. "They were suffering under the sanctions. They wanted better relations, and they wanted to test out the Trump administration."

Keen observers of US politics—though not always skilled ones—

the North Koreans saw a change maker in Trump, who might ultimately play to their advantage.

"They saw change, but also they saw an opportunity," Yun said.
"They felt 'Trump is unpredictable, and so maybe he's not going to be
the same old, same old.' So I do think they saw an opportunity."[9]

FIRST SETBACK:
THE KIM JONG NAM ASSASSINATION

Plans for Yun's first meeting with his North Korean diplomats pro-
ceeded very quickly. In February 2017, less than a month after Trump's
inauguration, Yun received permission from Secretary of State Rex
Tillerson—and ultimately President Trump—to meet with North
Korean diplomats in New York. It would be his first meeting with
his North Korean counterparts since he had been appointed special
representative for North Korea policy. The potential stakes were high.
Reeling under the sanctions, how much would North Korea be willing
to give up in return for sanctions relief?

Within days of the planned meeting, those high hopes were
crushed. On February 13, 2017, Kim Jong Nam, half brother to the
North Korean leader via their common father, Kim Jong Il, was attacked in Kuala Lumpur International Airport. Kim had been exiled
from North Korea for years, suspected by his half brother of being not only a competitor for power but also a spy for Washington.
That day, he was walking through the airport's Terminal 2 to board
a flight to his adoptive home in the Macau Special Administrative
Region.

Security camera footage from the airport showed two women approaching him, one coming from behind and rubbing something on
his face. The two women then quickly washed their hands in an airport
bathroom and fled. Alarmed, Kim ran to the airport's medical clinic to

seek help. He collapsed shortly after and died twenty minutes later in an ambulance.

Though the immediate cause of death was suffocation, Malaysian investigators would later identify the murder weapon as VX, one of the deadliest nerve agents ever manufactured—so powerful that the United Nations classifies it as a weapon of mass destruction.[10]

North Korea—specifically, Kim Jong Un himself—came under immediate suspicion among close observers of North Korean affairs.

"That's his half brother," noted Sue Mi Terry, who previously served as a CIA analyst on North Korea. "You cannot do something like that without Kim's order."[11]

Kim Jong Un viewed his half brother as a direct competitor to the throne. As the elder son of the late North Korean leader Kim Jong Il, Kim Jong Nam was, by right, in line ahead of Kim Jong Un. The North Korean leader would be an immediate beneficiary of his half brother's "removal."

"Kim Jong Nam was the one and only person who can really legitimately threaten Kim's rule," said Terry.

Adding to his precarious position, Kim Jong Nam had himself made critical comments in public about the North Korean leadership.

"When Kim Jong Nam gave an interview with the Japanese media criticizing Kim Jong Un and [North Korea's] dynastic succession, I just thought his fate was sealed then," Terry said.[12]

US intelligence soon assessed that Kim had been assassinated by North Korea, under orders from Kim Jong Un himself. The brutal assassination of a private citizen on foreign soil alarmed the international community. Special Representative Yun's planned meeting in New York was canceled.

"When they killed [Kim Jong Nam] in Kuala Lumpur, that visit was off," he told me with almost sarcastic understatement. "But then we continued our contacts, and they continued to want to meet with me."[13]

SECOND SETBACK: OTTO WARMBIER

Three months later, the talks were on again, this time slated for Oslo, Norway. Given the murder of Kim Jong Nam and the slew of missile tests, Yun told the North Koreans that they needed to make a sign of good faith—and quickly. "I told them that without getting the US prisoners out, that I would find it very difficult to do anything else for them," he told me.[14]

Among the Americans detained in North Korea at the time was a twenty-two-year-old University of Virginia student, Otto Warmbier. Warmbier had been detained in January 2016, accused of attempting to steal a North Korean political banner from his hotel in Pyongyang. The next month, he was paraded in front of North Korean state media for an absurd show trial. His appearance in court included a dramatic and tearful confession. In a videotape obtained from North Korea exclusively by my CNN colleague Will Ripley, Warmbier, shouting through tears, declared, "I entirely beg you, the people and government of the DPRK, for your forgiveness. Please, I have made the worst mistake of my life."

The confession was certainly coerced, his melodramatic performance a possible attempt to satisfy a North Korean government that has always conditioned the release of foreign prisoners on public admissions of guilt.

Looking to the heavens, his hands together, Warmbier said, "If you are there, please save this poor and innocent scapegoat."[15]

Despite the performance, Warmbier was sentenced to fifteen years in prison and hard labor. For Joseph Yun, Warmbier's release was a priority from the moment he took the job as special representative. He communicated frequently with Warmbier's parents, Fred and Cindy, and met with them in person. "They were distraught and frustrated," Yun told me.

Yun did his best to share as much information as he could with the Warmbiers. But one thing Yun had no information on was Otto's condition. The US government at the time had no reason to believe his health was in danger. Most previous US detainees had eventually left the country in good health.

"At that time, my North Korean interlocutors, who are all in the Ministry of Foreign Affairs, did not know Otto was that sick," he told me, his voice growing somber at the memories of what soon followed. "And so we agreed to meet again, about two or three weeks later, to talk again about how to get the prisoners out."

Inside prison, Warmbier's condition had taken a dramatic turn for the worse. When Yun met the next time with the North Koreans, they returned with shocking news. "They came back to me and said Otto was very sick, that he was in a virtual coma," Yun said. "We had had no idea."

The news was debilitating to Yun. Pressed by Yun, his North Korean contacts shared a confusing story of how the healthy young man had suddenly fallen into a coma, saying his health had declined suddenly and without warning the same day as his February trial. "According to them," Yun recalled, "on the day the trial finished—I mean, it was a one-day trial, from beginning to end—he was in a very agitated state."

His "agitated state," they claimed, had begun as he was being moved from the court to prison. That night, according to the North Koreans, he had a dinner of pork and spinach and had then been given a sedative to calm him down.

"When they checked back within two or three hours," Yun says they explained, "they found him in a vegetative state."

Yun immediately notified Secretary Tillerson, who asked him to travel to North Korea in person as soon as possible. After making preparations, including mobilizing an elite medical team to join him,

Yun contacted his North Korean counterparts. "I asked them, 'Can I come?'" he recalled. "They said I could come, and I could see Otto, but they would not release him."

Yun's immediate priority was to get onto the ground to assess Otto's health and then bring him home. The North Koreans, however, were eager to extract value from their foreign hostage, even as his life hung in the balance.

"To get him released," Yun recalled, "I had to agree to a couple of things: one, that I would pay $2 million in health care expenses, and two, that we would not—the American government would not—use Otto to criticize the North Korean government."

Ambassador Yun signed the agreements, though President Trump would later say the United States paid "no money" to North Korea to allow Warmbier's release.

"Of course I signed those agreements," he told me. "And then we came back, and Otto died about five days later. What I thought would be a confidence-building measure, more than anything else, made the situation more tense."[16]

More than two years later, I asked Yun if he or the US government knew what really happened to Warmbier.

"I don't think he was tortured, and the [American] doctor who went with me seemed to agree, that he was quite well taken care of physically, considering he was in a vegetative state," Yun told me. "The doctor felt that it could have been bad medicine. The sedative could have been bad."[17]

That might help explain why—in February 2019, at his second summit with Kim Jong Un in Hanoi—President Trump left open the possibility that Kim Jong Un had not intended to harm Warmbier.

"There is plausibility that it was an accident," Yun said. "There is plausibility to that, but of course, it is their fault that he was detained in the first place and got the ridiculous fifteen-year hard-labor sentence. So there's nothing that would abrogate North Korean responsibility."[18]

A more careful president might have cited lingering doubts about the cause, while still holding Pyongyang responsible for Warmbier's death. Instead, Trump latched on to the uncertainty to once again profess confidence in his "friend," Kim Jong Un.

For North Korea, in the tense summer of 2017, the bottom line remained the same. Twice in four months, the United States and North Korea had reached the doorstep of progress only to retreat, driven back by brazen acts by the North Korean regime.

"THIS IS HOW WAR STARTS"

As the State Department, Department of Defense, and National Security Council wrestled with how to balance the president's sudden interest in holding a historic summit with the North Korean leader with his threats of military action, the relationship between the two nations entered a dire period. In both Washington and Seoul, there was grave concern about the mounting danger of military conflict.

On September 3, 2017, North Korea conducted its sixth and largest nuclear test. Pyongyang claimed for the first time to have detonated a hydrogen or thermonuclear bomb, a weapon an order of magnitude larger than those it had previously tested. Photographs by US surveillance satellites showed landslides and other evidence of a massive explosion, to a far greater degree than those generated by earlier nuclear tests. Various estimates put the weapon's explosive yield at or above 250 kilotons, ten times as large as any previous North Korean nuclear test and more than sixteen times as large as the atomic bomb dropped on Hiroshima in 1945.

North Korea was also demonstrating progress in its ballistic missile program. Over a tense ten-month period, it fired twenty-three missiles in sixteen separate tests. Weeks before the nuclear test, it had conducted its first successful test of an intercontinental ballistic missile, or ICBM, which it claimed could reach "anywhere in the world."[19] In November, it tested an ICBM once again. Pyongyang now had a plausible capability of striking the US mainland with a nuclear weapon.

"The worst was around September, October, November of 2017, when they did their last nuclear test and the ICBM test," Ambassador Yun told me. "It became very dark."[20]

President Obama's warning to Trump during the transition was bearing itself out.

President Trump's public threats against the North were not all bluster. Inside the Defense Department and the National Security Council, there were private discussions of military options for North Korea. Trump administration officials began raising the seemingly tantalizing possibility of a limited military strike that could impose costs for North Korean provocations without leading to all-out war. That course came to be known glibly as a "bloody-nose strike."

No military official I spoke to at the time believed that a bloody-nose strike was realistic. What the United States viewed as a limited strike might very likely be viewed by North Korea as the first salvo of a war intended to destroy the regime. Moreover, given Seoul's proximity to the North Korean border and the enormous array of artillery pieces and rocket launchers aimed at the South Korean capital, the human costs of even a limited exchange would be devastating. One US military official briefed on the intelligence assessments of a "limited" conflict told me the estimated death toll rose to the tens of thousands.

The first days of January 2018 would prove even darker. On January 2, President Trump delivered another alarming public threat to Kim. In a tweet that was colorful even by his own standards, Trump wrote, "North Korean Leader Kim Jong Un just stated that the 'Nuclear Button is on his desk at all times.' Will someone from his depleted and food starved regime please inform him that I too have a Nuclear Button, but it is a much bigger & more powerful one than his, and my button works!"

Were the United States and North Korea hurtling toward war? Eleven days later, an entirely unplanned event made that prospect feel alarmingly close. On January 13, 2018, a short but alarming text message went out across the state of Hawaii. In all caps, the message announced, "BALLISTIC MISSILE THREAT INBOUND TO HAWAII. SEEK IMMEDIATE SHELTER. THIS IS NOT A DRILL."[21] Television and radio stations interrupted their broadcasts with the same message. Those fourteen words sent thousands of residents and vacationers into a panic.

Hawaii had been well aware of the growing tensions between the United States and North Korea. In the past, Pyongyang had threatened Hawaii and the "U.S. imperialist aggressor troops" based there.[22] In the weeks leading up to the alert, Hawaii officials had been carefully preparing residents and visitors for how to respond, airing ads encouraging them to "get inside, stay inside" in the event of an attack. State authorities had tested a Cold War–era warning siren for the first time in decades and set up the emergency text alert system.[23]

That frightening January 13 text warning would turn out to have been a mistake. State officials would later explain that an employee had "pushed the wrong button." The Hawaii Emergency Management Agency tweeted out a correction within minutes. "NO missile threat to Hawaii," the tweet read. However, it would take thirty-eight minutes for authorities to send a second text message to all of the islands' residents confirming the false alarm.[24]

The false alarm exposed severe deficiencies in Hawaii's public alert system, leading Hawaii's governor to promise an overhaul. But it also raised broader questions about the entire country's ability to warn the public quickly and accurately in the event of a real attack.

When the incoming missile alert rocked the state of Hawaii, President Trump was on a golf course in Florida, nearly five thousand miles away. Riding behind him in a golf cart were two staffers who never left his side: a member of the national security staff and a military aide carrying the so-called nuclear football, the briefcase containing a mobile command system that allows the president to launch a nuclear attack when in transit.

The national security staffer received a call from the Situation Room in the White House with news that something had triggered Hawaii's missile warning system and that the entire state was now on alert. The staffer told me he still remembers the grave look on the military aide's face. A sobering thought occurred to him: he might be about to witness the first-ever use of that mobile missile launch system.

Receiving the news, this staffer said, Trump was angry. He wanted to know why the military did not yet know if this was a real incoming missile, or a false alarm. His anger was understandable. If the United States didn't know for sure that a missile was on its way, how could he, the president, decide how to respond? Trump and his golfing entourage left the course immediately and returned to the clubhouse. By then, his staff had received another call informing them that the missile warning was a false alarm. The frustrated but relieved President Trump turned on Fox News to watch its coverage.

US officials were not the only ones who took sober note of the false alarm. According to Ambassador Yun, Hawaii's experience sparked deep fears in Pyongyang. "I think they got a real scare when there was a false alarm of a missile going to Hawaii," he said. "North Koreans realized that if it happened to them, they don't have a backup system, to tell quickly whether it was a false alarm or not."

And if neither the United States nor North Korea had a reliable means to detect an impending attack and alert their public to it, what were the chances one or both countries might make a fatal error? Another false alarm could spark a real war.

"I mean, this is how war starts, not because Trump gets up one morning and presses a button but because of accidents," Yun said.[25]

That was where the United States stood during that nervous winter: with two nuclear-armed powers fearing they were on a path to war and with a president still convinced that he alone could balance his public threats of military action with his private desire for groundbreaking presidential diplomacy.

SOUTH KOREA STEPS IN

No one was more concerned about a march toward war than South Korea. With its capital, the hub of its world-class economy, situated just thirty miles from the North Korean border, even a limited conflict carried the prospect of devastating human and economic losses. Thousands of US soldiers and private citizens were also at risk. An exchange limited to conventional weapons or conventional weapons coupled with chemical weapons (of which the North has vast stockpiles) carried a potential death toll in the tens of thousands.

"There is no question that the South Koreans very much have the goal of denuclearizing North Korea, but their higher priority is no war, you know?" said Ambassador Yun.

South Korean leaders now had a new variable to add to a deadly serious calculus: Donald Trump. His incendiary public threats of "fire and fury" and casual consideration of a "bloody-nose" military strike few believed to be realistic were too much for the South Korean government. "That's really when the South Koreans stepped in," Yun recalled.

In January 2018, Seoul sent a delegation to Washington to inform Trump that North Korea was ready to talk—and not just to restart limited nuclear negotiations but to discuss full denuclearization. "They said North Korea would agree to denuclearize and that they wanted to meet Trump," Yun said. "And so Trump agreed."[26]

What's remarkable is that South Korea, the United States' ally, and North Korea were coordinating Kim's outreach to Trump, according to US officials involved. Their intention was drawing Trump to the negotiating table while exaggerating expectations of what North Korea was willing to give up.

"They were in cahoots," one former Trump administration official told me. "I think Kim was leading Trump on, as, most likely, were the South Koreans."

The immediate result was positive: the United States and North Korea retreated from the precipice of war. In the short term, that served everyone's interests. However, in the medium and longer term, Pyongyang and Seoul created an illusion of denuclearization that was almost certainly not going to become a reality. To some degree, Trump was being played by both the ally and the adversary.

A CHANGE IN TONE

Around the same time, the North Korean leader was beginning to strike a more conciliatory public tone. In his annual New Year's speech, Kim expressed both confidence in his country's nuclear progress—including his infamous reference to his nuclear launch button being "always on the desk in my office"—and openness to a change in direction with South Korea. Appearing in a Western-style suit and tie rather than his favored collarless traditional tunic, Kim said he would send a North Korean delegation to the upcoming Winter Olympics, to be hosted by South Korea in Pyeongchang in February.

Weeks earlier, South Korean president Moon Jae In had issued a public invitation to the North, saying, "I hope that North Korea will also participate, which will provide a very good opportunity for inter-Korean peace and reconciliation."[27] Kim was now wishing the South a successful Olympics.[28]

Had Trump's "maximum-pressure" campaign forced Kim's change of heart? Or was the difference the North's nuclear progress?

President Trump and his allies would claim sole responsibility for bringing North Korea to heel. But other North Korea watchers saw a different dynamic. With its hydrogen bomb test in September 2017, North Korea had proven its mastery of nuclear weapons. With its ICBM tests, it had further proven its capability to deliver nuclear warheads to targets near and far. Kim Jong Un had, in effect, achieved the goal his father and grandfather had dreamed of for decades but never realized: establishing North Korea as a nuclear power.

"I myself tend to believe that North Koreans were operating in their time schedule," Ambassador Yun said, "which is they had shown nuclear capacity through the September nuclear test. They had shown ICBM capability with their last ICBM test in November, and I think they felt the time was right. They were operating on their own schedule, and certainly, sanctions by themselves were not really going to bring them down."[29]

Sue Mi Terry believes that Trump and Kim misread each other. Trump believed that his "maximum-pressure" campaign had given him leverage, almost singlehandedly moving Kim. Kim believed that progress in North Korea's nuclear program had given him leverage, almost singlehandedly moving Trump. "They misjudged each other," she said. "Trump thinks it's all maximum pressure that brought Kim Jong Un to the table. The fact that North Korea got its nuclear program about ninety to ninety-five percent completed made Kim think that he had leverage, if he sat down with the United States."[30]

Regardless, the conflict between the two nuclear powers—one superpower and one upstart—was now moving to the negotiating table.

THE ANSWER

At the end of his first year in office, Trump's "fire and fury" gamble appeared to have paid off. The United States and North Korea had marched disturbingly close to the brink of military conflict but retreated safely and subsequently embarked on a path to negotiation. Members of Trump's own negotiating team questioned whether it was Trump's threats and "maximum-pressure" campaign or North Korea's satisfaction with its nuclear progress that had brought Pyongyang to the negotiating table. But the end result was the same.

The two sides, with the support of the United States' ally South Korea, were laying the groundwork for unprecedented talks between their two leaders and hopes at least of progress toward peace.

7

"Falling in Love": North Korea, Part Two

THE QUESTION

WHO PLAYED WHOM?

One year into his term, President Trump reversed course with North Korea, exchanging "fire and fury" for summit diplomacy with Kim Jong Un. It was a novel and risky approach to a defining test of his foreign policy. Normally, such a summit would follow lengthy negotiations at the working level. Summits are where agreements are signed, not negotiated. And normally, each party would demand concessions to match its own. But Trump is not a normal president, and neither were those negotiations.

Would Trump charm Kim into recalculating his country's core interests? Or would it work the other way around? Would Kim play Trump?

Beginning in 2018, a geopolitical melodrama played out between the US president and one of the world's most notorious dictators. Covering the story for CNN, I had a front-row seat for all three acts: in Singapore, in Hanoi, and then in the demilitarized zone on the North and South Korean border. Those were enormous stories, carrying the hope, at least, of redefining one of the most precarious and dangerous relationships in the world. As with every other national security challenge, however, Trump's approach was built less on a formal national security strategy and process than on his gut feelings and his personal relationship with the leader of the other party. Could Trump singlehandedly move Kim, as he hoped to do with Putin, Xi, Erdoğan, Supreme Leader Ali Khamenei of Iran, and others?

ACT ONE: SINGAPORE

The first meeting was meant to be a table setter—a chance to build the relationship between Kim and Trump, who insisted he could engineer an agreement through sheer force of personality and the "art of the deal."

Yet at that crucial moment, the two sides had not even agreed on what exactly was under negotiation. The United States had set the lofty goal of North Korea's "complete, verifiable and irreversible denuclearization." To the United States, that meant that North Korea would dismantle its nuclear facilities to the extent that those facilities could not be reactivated if North Korea ever reneged on a deal. To verify its compliance, any agreement would have to allow regular inspections of those dismantled facilities. Oddly enough, that had been the exact standard contained in the 2015 nuclear agreement with Iran, from which President Trump had withdrawn in May 2018, just one month before the Singapore summit.

To North Korea, denuclearization applies not just to itself but to the entire peninsula. That is, it would apply not only to Pyongyang but to South Korea and to US forces deployed in the South. The United States has not stationed nuclear weapons in the country since 1992, but Kim sees the entire US deployment as a nuclear threat. So any agreement on denuclearization would require both the dismantling of its program and the removal of all US forces.[1]

Also still undefined was the extent of North Korea's nuclear program. Normally, before such talks, North Korea would be expected to deliver an accounting of its nuclear weapons and facilities, to then define what and how much it would be willing to give up. The United States would have to do no such accounting.

Trump and Kim would get their photo op in Singapore, shaking hands with awkward smiles in front of an array of perfectly ironed US and North Korean flags, but the summit would settle none of the outstanding issues. And in their joint statement, North Korea seemed to have gotten exactly the language it wanted: "Chairman Kim Jong Un reaffirmed his firm and unwavering commitment to complete denuclearization *of the Korean Peninsula.*" (Author's italics.)[2]

In the end, this first face-to-face meeting, though unprecedented, had delivered no concrete agreement or concessions, no accounting of North Korean weapons, no road map to peace.

Diplomacy, rather than war, was progress in its own right. Only nine months before the Singapore summit, President Trump had stood at the UN General Assembly and shocked world leaders by threatening war with North Korea, while dismissing Kim in demeaning terms as "Rocket Man":

The United States has great strength and patience, but if it is forced to defend itself or its allies, we will have no choice but to totally destroy North Korea. Rocket Man is on a suicide mission for himself and for his regime. The United States is ready, willing and able, but hopefully this will not be necessary. That's what the United Nations is all about; that's what the United Nations is for. Let's see how they do.[3]

Contrast Trump's threat to "totally destroy" North Korea with his comments weeks after the Singapore summit, when he explained his new relationship with the North Korean leader to rallygoers in West Virginia this way: "I was really being tough—and so was he. And we would go back and forth. And then we fell in love, okay?" Trump told the audience, who laughed and cheered in response. "No, really—he wrote me beautiful letters, and they're great letters."[4]

A summit between the US and North Korean leaders less than a year after the UN General Assembly was a remarkable turn of events. However, the personal goodwill—the budding "love" affair between Trump and Kim—would have value only if that goodwill delivered concrete progress. Would the talks themselves become the aim of the talks?

ACT TWO: HANOI

Donald Trump's February 2019 summit in Hanoi with Kim Jong Un— his second face-to-face meeting with the North Korean dictator— appeared hobbled before the US president even landed in Vietnam. His secretary of state, Mike Pompeo, had arrived earlier, expecting to meet with the top North Korean negotiator, Vice Chairman of the Central Committee of the Workers' Party of Korea Kim Yong Chol, before the leaders' arrival. After weeks of working-level talks had yielded less progress than the United States had hoped for, Pompeo wanted to gauge North Korea's willingness to make concrete progress when Kim Jong Un and Donald Trump met. But Kim Yong Chol, ever the dour negotiator, had refused. Pompeo waited several hours into the night, hoping that the North Korean vice chairman would change his mind and growing increasingly frustrated. It was a demeaning snub for Secretary Pompeo and, it turned out, a harbinger of disappointing things to come.

North Korean negotiators had played this game before. Like Russian president Vladimir Putin, North Korean officials reveled in keeping their US counterparts waiting. It seemed to be a transparent power play to demonstrate who had the upper hand.

North Korea's hardball tactics contrasted with the Trump administration's more accommodating posture entering the talks. In the days leading up to the Hanoi summit, the Trump administration weighed softening US demands to help ease the way to some sort of an agreement. In particular, US negotiators considered dropping the US demand that North Korea provide a full accounting of its nuclear weapons and missile program as a prerequisite for any US concessions. The United States had been pressing North Korea since the summit in Singapore to give a full accounting of its weapons programs, to no avail. That failure made any potential agreement unusual; such an accounting was normally the first step in any such negotiations. In the simplest terms, if one side didn't know exactly what weapons the other side held, how could it gauge the value of what the other side was giving up?

More broadly, US intelligence had assessed that North Korea would never give up its nuclear program. The Defense Intelligence Agency had advised the Trump administration that Kim Jong Un had no intention of submitting to full denuclearization.[5] In the view of the North, nuclear weapons were essential to its survival. But this was intelligence that the president either did not or was not willing to believe, a pattern he would replicate with other intelligence assessments, most notably on Russian interference in the 2016 election.

Behind the scenes, some more cautious US officials were tempering expectations. Leading up to the leaders' summit, working-level talks between US and North Korean negotiators had yielded little progress. North Korean officials even threatened to cancel the summit altogether, a development that would have been deeply embarrassing for President Trump.

Hanoi was a remarkable setting for the summit. The leader of the free world was meeting with the leader of a hostile nation without preconditions for a second time, and doing so close to the other's turf, traveling from the United States all the way to East Asia and to Vietnam, which, like North Korea, is a Communist country, at least in name. Trump was again abandoning one of the ground rules of diplomacy: *Always meet on neutral ground.*

The city of Hanoi was relishing the attention. Streets were decked out with banners commemorating the visit. Local vendors were doing good business in Trump-Kim portraits and T-shirts. Trump himself was hoping for the United States to cash in itself on the visit to Vietnam. With great fanfare, he announced that Vietnam had promised to purchase more than $20 billion worth of Boeing jets and technology.

"We are going to be signing some very big trade deals," the president said of Vietnam after his bilateral meeting with Vietnamese president Nguyen Phu Trong. He claimed that Vietnam would be "buying a lot of different products from the United States . . . which we appreciate."[6]

Two days after the Pompeo snub, North Korean negotiators abruptly reversed course. In a scene described to me and my CNN colleagues by multiple US officials, as the talks were coming to a close, a North Korean official rushed over to the US delegation. North Korea's first vice minister of foreign affairs, Choe Son Hui, brought the US team a message from Kim Jong Un himself. Contained in the message was a last-ditch proposal—a "Hail Mary," as one official described it to me—for some US sanctions relief in return for the dismantling of the Yongbyon nuclear complex.

At issue throughout the talks had been a shared definition of what exactly comprised the sprawling Yongbyon nuclear complex. What the two sides agreed was within the site—and what was not—would determine exactly how much nuclear production capability Pyongyang was really sacrificing. The eleventh-hour message from Kim did not specify whether North Korea accepted the US definition of the complex's extent. So US negotiators asked for clarity. Choe returned to her delegation and then rushed back with the answer: Chairman Kim meant everything on the site of the complex. The US side remained unconvinced and indicated that President Trump did not want to resume negotiations.

Asked about the North Koreans' diplomatic "Hail Mary" before departing Hanoi, President Trump said, "We had to have more than that. We had to have more than that because there are other things that you haven't talked about, that you haven't written about, that we found."[7]

Trump appeared to be referencing US intelligence that North Korea had expanded facilities at Yongbyon even as negotiations were under way. That was one early sign that Pyongyang might be taking advantage of the negotiations and Trump.

The North Koreans' last-ditch offer also left Washington and Pyongyang at odds over what sanctions relief the United States would grant in return. That was at the core of the negotiations: how much of its nuclear program would North Korea give up in return for the US easing its "maximum-pressure" campaign.

In what Trump and his aides would dub "the walk," the president said he had walked away from a bad deal. "Sometimes you have to walk," he said during his end-of-summit news conference. "This was just one of those times."[8]

Intelligence officials and other diplomats involved in the negotiations claimed a rare victory in warning the president away from a bad deal. Together, their voices had amounted to a chorus of skepticism. "I think certainly a number of people ganged up, including Pompeo and Bolton," Ambassador Yun told me. "They ganged up to say that that was not enough."[9]

Here the president listened. In public, however, Trump administration officials had a different message. They said North Korea's last-minute offer proved that Kim was still interested, even eager, to come to an agreement. They insisted that even after North Korea contradicted the administration's line. Soon after the summit, North Korean foreign minister Ri Yong Ho described his side's offer as final, stating that it would "never be changed."

When confronted with that statement in an interview with *USA Today*, Secretary of State Mike Pompeo characteristically dismissed the basis of the question as false: "That's not what the North Koreans said. Don't say things that aren't true. . . . Show me the quote from the North Koreans that said this was their one and only offer. Where'd you get that?" The *USA Today* article continued:

After he was read a quote from Foreign Minister Ri Yong Ho . . . Pompeo fell silent for about six seconds. Then he countered, "What they said is they're prepared to continue conversations with us and that's what we intend to do."[10]

Administration officials repeatedly insisted to me and my colleagues that it was all just a matter of time. They were confident that the president's negotiating skills would soon carry the day.

Even with the failure of the Hanoi summit, President Trump again showered Kim with unlikely praise. At the same press conference in which he boasted of walking away from a bad deal, Trump appeared to gift Kim a free pass on the death of Otto Warmbier.

In comments reminiscent of his Helsinki moment with Vladimir Putin, Trump said he did not hold the North Korean leader responsible for Warmbier's death, accepting Kim's personal denial after the two leaders discussed the matter privately. "He felt badly about it," Trump said. "... He tells me that he didn't know about it, and I will take him at his word."[11]

Making matters worse, only four months earlier, he had accepted the denial of another authoritarian leader of another killing. In the weeks after Saudi agents brutally murdered Jamal Khashoggi in the Saudi Consulate in Istanbul in October 2018, Trump tweeted, "Just spoke with the Crown Prince of Saudi Arabia who totally denied any knowledge of what took place in their Turkish Consulate."

He would go on to compare the suspicion of Crown Prince Mohammed bin Salman's involvement to the allegations against Supreme Court nominee Brett Kavanaugh. In an interview with the Associated Press in October 2018, he said, "Here we go again with, you know, you're guilty until proven innocent. I don't like that. We just went through that with Justice Kavanaugh and he was innocent all the way as far as I'm concerned."[12]

US intelligence would conclude otherwise: that the murder had likely taken place on the orders of the crown prince (known widely by his initials, MBS). Even as news of that assessment became public, Trump continued to take MBS's word. In an interview with Fox News in November that year, he said Prince Mohammed had told him "maybe five times" that he had no involvement. When pressed by Fox News anchor Chris Wallace about what he would do if he discovered that the crown prince had lied, Trump replied, "Will anybody really know?"[13] Later, he would focus less on professing MBS's innocence than on trumpeting the importance of the two countries' relationship, arguing that Saudi Arabia was too close an ally to break with over Khashoggi.

The pattern was clear: when convenient, the president was willing to look the other way when certain allies or adversaries committed horrible crimes. Mohammed bin Salman "totally denied" ordering the murder of Khashoggi. Putin gave an "extremely strong" denial of interfering in the 2016 election. Kim "didn't know about" Otto Warmbier.

Trump's defense of Kim was too much, even for some of the president's most ardent Republican supporters. On February 18, 2019, Nikki Haley, Trump's former ambassador to the United Nations, tweeted, "Americans know the cruelty that was placed on Otto Warmbier by the North Korean regime. Our hearts are with the Warmbier family for their strength and courage. We will never forget Otto."

Most biting were the words of Warmbier's heartbroken parents, Fred and Cindy, who on March 1 shared this statement with CNN: "We have been respectful during this summit process. Now we must speak out. Kim and his evil regime are responsible for the death of our son Otto. Kim and his evil regime are responsible for unimaginable cruelty and inhumanity. No excuses or lavish praise can change that. Thank you."[14]

It was an odd and entirely unnecessary concession to Kim delivered for nothing in return. And one more Trump-Kim summit had ended without progress on denuclearization.

ACT THREE: THE DMZ

The third act of the Trump-Kim summit drama would take place on the most remarkable stage and on a timeline built for maximum impact. In June 2019, in advance of the G20 summit in Osaka, news outlets including CNN were given a tantalizing heads-up by the White House: the president, we were told, might make an additional stop during his Asia trip, in South Korea. Logistically, that meant "get your camera crews, hotel rooms, and visas ready." Substantively, Trump appeared to be planning his most dramatic diplomatic moment yet: a third summit with Kim right on the Korean Peninsula.

As a journalist, my heart pumped at the possibility. The death of Kim Jong Un's grandfather Kim Il Sung had been one of the first stories I had filed as a foreign correspondent based in Hong Kong. Since then, I had worked on the standoff between Pyongyang and Washington for twenty-five years, as a correspondent in Asia and Washington and as a US diplomat in Beijing. A Trump-Kim summit on the peninsula, perhaps at the DMZ, would be an unforgettable event to witness.

As the G20 meeting ground on, President Trump kept the traveling US media in limbo. For days, there was no confirmation either way and there were occasional hints that the summit was on and then off.

On June 28, Trump tweeted a bold invitation: "After some very important meetings, including my meeting with President Xi of China, I will be leaving Japan for South Korea (with President Moon). While there, if Chairman Kim of North Korea sees this, I would meet him at the Border/DMZ just to shake his hand and say Hello(?)!"

"I just thought of it this morning," Trump told reporters in Japan. "I just put out a feeler because I don't know where he is right now. He may not be in North Korea."[15]

A senior US official told CNN at the time that administration officials planning the president's overseas trip first learned of Trump's invitation to Kim when everyone else had, after Trump's tweet.[16] However, that claim was later contradicted by news of the president's own words earlier in the week. In fact, Trump had mentioned the possibility of meeting Kim at the DMZ in an interview with The Hill website four days before, though the White House had asked the newspaper to delay publishing the information, citing concerns about security.[17]

Regardless, the plan was now public. And on Sunday, June 30, the stage was set. Trump and Kim would make history at a border that had separated North and South Korea since the armistice ceasing hostilities nearly sixty-six years before. The war wasn't officially over; the two sides had never signed a formal peace treaty. And through the decades, they had traded cross-border gunfire, artillery fire, and armed raids. North Korea had sunk a South Korean Navy ship and carried out terror attacks, leaving hundreds dead. Just nineteen months before, a North Korean soldier had defected across the DMZ in a bold escape, shot five times by North Korean soldiers in pursuit. Now Trump and Kim would bring their mutual flair for the dramatic to the most heavily defended frontier in the world.

Our team—producer Shelby Vest, Seoul producers David Hawley and Yoonjung Seo, photojournalist Paul Devitt, Seoul correspondent Paula Hancocks, and I—drove up to the border from Seoul early that morning. Despite the array of defenses on both sides of the 38th parallel, the South Korean side has become a tourist destination, complete with a café, public restrooms, a sculpture garden, and even carnival rides for children. We staked out a position backed up against the first line of barbed-wire fences, a few hundred yards from the Freedom Bridge, which leads from South Korean territory to Panmunjom village, where Trump and Kim would meet later that day.

Panmunjom resembles a movie set. Soldiers from the North and South stare at each other across the frontier, separated only by a foot-high stone curb marking the border. A handful of meticulously preserved wooden huts, including the building where the two sides signed the 1953 armistice, are arrayed on either side. President Trump knows how to stage a dramatic moment—and that one certainly qualified.

CNN decided to broadcast the summit live around the world and asked me to anchor the coverage. The White House provided only the barest of details on the talks. The truth seemed to be that the format and schedule would be decided by Trump and Kim in the moment. It wasn't even clear that the meeting would take place until the president confirmed it—again with a tweet—a little more than an hour before he would arrive at the DMZ.

Covering this would be a challenge as an anchor but the most satisfying one for me: witnessing and reporting the news as it happens. My focus was not only on the spectacle but on the outcome. The world had already witnessed two summits heavy on style and short on substance. Would this one be different?

Early that afternoon, I heard the roar of engines in the distance and looked up to see a line of helicopters carrying the president and the traveling media. The olive drab choppers looked more like a military formation than a diplomatic mission. Yet in a few minutes, they would land in Panmunjom for a meeting few could have predicted years, months, or even days before.

The president's helicopter touched down on a landing pad a short distance from the border, where he was greeted by the US commander in charge of forces deployed to the DMZ. Trump listened quietly to a businesslike report on conditions at the border, the president's hair blowing wildly in the wind. On the cusp of making history, he could not avoid a swipe at media coverage of the nuclear negotiations. "When they say there's been no difference, there's been a tremendous difference," he said. "I say that for the press, they have no appreciation for what is being done, none."[18]

Soon after, he had his moment: he and the North Korean leader greeted each other on the South Korean side of the border with broad smiles and a warm handshake. But was that all the drama Trump had planned? As he and Kim chatted and walked, it became evident that they had more in store. At 3:45 p.m., President Trump approached the low line of bricks marking the border between North and South. "Would you like me to step across?" Trump asked Kim as they shook hands. "I am OK with it."

And across he went, taking twenty steps into perhaps the most reclusive country in the world. Trump and Kim spent just over a minute on the other side, patting each other on the back and smiling broadly. "I never expected to meet you at this place," Kim told Trump through his interpreter, exuding what appeared to be genuine delight.

After stepping back into South Korea, Trump said he was "proud" to have crossed the border and raised the possibility of inviting Kim to the White House. The North Korean leader cited his "excellent relationship" with Trump, admitting he had been surprised by the president's invitation to meet.

With their historic photo opportunity complete, the two men retreated into Freedom House for a sit-down meeting. Administration officials had told reporters not to expect the leaders to meet for more than a few minutes, but the discussion went on for nearly an hour. Inside the room was a large contingent of the president's advisors—some expected, such as Treasury Secretary Steve Mnuchin and lead negotiator Stephen Biegun; others less so, including his daughter Ivanka Trump and son-in-law, Jared Kushner.

The two leaders appeared genuinely at ease with each other, yet it was not clear what they intended to accomplish. Neither side made any new commitments. Afterward, Trump said he had not made any new demands for Pyongyang to dismantle its nuclear weapons program.[19]

ONE + TWO + THREE = ZERO

Over twelve months and nineteen days, I had covered three "historic" summits between Trump and Kim in three different Asian countries. Each presented a dramatic backdrop: Singapore as the crossroads of Asia, Hanoi as the heart of a former US enemy, and then across the DMZ into North Korea. Each had delivered overwhelming pageantry and underwhelming progress. What had changed? North Korea had made no commitments to shrink its nuclear program. The United States had made no promises to soften sanctions. Pyongyang had still not provided even an accounting of its nuclear weapons program, and the United States appeared not to have made any firm demand for one as a prerequisite for further talks. More disturbing, US intelligence continued to assess that North Korea was in fact expanding its nuclear program, even as the talks were going on.

In the weeks that followed Trump's twenty steps into history, North Korea restarted ballistic missile tests. In one particularly busy period in the late summer and early fall, Pyongyang conducted twelve separate tests. Trump dismissed each one as inconsequential, even though those short-range missiles still threatened not only US allies South Korea and Japan but also US military bases in the region. In the fall of 2019, North Korea tested a submarine-launched missile, making further progress on a capability to deploy nuclear-capable missiles on submarines, which are far harder to track than land-based launchers.

The broader pattern in the negotiations was focus on the talks themselves over concrete progress. Intelligence analyst Sue Mi Terry blamed the lack of progress on Trump placing personality over policy making: "Kim and Trump met three times. We got nowhere because we don't even have an agreed-upon definition on denuclearization. Never mind a road map, timeline or anything."[20]

Still Trump continued to make concessions to Kim. Even the summits themselves were concessions of a kind. Kim Jong Un, like his father and grandfather before him, was desperate for recognition by the United States as a power to be reckoned with. A face-to-face meeting with the US president was a long-held goal—an end in and of itself. For Trump to agree to one such summit was a remarkable achievement. For him to grant three over the course of a year was likely more than Kim could have hoped for.

THE MILITARY'S PRICE

But the summits were not the only concessions President Trump delivered to Kim. Beginning in June 2018, just after his first summit in Singapore, Trump surprised even his own seniormost military officials by announcing the suspension of large-scale military exercises with South Korea. The exercises—bearing code names such as "Key Resolve" and "Foal Eagle"—had taken place every spring for years and involved thousands of troops from all branches of the US and South Korean military services. US and South Korean military officials considered them essential training to prepare for and deter a North Korean invasion.

President Trump had a different view. He described the exercises—which he called "war games," a term the US military intentionally avoided—as a waste of money and an unnecessary provocation.

"We will be stopping the war games, which will save us a tremendous amount of money," he said in his postsummit news conference in Singapore, in which he also accused ally South Korea of not sharing the costs. ". . . We have to talk to them. We have to talk to many countries about treating us fairly."[21]

Trump went on to cite his own expertise as owner of a private jet as contributing to his decision to cancel the exercises, which normally involved US aircraft based as far away as Guam.

"We fly in bombers from Guam," Trump said. "I said it when I first started, I said, 'Where do the bombers come from? Guam. Nearby.' I said, 'Oh great, nearby, where is nearby?' Six and a half hours. Six and a half hours. That's a long time for these big massive planes to be flying to South Korea to practice and then drop bombs all over the place and then go back to Guam.

"I know a lot about airplanes," he continued. "It's very expensive. I didn't like it."

He then cited another reason for canceling the exercises: to avoid upsetting Kim Jong Un. "I think it is very provocative."[22]

Prior to Trump, those exercises were, by design, as predictable and as routine as possible. The routine was essential to deterrence. Under Trump, several were canceled without warning. Military officials, aware of their importance, tried different ways to preserve them. One exercise was renamed to appear smaller to the president, a senior military official told me. In the fall of 2019, when the president was again demanding cancellations, Secretary of Defense Mark Esper attempted to call Secretary of State Mike Pompeo to seek his support in restoring the exercises, this same official said, but Secretary Pompeo refused to take Secretary Esper's call and didn't call back.

US military commanders are laser-focused on readiness. And none more so than those commanding forces on the Korean Peninsula, where "Fight tonight" is more than just a motto.

Every US military exercise is vetted through multiple levels of US military leadership. And leaders at every one of those levels—from field commanders to the seniormost Pentagon officials—must be in agreement before an exercise moves forward. US military exercises in South Korea are some of the most highly vetted, as a result of the tension on the Korean Peninsula and the severity of the threat. Given the fact that North and South Korea technically remain at war, reducing the risk of miscommunication is of particular concern. Planning such exercises is a deliberately thorough process. But in the age of Trump, no process is fixed.

If an exercise is to be canceled, normally the president would make such a decision in consultation with the Pentagon, US commanders in the region, and South Korea. When he made his announcement in Singapore canceling the exercises, however, those commanders heard the news for the first time as the words left the president's mouth.

The South Korean Ministry of National Defense issued a short statement indicating that it was seeking confirmation from the United States. US forces in South Korea said that they were still moving forward with planning for the exercises. The Pentagon, for its part, issued a statement saying simply that it would do what the president said.

"We are working to fulfill the President's guidance. The Department of Defense is aligned and continues to work with the White House to ensure we provide options that meet the President's intent," Pentagon spokesman Marine Corps lieutenant colonel Christopher Logan said.[23]

Two months later, Secretary of Defense Mattis seemed to register his opposition by stating that future large-scale exercises would go ahead as per normal. "We took the step to suspend several of the largest exercises as a good-faith measure coming out of the Singapore summit," he told reporters at the Pentagon. "We have no plans at this time to suspend any more exercises. We will work very closely, as I said, with the Secretary of State and what he needs done."[24]

The very next day, Mattis's words drew a rebuttal from Trump himself in a series of tweets that the president headlined in all caps as a "Statement from the White House."

The tweets read, in part, ". . . the President believes that his relationship with Kim Jong Un is a very good and warm one, and there is no reason at this time to be spending large amounts of money on joint U.S.-South Korea war games." He continued, "Besides, the President can instantly start the joint exercises again with South Korea, and Japan, if he so chooses. If he does, they will be far bigger than ever before."

Trump's downplaying of military readiness echoed his later downplaying of preparedness for a global pandemic. As the coronavirus outbreak worsened in early 2020, the president defended his earlier proposed cuts to the CDC budget by arguing—as he did with exercises on the Korean Peninsula—that he could easily ramp up resources whenever he wanted.

"I'm a business person. I don't like having thousands of people around when you don't need them," he said. "When we need them, we can get them back very quickly."[25]

In each case, the people closest to the problem, whether the nation's seniormost military officials or its health experts, expressed a very different view of preparedness. They argued that the threats—whether a North Korean invasion or a pandemic—required preparation over time: training, storing up resources, having plans in place, and updating them when new information became available. But in each case, the president chose to downplay or ignore them.

Throughout his love affair with Kim, Trump would continue to downplay military readiness. After the second summit in Hanoi in February 2019, Trump again suspended large-scale military exercises. "I was telling the generals, I said, 'Look, you know, exercising is fun and it's nice and they play the war games,'" he said. "And I'm not saying it's not necessary because at some levels it is, but at other levels it's not."[26]

The official announcement from the Pentagon—canceling the "Foal Eagle" and "Key Resolve" exercises—came soon after, citing acting secretary of defense Patrick Shanahan and South Korean minister of national defense Jeong Kyeong Doo. "The Minister and Secretary made clear that the Alliance decision to adapt our training program reflected our desire to reduce tension and support our diplomatic efforts to achieve complete denuclearization of the Korean Peninsula in a final, fully verified manner," the statement said.[27]

Shanahan's predecessor, Secretary Mattis, had left by then, resigning from his post in December 2018 following President Trump's snap decision to withdraw US troops from Syria. In his resignation letter, addressed to President Trump, Mattis noted his "core belief" in the necessity and importance of the United States' alliances:

> One core belief I have always held is that our strength as a nation is inextricably linked to the strength of our unique and comprehensive system of alliances and partnerships. While the US remains the indispensable nation in the free world, we cannot protect our interests or serve that role effectively without maintaining strong alliances and showing respect to those allies.[28]

Mattis did not name Syria or South Korea explicitly, but officials close to him told me at the time that the president's decisions regarding both Syria and South Korea had factored into his decision to go. The Syrian withdrawal had been the last straw. It was a remarkable moment: the seniormost military official in the country, a decorated former marine general appointed by Trump and repeatedly praised as one of *his* generals, was accusing the president of abandoning US allies.

Over the months that followed, the United States continued to cancel or shrink long-held joint military exercises with South Korea. US military commanders, already concerned in private, began to share their concerns publicly that by canceling the exercises, the president was undermining military readiness.

Testifying before the Senate Armed Services Committee in September 2018, army general Robert Abrams, who led Army Forces Command, acknowledged as much, telling lawmakers, "I think there is certainly degradation to the readiness of the force. That's a key exercise to maintain continuity and to continue to practice our interoperability, and so there was a slight degradation."

He did describe the president's decision as a "prudent risk if we're willing to make the effort to change the relationship" with North Korea.[29]

SOUTH KOREA'S PRICE

Left in the middle of Trump's diplomatic flirtation with Kim was US ally South Korea.

"South Korea is savvy enough to know that this is very specific to Trump himself," said Sue Mi Terry. "They talk to everybody else. They've dealt with Democrats, Republicans. So they know this is not a normal thing."[30]

In November 2019, at the very same time that the House was considering impeaching him for withholding military aid from Ukraine in return for political favors, President Trump called into question US military support for another ally at war. In negotiations with South Korea, Trump summarily demanded that Seoul immediately increase its contribution to the costs of the deployment of US forces on the Korean Peninsula fivefold. When South Korean officials balked at the number, US officials walked out of the room—a remarkable rebuke to one of the United States' closest allies in the world.

Trump's demand was reminiscent of his demand that European allies increase their financial contributions to the NATO alliance. However, he was demanding that South Korea increase its payments by a far greater amount and at a time when its enemy North Korea was rapidly building its nuclear and missile capabilities. It was a brazen demand that left South Korean officials feeling outraged and betrayed.

Behind the scenes, military officials told me, Trump was backing his demand with an alarming threat. If Seoul did not pay up, the National Security Council instructed its negotiators to hint to South Korean officials that the president could withdraw some US forces from the peninsula. Specifically, the threat involved the removal of an entire brigade combat team, comprising some 4,000 US soldiers—about one in seven of the nearly 28,500 US soldiers, sailors, airmen, and marines based there.

"It's extortion," said Sue Mi Terry, who covered North Korea as an intelligence analyst for the CIA and National Security Council. "It's not how you treat a friend."

Terry was traveling in South Korea at the time of the threat, meeting with South Korean government officials, who expressed alarm at the president's hardball tactics. "When you meet the Koreans, they're like, 'Do you understand we sent three hundred thousand troops to Vietnam? Five thousand were killed,'" she recalled. "This is a blood alliance, right? An alliance forged in blood."[31]

The "maximum-pressure" campaign, waged under the direction of the White House, was juxtaposed against the latest public chapter in President Trump's charm offensive toward the North Korean dictator Kim Jong Un. When North Korean state media—in particularly bombastic rhetoric—called Joe Biden a "rabid dog" who should be "beaten to death with a stick," Trump did not convincingly defend his fellow American, a former vice president of the United States, tweeting instead, "Mr. Chairman, Joe Biden may be Sleepy and Very Slow, but he is not a 'rabid dog.' He is actually somewhat better than that, but I am the only one who can get you where you have to be. You should act quickly, get the deal done. See you soon!"

Yet as he soft-pedaled his response to Kim, Trump continued to pressure South Korea, which struck several of his advisors as a particularly strange choice of target. South Korea has the eighth largest military budget in the world and is the third largest purchaser of American weapons.[32] Unlike many NATO countries, South Korea spends well over 2 percent of its GDP on defense.

"So they think it's insane," Terry told me. "It's something that they can't even begin to negotiate."[33]

When the South Korean newspaper *The Chosun Ilbo* reported that the United States had threatened to remove some US troops in response, Pentagon spokesman Jonathan Hoffman released a statement saying, "There is absolutely no truth to the Chosun Ilbo report that the U.S. Department of Defense is currently considering removing any troops from the Korean Peninsula."[34] According to Terry, however, many South Korean officials believed the threat was real. "They expressed a very high level of alarm and they have the sense that the US—or that President Trump—no longer sees them as key," she said.[35]

The dispute with South Korea had disturbing parallels to the president's decision to withhold military assistance from Ukraine. Again, here was a US ally that was depending on US assistance to defend itself from a dangerous adversary. No one in the US Department of Defense, the State Department, or even Trump's own National Security Council supported withholding aid. Many officials voiced strong opposition. But to get the money he wanted from Seoul, everything seemed to be on the table.

Inside the Pentagon, as one senior US military commander described it to me, the US military was being presented with another "hill to die on." It had faced similar moments before: in South Korea, with the cancellation of vital military exercises, and in Syria, with two sudden presidential orders to withdraw US troops. Would they stand up to the president this time? And if not here and now, then when and where? The decisions *are* the president's. He is the commander in chief. Military leaders are required to follow his orders. However, determining the line marking the presidential decisions that go too far—the orders they will not follow or attempt to reverse—has proven deeply difficult for men and women in uniform. Is the line the cancellation of one crucial military exercise? Or the cancellation of several? Is the line the withdrawal of some US forces an ally depends on? Or all of them? In South Korea, no single questionable decision or collection of questionable decisions seemed to define that line.

Trump's harsh dealings with Seoul, especially juxtaposed against his seemingly endless patience with Pyongyang, sparked growing fears the president was doing long-term damage to the alliance with South Korea.

"You've got talk about pulling out a brigade now. What would happen if he's reelected?" said Terry. "I don't think the alliance would be able to deal with five more years of this."

In the midst of the coronavirus pandemic in early 2020, the president would play hardball with South Korea once again. On April 1, the United States furloughed thousands of South Koreans who work on US bases, after Seoul and Washington failed again to reach a new cost-sharing agreement. The commander of US troops in South Korea called these employees "vital" to the mission and the US–South Korea alliance.

There are broader dangers to Trump's undermining of the United States' relationship with South Korea. Terry is concerned that a widening gap between the two allies will lead the South to move closer to other players in the region, even China.

"When you talk to the South Koreans, they are in the middle of US and China," Terry said. "China is South Korea's number one trading partner. Their trade volume is more than US, South Korea, and Japan combined. South Korea is already pursuing a hedging policy between the US and China."[36]

A slow drift away from the United States and toward China would have consequences for the United States across the entire region. The United States' alliance with South Korea—and its force presence there—is intended not just to defend the South from the North but to project US influence throughout Asia. The United States' position as an Asian regional power depends, in large part, on the strength of its alliances with its two principal allies in the region: South Korea and Japan. Each hosts large contingents of US forces, and each country's military serves as an essential piece of the US military deterrent against China. Weakening those links weakens the United States and strengthens China.

"It is almost irreversible harm," Terry said.[37]

South Korea is of particular importance to the balance of power between the US and China. North Korea is China's only ally in the world. And so Beijing views the deployment of US forces on the Korean Peninsula as the equivalent of a US military presence on its own border. Removing or reducing the deployment and widening the gap between the United States and South Korean governments weakens the United States' position against Beijing as much as Pyongyang. This is another example of "America First" undermining its own agenda.

NORTH KOREA'S PROGRESS

While South Korea suffered under Trump, North Korea gave little ground. Trump's concessions on military exercises failed to generate reciprocal concessions from North Korea on its nuclear program. And that was the inherent problem: Trump was ceding important ground to Kim without receiving in return anything on his principal demand of denuclearization.

In November 2019, the International Atomic Energy Agency expressed its alarm at North Korea's continuing nuclear activities. Noting that North Korea—nearly two years into President Trump's diplomatic efforts—was still in violation of UN Security Council resolutions regarding its nuclear and missile programs, the IAEA's acting director,

Cornel Feruta, demanded that Pyongyang take immediate action to curtail its program.

"The DPRK's nuclear activities remain a cause for serious concern. The continuation of that programme is a clear violation of relevant UN Security Council resolutions and is deeply regrettable," said Feruta in September 2019. ". . . I call upon the DPRK to comply fully with its obligations under relevant UN Security Council resolutions, to cooperate promptly with the Agency and to resolve all outstanding issues."[38]

Feruta noted that the IAEA stood ready to monitor any potential nuclear agreement, a mission it had not yet been asked to fulfill given the absence of concrete progress. "The Agency remains ready to play an essential role in verifying the DPRK's nuclear programme if a political agreement is reached among countries concerned," he said.[39]

Which side was winning the standoff? As President Trump entered the fourth year of his term, North Korea appeared increasingly emboldened. Kim had achieved what his father and grandfather had not: North Korea was a nuclear power.

"One thing that is misunderstood on both sides is that the North Korean elite—they feel they have hugely succeeded in their weapons development," Ambassador Yun told me.

That success created a new confidence inside the North Korean leadership and a new dynamic in any nuclear negotiations going forward.

"The price has gone up," Yun continued. "And the problem is that that view is not shared by the Americans, and Americans want to pay the price Americans are used to pay. This is why the whole thing is stuck.

"Whose side is time on?" he asked. "Everyone used to say that time is on the American side. And again, that's very debatable, because as time elapses, you're going to have North Koreans accumulate more and more weapons. And so the price keeps on going up."[40]

DREAMING OF THE NOBEL PEACE PRIZE

Current and former Trump administration officials who have interacted with Trump on North Korea say Trump recognizes the change in Pyongyang's posture and has made substantive adjustments as a result. "I think he has an understanding of it. I think more than people give him credit for," Yun told me.

One key lesson is that he cannot singlehandedly negotiate progress in the relationship in his personal encounters with Kim Jong Un. "I think this is a lesson he learned from Hanoi, which is that you cannot do all negotiations at a summit setting," Yun said. "There are too many details and too many entrenched positions that have to be met, and I think that's the lesson he learned, and if there is a next summit, he is determined to go in with an agreement largely in place."[41]

"Having dealt with Kim for two years now, he probably finally realized that it's not going to be so easy," Sue Mi Terry agreed. "He probably has a little more realistic expectations now."[42]

If so, Trump was learning what his closest advisors had been telling him from the beginning: that summits are where agreements are signed, not negotiated. Still, he continues to see the summits as "wins" in their own right.

"I believe he takes great pride in this issue," Yun said. "He takes pride that he has accomplished something. He keeps mentioning otherwise we'd be in a war."

North Korea is a matter of such personal pride for Trump that he has a deep personal desire for international recognition for his efforts.

And he wants that recognition bestowed on him in a very tangible way: the Nobel Peace Prize.

"You cannot underestimate that he wants to win a Nobel Peace Prize," Yun told me. "He felt [President] Obama had won a Nobel Peace Prize for doing nothing and that he deserves to win, and North Korea is going to be his ticket."

His desire for such recognition leads some current and former Trump administration officials to fear he will give up too much in pursuit of that personal goal. "Too much would include, in my view, giving up all the sanctions before denuclearization is completed," Yun cautioned. "Giving up too much is removing US troops from South Korea. Giving up too much would be disestablishing what's called UN command. Giving up too much would be recognizing North Korea as a nuclear weapon state."

What about the Trump administration's original standard for success in these negotiations? The four words repeated ad infinitum at the start of the talks—"Complete, verifiable, irreversible denuclearization"—have faded into memory.

"It was always a dream from the beginning that we will get complete denuclearization before we do anything. That was always a dream," Yun told me. "Will they ever give it up? I don't think they'll give it up."

That does not mean all hope for progress is lost or that the value of negotiations has disappeared. The standard is, as always, what you get in return.

"Is it worth having a negotiating process established, so you get to [denuclearization] then little by little?" asked Yun. "You don't know where you're going to go to, but if the situation improves, it is possible that you could have a substantial denuclearization, maybe even complete denuclearization many years down the road.

"These are all possibilities," he concluded. "But we are not going to have complete denuclearization anytime I can see in the future."[43]

THE ANSWER

President Trump made a gamble on North Korea. He believed that by building a personal relationship with Kim, coupled with economic sanctions, he could cajole North Korea into making concessions on its nuclear program. At the end of four years of summit diplomacy and maximum pressure, that gamble has not paid off. In fact, there is evidence that North Korea used that time to expand, rather than freeze, its nuclear program. Trump now risks suffering the same fate as his predecessors, who watched North Korea meet diplomatic outreach with further delays and cheating.

In this sense, it may end up being Kim who played Trump, not the other way around.

8

"Retreat, Reverse, Repeat": Syria

IS THE UNITED STATES IN OR OUT OF THE MIDDLE EAST?

Donald Trump ran as the candidate who would both restore respect for the United States abroad and end the United States' "endless wars." In practice, those two ambitious campaign promises often contradicted themselves. The deployment of US forces to Syria to fight ISIS—a deployment Trump himself expanded as president—put this contradiction in plain view.

How would the United States restore the respect of its allies in the region, including the Syrian Kurds, and its adversaries, led by Russia and Iran, if it abandoned those allies and ceded territory to those adversaries? How would Trump avoid repeating the mistake of President Obama's own swift withdrawal from Iraq but also make good on his promise to bring US troops home?

In late December 2018, I received a panicked phone call from a senior Trump administration official. It was less than a week before Christmas, normally a slow news period during any other time but the Trump era. The president had just tweeted out a major policy reversal in what was then the hottest and deadliest battlefield for the United States abroad: Syria.

"We have defeated ISIS in Syria, my only reason for being there during the Trump Presidency," read his December 19 tweet. That statement from the commander in chief—consisting of just sixteen words and delivered, as so often with President Trump, via his favorite social media platform—summarily reversed stated US policy. And it did so as the battle against ISIS was in one of its most crucial periods, catching the Pentagon, Central Command, US forces in Syria, several senior White House advisors, and the world off guard.

One of those caught off guard was the man the president had designated as his point man on Syria, the special presidential envoy for the Global Coalition to Counter ISIL, Brett McGurk. McGurk was one of the longest-serving US officials in the Middle East. He had been appointed to the post by President Obama in 2015 after serving as deputy to his predecessor, John Allen, since 2014. President Trump had retained him at the start of his term, making him a rare holdover between the Obama and Trump administrations and one who made the transition with unusual staying power. The fight against ISIS had been proceeding rapidly and effectively, an almost unqualified national security success for President Trump.

McGurk was on the phone with me that night, expressing alarm and frustration. Trump's announcement, he said, was "a complete reversal done without deliberation and no consideration of the risks."

In the hours immediately following the president's tweet, McGurk was fielding panicked phone calls from US allies in Syria and across the region.

"They're shocked and bewildered," he said. The Syrian Democratic Forces (SDF), which was militarily led by the mostly Kurdish People's Protection Units, or YPG, had been the tip of the spear against ISIS, backed by a relatively small contingent of US Special Forces. Their leaders were now incredulous. "They don't believe this is happening."

The withdrawal via tweet contradicted not only the stated US policy but also the message senior US officials in the region had been delivering to their partners in the weeks just prior. Then national security advisor John Bolton, McGurk told me, had instructed him and his colleagues to meet with coalition partners to assure them that the United States would be staying in Syria until Iran was out of the country. In sixteen words, Trump had rendered those assurances meaningless.

The timing was critical. McGurk described the current state of play on the ground as a "Tora Bora situation." That is, US forces were then as close to surrounding and capturing ISIS leader Abu Bakr al-Baghdadi in Syria as they had been to Osama bin Laden in the months after the US invasion of Afghanistan. Bin Laden had gotten away then when US forces retreated. McGurk feared that a sudden US withdrawal from Syria might allow al-Baghdadi the same free passage to safety.

According to McGurk, the latest US intelligence indicated that al-Baghdadi and his senior commanders were trapped in a tiny pocket in central Syria. That assessment was based, in part, on the vigorous defense ISIS fighters were mounting in the area. They were attacking US and Syrian forces with suicide bombers, an indication, US intelligence believed, that they were willing to die in order to defend the ISIS leader himself.

Upon learning of the president's surprise announcement, the United States' Syrian allies believed the US was abandoning them to four separate adversaries: Syrian government forces, their Russian allies, their

Iranian allies, and Turkey, which had been looking for an opportunity to invade Syria, attack the Kurds, and create a wide buffer zone in northern Syria.

President Trump claimed, without basis, that Russia would somehow lose out from the departure of US forces, but McGurk, Trump's own seniormost advisor on the anti-ISIS campaign, said the opposite was true.

"Russia loves this," McGurk said, adding that the withdrawal would send a message to US allies across the region: "If Americans are your friends, they'll abandon you."

That was a message Russia had been spreading across the region for years—it had been propaganda intended to discourage forces in the region from allying with the United States. Now Trump had gifted Moscow with even more propaganda ammunition.

Once again, the president's Syria withdrawal order—the first of two he would issue via Twitter in less than a year—followed a familiar pattern in policy making under Trump: no consultation with senior advisors, no warning to US commanders or US partners on the ground, no discernible policy process at all.

Trump had not upset the national security process, his advisors said, he had destroyed it.

"National security decision making has basically stopped working," McGurk told me. "Decisions are now made on a whim on phone calls."

THE FIRST ERDOĞAN PHONE CALL AND WITHDRAWAL

The phone call in question this time had been with the Turkish leader Recep Tayyip Erdoğan, five days before Trump's tweet.

"Okay, it's all yours. We are done," Trump had told the Turkish president.

Those words—precipitating the immediate drawdown of a US military deployment years in the making—came at the very end of a phone call with Erdoğan. And accounts of the conversation show that it was Erdoğan who had lobbied Trump to withdraw US forces from Syria. In fact, Erdoğan had been hoping and pushing for US forces to withdraw for some time, allowing Turkey to establish control in northern Syria. His argument to Trump was that ISIS had already effectively been defeated there. In the end, all Trump demanded from Erdoğan in return was an assurance that Turkey would continue the fight. Erdoğan responded by giving Trump his "word." "In fact, as your friend, I give you my word in this,'" he told Trump, according to a senior White House official who spoke to CNN.[1]

To seal his victory, Erdoğan shared his account of this private conversation with Trump with the public soon after the call. In a speech broadcast nationally in Turkey, Erdoğan matter-of-factly said that Trump had made the decision based on that promise from Erdoğan himself.

"During a conversation I had with Mr. Trump—he said 'ISIS, can you clear ISIS from this area?'" Erdoğan said. "We did it before, and we can again as long as we have logistic support from you. And so they began pulling out.

"Within the framework of the phone call we had with Mr. Trump, we have started preparing plans for operations to clear the ISIS elements still within Syria."[2]

Trump's summary withdrawal was too much for many US military officials, including the most senior one. One day later, Trump's tweet claimed its first victim.

Deputy Assistant Secretary of Defense for the Middle East Mick Mulroy was in the dark, literally and figuratively, when the news broke, under general anesthesia for a medical procedure. Like McGurk, Mulroy, who was in charge of developing and coordinating US policy for fifteen countries across the region, including Syria, had not been consulted in advance.

When Mulroy came to the next morning, his doctor told him he had some unfortunate news to deliver. "'Mick, bad news,'" he said. "So I'm like 'Oh, crap, that's not what you want to hear.'

"'Did you find something?' He says, 'No, no, no, you're good. But your boss just quit, while you were under.' So I said, 'What boss? Trump?' He says, 'No, Mattis.'

"I was like, 'Oh, crap,'" Mulroy said.

That morning, without warning any of his senior staff, Defense Secretary Jim Mattis had submitted a letter of resignation to President Trump. "I'm sure that he thought about it and actually planned, he just didn't share it with us," Mulroy said.[3]

Writing like the career soldier he was before he shed his uniform to take on the job as secretary of defense, Mattis began with a thank-you, not to the president but to the men and women he had served with in the Pentagon: "I have been privileged to serve as our country's 26th Secretary of Defense which has allowed me to serve alongside our men and women of the Department in defense of our citizens and our ideals."

After citing issues he said he was proud to have made progress on during his nearly two years in his post, including "a more sound budgetary footing, improving readiness and lethality in our forces, and reforming the Department's business practices for greater performance," he went on to the core of his disagreement with Trump.

First, he made clear that he felt the United States had inexcusably abandoned its Syrian Kurdish allies:

One core belief I have always held is that our strength as a nation is inextricably linked to the strength of our unique and comprehensive system of alliances and partnerships. While the US remains the indispensable nation in the free world, we cannot protect our interests or serve that role effectively without maintaining strong alliances and showing respect to those allies.

Equally pointedly, he seemed to be arguing that, in addition to letting down America's allies, the president was in effect aiding the enemy:

Similarly, I believe we must be resolute and unambiguous in our approach to those countries whose strategic interests are increasingly in tension with ours. It is clear that China and Russia, for example, want to shape a world consistent with their authoritarian model—gaining veto authority over other nations' economic, diplomatic, and security decisions—to promote their own interests at the expense of their neighbors, America and our allies. That is why we must use all the tools of American power to provide for the common defense.

In a final flourish, he cited his decades of experience in the military. Though not explicitly accusing the president of lacking similar background, the difference seemed clear: he knew what he was talking about:

My views on treating allies with respect and also being clear-eyed about both malign actors and strategic competitors are strongly held and informed by over four decades of immersion in these issues. We must do everything possible to advance an international order that is most conducive to our security, prosperity and values, and we are strengthened in this effort by the solidarity of our alliances.

Because you have the right to have a Secretary of Defense

whose views are better aligned with yours on these and other subjects, I believe it is right for me to step down from my position.[4]

"He found it to be unacceptable," Mulroy later explained. "This idea that we would abandon a partner force, and not just a partner force, but a partner force that fought and did most of the dying. And I think that sentiment is universal inside the [Department of Defense], especially the uniformed folks."[5]

For US service members who had fought alongside the Kurds, the president's decision was particularly devastating. The United States was abandoning its brothers and sisters in arms. (In the case of Kurdish forces, which are made up of significant numbers of both male and female fighters and commanders, "brothers and sisters" is not political correctness but fact.)

For Mulroy, the situation was personal. In his role at the Pentagon, he had visited the battlefields repeatedly and knew the Kurdish commanders well. As a former US Marine, he had fought alongside the Kurds in Iraq and Syria on multiple deployments. I had witnessed the Kurds in action as well. As we would discover, Mulroy and I had entered Iraq during the 2003 invasion in the same unit of Green Berets—me as an embedded reporter, Mulroy as a CIA operative— that was advising and assisting Iraqi Kurds. The fight against ISIS in Syria depended on local Kurdish fighters to win.

"It's pretty emotional," Mulroy told me. "Quite frankly, even trying to repeat it is an emotional thing. And it really struck, especially the [special operations] guys who had been out there fighting alongside them."

At his desk in the Pentagon, still somewhat unfamiliar territory for someone who had spent years fighting in the field, Mulroy was flooded with outraged messages from US commanders. "'You got to stop this. This isn't right. We can't leave these people to get slaughtered,'" Mulroy recalled hearing from them.

And their concerns extended beyond Kurdish fighters to what the US withdrawal would mean for Kurdish civilians in northern Syria. "This isn't just about the YPG [the mostly Kurdish militia]," Mulroy said. "They [ISIS] were forcibly moving Kurdish populations, families."

Mulroy's Kurdish contacts on the ground were expressing genuine fear. We've been abandoned again, they told him. "We were in the same place at the same time, a lot of [my] Kurdish friends," Mulroy recalled. "And they all reached out to me at the same time. One of the themes was, 'We know it isn't the Department of Defense. We know it isn't you personally. We know that you'd stay with us, period. But this is a travesty.'"

In the midst of boiling fear and resentment, the commander of the Syrian Kurdish military forces, Mazloum Abdi, sent an email to members of the US military who had fought along with him. Even as his forces faced the very real danger of slaughter at the hands of Turkish, Syrian, Russian, and Iranian forces, Mazloum expressed forgiveness to members of the US military.

"Mazloum essentially absolved the soldiers of the decision of the president," Mulroy remembered. "He said, 'I know that you guys would stand with us to the end. And we know it wasn't you, so don't take that guilt.'

"It was a pretty emotional letter," Mulroy continued. "As it went around, I thought, 'Damn.' It spoke more than any American can actually say about the connection between the forces. So it was tough."[6]

Beyond abandoning a close ally in the midst of battle, Mulroy and other senior Pentagon leaders believed the president was abandoning core US national security interests. The United States' partnership with Syrian Kurds had reaped enormous rewards on the battlefield.

In a matter of months, US and Kurdish forces had reduced the ISIS caliphate to virtually nothing.

Between 2017 and 2019, according to Pentagon estimates, the United States and its partners had killed tens of thousands of ISIS fighters in Syria and Iraq and captured some thirty thousand. ISIS territory, which at its peak had encompassed thousands of square miles across Iraq and Syria, had been whittled down to a few disparate pockets. And the United States had achieved that remarkable progress in Syria, which had been the site of the ISIS caliphate's capital, Raqqa, with just a few hundred US soldiers and marines on the ground.

"This is actually the model for how to do this stuff," said Mulroy. "It's not the fourteen thousand troops like in Afghanistan. It's about two thousand. And it's with a significantly capable partner force, using US enablers. We just provided them what they needed to beat ISIS, and then the enablers were all controlled by the United States."[7]

The strategy of augmenting a capable local fighting force, in this case the Syrian Kurds, with a small number of US forces, mostly special operations troops, had been gaining purchase in the US military for years, driven by the enormous human and financial costs of the much larger US deployments during and after the invasions of Iraq and Afghanistan. Early in his term, President Trump had embraced the strategy and, at times, backed it with greater resources and freedom of decision making for the military. And it had worked: the gains against ISIS had accelerated under Trump.

THREE PILLARS OF NATIONAL DEFENSE

The fact is, the US strategy—President Trump's strategy—would not have worked without the Syrian Kurds. They did the bulk of the fighting against ISIS, and, in the view of US soldiers who fought alongside them, they were good at it.

"The YPG [the mostly Kurdish militia] was the only experienced battlefield leadership cadre that could have done what they did within the Syrian Democratic Forces [the larger alliance of antigovernment forces in Syria, backed by the US]," Mick Mulroy told me.

Not for the first time, the president's decision directly contradicted his own administration's National Defense Strategy, the annually updated document that identifies US national security priorities around the globe.

"If you look at the National Defense Strategy, one of the pillars is partners," Mulroy said. "There's only three pillars: Make a more lethal force; Fix the actual bureaucracy and the administrative part of the Pentagon; and Build strong partners and keep them."

For previous presidents, the National Defense Strategy has been the most detailed public document of their administration's priorities and strategies for achieving them. The NDS is a blueprint for keeping the country safe. Trump, however, repeatedly ignored his own administration's blueprint. As Mulroy told me earlier in this book, it wasn't clear to many of his advisors that he had even read it. "So here's a partner that we would hold up as a model, and these precipitous decisions to withdraw run totally counter to what has been a core part of our Middle East plan for decades. You're certainly not going to inspire a lot of faith in potential partners if you do things like this."

In the Syrian Kurds, the United States had found the right partner in the right place at the right time and one that fought like few others. US soldiers will not hesitate to disparage partner forces who do not carry their weight on the battlefield. In dozens of embeds with the US military in Iraq and Afghanistan, I've heard tales of the best and the worst of those partners in action. US service members unanimously place the Syrian Kurds among the best.

"It's one of the few partner forces where you can absolutely count on them sticking in a fighting position with you, to the end," Mulroy said. "And I imagine it's a sentiment shared by a lot of people who have spent time with them."

The US and the Kurds shared more than combat acumen; they shared values.

"You quickly become part of their unit," Mulroy told me. "For some reason, they just seem to have a connection to our way of thinking. I mean, it's not just that they like us because we're a strong partner and they're the smallest in the region. They have female generals. The second in command under [SDF commander] Mazloum is a female. And they have female fighting units. And if you're a religious minority, where do you go in that region? You go to the Kurdish region. Why? Because they're okay with it and actually protect you.

"They're not perfect. They're a little mafioso up there, too," he cautioned. "But all things considered, they have an affinity for our kind of progressive way of thinking."[8]

Like few other decisions during this presidency, Trump's Syria withdrawal order sparked deep and bipartisan alarm at home, even among some of his closest and most loyal allies. "I'm pretty annoyed," Republican senator Lindsey Graham told my CNN colleague Manu Raju before delivering a biting criticism for a Republican lawmaker, describing Trump's decision as "Obama-like."

Graham's quip was an apparent reference to President Obama's 2011 decision to withdraw US forces from Iraq, a move that even Obama administration officials later acknowledged had helped fuel the rise of ISIS in Iraq and Syria. Obama had been forced to reverse his withdrawal order, redeploying some forces to Iraq and later to Syria to fight. Graham went on to demand that Trump and his administration "explain their policy, not in a tweet, but before Congress answering questions."[9]

Other Republican lawmakers expressed less restrained outrage.

"I've never seen a decision like this since I've been here in 12 years,"

Senator Robert Corker, the outgoing chairman of the Senate Foreign Relations Committee, told reporters. "It is hard to imagine that any president would wake up and make this kind of decision, with little communication, with this little preparation."[10]

GOP representative Adam Kinzinger, a veteran of Afghanistan, went on Trump-friendly Fox News to make an appeal to Trump: "I have no idea what went into this," he said. "I can almost guarantee you that none of his advisors said this was a good idea. I know he's been playing golf with Rand Paul and maybe Rand has tried to convince him of this, but the people that know things about foreign policy and the devastating impact of repeating 2011 again, I'm sure were shocked, as I was by this. It is frightening."

Addressing his comments directly to Trump, he added, "I implore the president to reconsider this. There is no shame in reconsidering this. There is some damage that is going to have been done regardless, but much less than is going to be done if you bring everybody home."[11]

★ ★ ★

BUT WAS THE PRESIDENT REALLY BRINGING EVERYBODY HOME? Trump was the commander in chief, and the Pentagon had a direct order from him to withdraw forces, though now with Mattis's departure under a new acting defense secretary. Behind the scenes, however, defense officials were asking questions. They had been here before with him. Was the president serious? If so, was he serious about removing *all* two thousand US service members? And if so, by when exactly?

"That was one of the conversations we had up front," Mulroy recalled. "Did the president tell us we had to have a certain number by a certain time? And the answer was no."[12]

The lack of clarity and lack of a formal plan from the White House were not new. It had become the norm. And in that lack of clarity, US military leaders deeply opposed to abandoning their Kurdish allies and undermining a highly successful US counterterrorism mission saw an opportunity. Could they find a way to reduce the number of troops while maintaining a credible fighting force? In the simplest terms, could they give the president some, but not all, of what he wanted?

"They just wanted to show progress toward withdrawal. And we could," said Mulroy. "We could show him that we did withdraw. But we still had enough capabilities to maintain our relationship."

Their solution was to reduce the US fighting force somewhat—to about one thousand service members—but not to zero, as the president had ordered in his tweet. Pentagon officials suspected that they had something to their advantage: the president's fleeting attention span. Given time, they hoped, Trump would just forget about Syria.

"We did significantly reduce our presence," said Mulroy. "And then the president just seemed to have moved on to other issues and never asked about it."[13]

The president "just seemed to have moved on."

THE SECOND ERDOĞAN
PHONE CALL AND WITHDRAWAL

President Trump "moved on" from Syria for nearly ten months. During that time, a reduced US force of just over one thousand soldiers continued to partner with the SDF and continued to roll back ISIS territory and kill and capture thousands of ISIS fighters. By March 2019, the Pentagon would declare all of ISIS territory in Syria recaptured. By October 2019, ISIS's few remaining fighters and their leader, Abu Bakr al-Baghdadi, were hiding in shrinking pockets of territory, often located in no-man's-land between territories controlled by other forces.

US policy in Syria was working. The United States and the Syrian

Kurds were winning the war. Then, on October 6, 2019, President Trump got on the phone with Turkish president Erdoğan once more.

"What happens is these phone calls that he does with world leaders, which of course he should do, that's what presidents do, that is what causes a significant adjustment in the strategy, usually," said Mick Mulroy.[14]

In the case of that conversation, Syria wasn't even the original purpose of the call. Trump had agreed to it primarily to smooth over Erdoğan's pique at not securing a one-on-one meeting with Trump at the UN General Assembly in New York the month before.

At the United Nations, Erdoğan had wanted to discuss his interest in establishing what Turkey described as a "safe zone" inside Syria along the Turkish border. US officials throughout the government viewed the Turkish plan with skepticism or outright disdain, believing that Turkey's real intention was to launch a broad offensive against Syrian Kurds, including the United States' partner in the fight against ISIS, the Syrian Democratic Forces.

On the phone, Erdoğan made his case. Trump in turn warned Turkey against anything but a limited incursion, vowing that if Turkey mounted a full-scale invasion, the United States would leave Syria altogether. Trouble was, that was exactly what Erdoğan wanted, and so that was what he vowed to do, leading the president, in a bizarre instance of negotiating retreat, to give Erdoğan even more than he had asked for.

Soon after the call, the White House issued a statement announcing the complete withdrawal of US forces from the border area, characterizing Turkey's invasion as inevitable: "Turkey will soon be moving forward with its long-planned operation into Northern Syria. The United States Armed Forces will not support or be involved in the operation, and United States forces, having defeated the ISIS territorial 'Caliphate,' will no longer be in the immediate area."[15]

With the United States' withdrawal from the north, Erdoğan made clear that Turkey was now ready to follow through on its invasion plans, saying it had "completed our preparations and action plan" and was ready to launch a "ground and air operation" east of the Euphrates River to establish "peace" in the area.[16]

Regardless of his demand to Erdoğan during the call, by withdrawing US forces from the border area, Trump had given Turkey the green light to invade. US military leaders knew it. The Syrian Kurds knew it. And Turkey knew it. As Turkish forces massed on the border, Trump administration officials were left to issue limp protests.

A senior State Department official told reporters that the administration "would not support [the Turkish] operation in any way, shape or form," adding that Turkey in effect would now own the problem.

"If the Turks really want to go in and do this without our support, then they have to do all of it," the official told CNN. "They have to do things like deal with the [foreign terrorist fighters], which we have been doing; it has not been easy."[17]

And that was that: for the second time in ten months, the president had ordered a US retreat in Syria without consulting any of his senior advisors, the US military, US commanders in the region, or US allies. Trump's decision caught his entire administration off guard. At the Pentagon, Mick Mulroy recalls total surprise and deep frustration. "We find out that we're going to just withdraw from the northern part of Syria because of a conversation with President Erdoğan, when our whole plan, the security mechanism, was already worked out so we wouldn't have to do that," he said. "And we spend countless hours working with our counterparts to do that."

Trump's second call with Erdoğan jettisoned that policy and, perhaps, the entire US anti-ISIS mission in Syria. President Trump's second withdrawal order from Syria was, Pentagon officials thought, the final straw. "When he pulled out of the north, we thought we were all out," Mulroy recalled. "We thought for sure that time it was going to be, 'Okay, I told you this before, and now you didn't do it, and I'm telling you again.'"[18]

In effect, they thought the jig was up.

THE KURDS AND NORMANDY

At the root of the president's decision was his apparent acceptance of Erdoğan's view of the Syrian Kurds. Turkey characterized them as terrorists, grouping the YPG with other Kurdish groups that had waged a campaign of violence inside Turkey for years. That was not how the US military viewed the YPG.

"The YPG itself was not attacking Turkey," said Mulroy. "And I think we should have said that more often, because we just kind of did the party line—the Turkish party line—which is to say they were a 'legitimate security concern.' I don't think they're going to attack Turkey, period. They've got enough of their own issues to worry about."

Regardless, the US military had worked out a solution to placate Turkey. The plan, developed jointly by the Defense Department, the State Department, and Central Command, was for US and Turkish forces to conduct combined patrols in the border region.

"We said, 'Okay, we'll do combined patrols, air and ground, in this area on the border that you consider a threat, and we will continue the fight with the SDF against ISIS,'" Mulroy said. "I thought we had worked it out, and it was a lot of effort."

The idea was in part that Kurdish forces would never attack Turkish forces so long as they were patrolling alongside those of the United States. So US forces were, in effect, the Turks' bodyguards. Such patrols were a significant concession to Turkey and a loss for the Kurds.

"I thought we had it to a point where, if anything, it was unfair to the SDF because we asked them to dismantle several of their fighting positions," said Mulroy.

In retrospect, Mulroy suspects that Turkey took advantage of the joint patrols to prepare for its eventual invasion of northern Syria. In hindsight, the operations gave Turkish forces opportunities to do reconnaissance on the Kurds, their eventual targets. "If we're Turkey, we know we're not going to get shot at because we're with the Americans," he explained. "We want to fly over and look at all their defensive positions, better to do it with Americans. They're not going to shoot at us.

"And the coup de grâce would be that the Kurds actually dismantled several of their defensive positions, at our request," he added. "I don't know that this was Turkey's intent. But if Turkey were planning to do an invasion of a country, we could have been played the entire time."[19]

Turkey's invasion later that October was quick and devastating. My CNN colleagues inside Syria witnessed withering air strikes by Turkish warplanes and long columns of civilians fleeing the violence.

In Washington, the bipartisan outrage was even more intense than following Trump's first withdrawal order almost a year earlier. Trump ally Senator Lindsey Graham and his Democratic colleague Senator Chris Van Hollen sought to tie the president's hands, introducing legislation imposing sanctions on senior Turkish officials. "This unlawful and unwarranted attack against an American friend and partner threatens the lives and livelihoods of millions of civilians, many of whom have already fled from their homes elsewhere in Syria to find safety in this region," they said in a statement.[20]

Unmoved, President Trump came up with a novel way to justify his decision. At a press conference in Washington, he took aim at the Kurds, saying they were fighting for their own interests, not the United States. "Now the Kurds are fighting for their land, just so you understand," he said.

As if that weren't enough, he delved seventy years back in time to note—inexplicably—one time when the Kurds had not fought along-side the United States. "As somebody wrote in a very, very powerful article today, they didn't help us in the Second World War, they didn't help us with Normandy," he said.[21]

Trump was arguing that the Kurds, despite losing thousands in the fight against ISIS in Syria, were not the loyal allies their supporters claimed. In fact, to make his point, the president was actually mis-quoting the article he was referring to, an opinion piece by the conser-vative columnist Kurt Schlichter on Townhall titled "Critics Aghast as Trump Keeps Word About No More Wars."

Schlichter's point was that the Kurds were fighting alongside the United States not out of some romantic altruism but out of shared interests. He wrote, "The Kurds didn't show up for us at Normandy or Inchon or Khe Sanh or Kandahar. The Syrian Kurds allied with us in their homeland because we shared a common interest in wiping out the head-lopping freak show that was ISIS."[22]

It was a fair argument about shared interests, but Schlichter clearly wasn't disparaging the Kurds for not having fought in World War II (Normandy), or for that matter, in the Korean War (Inchon), the Viet-nam War (Khe Sanh), or the war in Afghanistan (Kandahar). That didn't stop the president from attacking the Kurds anyway.

Mulroy bristles even at Schlichter's argument. Fact is, he notes, the Kurds had been fighting—and dying—well beyond their own ter-ritory.

"Well, yeah, it was in their interest to remove ISIS from the Kurd-ish areas," he explained. "But they were way down into Sunni ar-eas. And they actually stayed down there even after the incursion by the Turks. So it's not just their interest. They're doing it as a partner. They've lost eleven thousand fighters. They have really borne the brunt of this."[23]

TRUMP AND THE OIL FIELDS

For the second time in a year, fearing the loss of the entire US operation in Syria, US military officials began looking for ways to water down the president's withdrawal order. At first, CENTCOM Commander Kenneth F. McKenzie, Jr., lobbied to keep the troops withdrawn from Syria in the region, so that they could be sent back quickly to conduct counterterror missions.

But military leaders had another idea: a way to cater to an objective they knew was close to the president's heart. They knew Trump viewed the deployment of US forces in the region, as in most corners of the globe, as at least partly transactional. So what could US forces take from Syria in return? Their answer was oil. They would lobby the president to redeploy US forces elsewhere in Syria to protect the oil fields there. There was a military objective in denying that oil revenue to other enemy forces on the ground. But, in reality, this was a stealth way to avoid abandoning Syria and the Syrian Kurds entirely.

"When Trump started talking about these oil fields and how we're taking the oil, which we're not, and I'm pretty sure that's against the law of armed conflict," recalled Mulroy, "we used it as a means to maintain a small presence there to be able to meet the minimum [force] requirement."

I asked Mulroy whether defense officials were, in effect, fooling the president into believing they were fulfilling his orders, when, in fact, they were going only as far as absolutely necessary.

"That's right. And you can see it play out," he replied. "If you look at his tweets, they were definitive about leaving. And then we didn't leave. And now we haven't left, we're still there, and that's a good thing."[24]

It was "a good thing" for the simple reason that every US official involved in Syria policy believed that a summary US withdrawal would enable ISIS to re-form and fight again.

"There is a significant concern, not only in DOD but in the intelligence community at large, that if you do leave, ISIS is sure to return," Mulroy told me. "And there's only so much you can expect the Kurds to do without our support."

Perhaps against the odds, the oil plan worked. US forces were still on the ground in Syria, though with a new stated focus: protecting the oil fields.

Their new mission—or continuation of their mission under different auspices—presented immediate challenges. One was the rules of engagement (ROE). If US forces were there to protect the oil fields, if necessary with the use of deadly force, could they also use deadly force to defend their Kurdish allies? In military-legal terms, could the Pentagon and Central Command extend the principle of "collective self-defense" to include the SDF? Under the existing ROE, US forces could of course use deadly force to defend themselves from enemy forces. But could a US soldier, say, shoot a Russian or Syrian soldier if he or she threatened someone in the SDF? Like so many other questions, that one went unanswered with any official policy decision.

After two orders by the president to withdraw, US forces were still on the ground in Syria. Yet their numbers were down again, to six hundred troops from a thousand, a decrease that significantly reduced their capabilities and scope. To his seniormost Syria advisors, the president's decisions were inexplicably undermining his own policy in Syria.

"What baffled me," Mick Mulroy told me, "and I'm not a political guy, is that this was the thing that this administration could have pointed to as a success. A foreign policy success in Syria, and a model for how it's done. And then everything, all the decisions, seem to run counter to their own interests because now it's going to be remembered for abandoning partners, placating Turkey."

The president himself had gotten in the way of his own success. And that created a disturbing dynamic for a nation at war against ISIS.

"The most challenging part was actually the policy decisions, not the enemy, which is a bad situation," Mulroy told me.[25]

The policy is more challenging than the enemy. That is Syria under President Trump.

THE ANSWER

In the span of ten months between December 2018 and October 2019, President Trump twice ordered the withdrawal of US forces from Syria and twice reversed his own orders—both times with no consultation with his senior advisors and no warning to US forces or US partners in theater. With each summary withdrawal, the US military cycled through stages of genuine alarm, attempts at alternatives short of the president's extremes, followed by the hope that those alternatives would satisfy the president enough for him to move on. Their tactics worked though the mission suffered.

And the president still managed to damage what could have been one of his most unqualified foreign policy successes—the defeat of ISIS—while enabling gains by parties invested in a US failure in Syria: the Syrian government, Russia, Iran, and Turkey.

9

Shifting Red Lines: Iran

WHAT HAS TRUMP GAINED WITH IRAN?

As a private citizen, Donald Trump sided with Barack Obama during one of the most controversial moments of his presidency: his decision not to enforce his so-called red line on Syria. President Obama had set the "red line" in 2012, when he had said in a speech that he would reconsider his opposition to military intervention in Syria if the Syrian regime used chemical weapons. In 2013, Syria did just that, killing more than a thousand Syrian civilians in a horrific attack using the deadly and powerful sarin gas. Obama considered a military response before retreating.

Based on his public comments at the time, Trump seemed to be on Obama's side. On September 3, 2013, he tweeted, "What I am saying is stay out of Syria." Two days later, he reiterated his opposition to military action, questioning President Obama's motivation for even considering it: "The only reason President Obama wants to attack Syria is to save face over his very dumb RED LINE statement. Do NOT attack Syria, fix U.S.A."

As president, however, Trump reversed himself. When

Syrian forces again used chemical weapons in a deadly attack on civilians in April 2017, Trump blamed Obama's failure to enforce his "red line" for having emboldened Syria to strike again. "These heinous actions by the Bashar al-Assad regime are a consequence of the past administration's weakness and irresolution. President Obama said in 2012 that he would establish a 'red line' against the use of chemical weapons and then did nothing," he said in a statement on April 4.[1]

Soon after, moved, he said, by pictures of the youngest victims of the chemical attack, Trump ordered a military strike, launching a wave of cruise missiles on Syrian military installations. He claimed credit for restoring US credibility. He was a president, he assured the American public, who would enforce his own red lines.

President Trump received praise from loyalists and critics for exacting punishment for a war crime. However, this attack was limited and the adversary relatively powerless to strike US interests.

What would he do when a far more powerful adversary tested the United States' resolve? Would he set a new red line with Iran?

On a Thursday in September 2018, a handful of mortar shells struck near the US Embassy in Baghdad's fortified Green Zone. One landed in a parking lot and another in the river, causing no casualties. The US military immediately suspected Iranian-backed Shia militias, which had recently released a statement threatening to attack "occupying forces" in Iraq. However, attacks like this one targeting US compounds in Iraq were relatively routine, usually causing limited damage.

US commanders in Baghdad informed the Pentagon of the attack, which was standard procedure. But none was alarmed. So officials at the Pentagon were surprised when they received a call from a senior official on the National Security Council demanding military options for the president to retaliate against Iran. That official said the president wanted to know immediately how and when the United States could respond.

"The NSC called us in on a Sunday," a former senior US official told me. "[The NSC official] was basically telling us we had to have military options against Iran, today, on that day."

Pentagon officials were dumbfounded. On a conference call with the White House, which included the vice chairman of the Joint Chiefs of Staff, General Paul Selva, and Undersecretary of Defense for Policy John Rood, Selva muted the line on the Pentagon's end and turned to his colleagues in disbelief.

"He said, 'Is this a joke? They really want us to propose direct military action into Iran, against Iran, based on this?'" the same former senior US official told me. "And I said, 'No, we've been dealing with this all morning. Have they spent any time in Iraq?' This is a constant thing."

When they got off the call, General Selva and Secretary Rood made it clear to their colleagues they would not be providing the White House with any military options unless directed explicitly by the president himself.

"There's no way we're going to provide the NSC military options for this," the former senior US official recalled their saying. "It just doesn't make sense."

That "urgent" request from the White House did not last. "It just died after that," the official remembered.

A handful of mortars. One forceful demand for military options. Then silence. It was just the first of many times the NSC would reach out to the Pentagon for military options against Iran, without warning and without the normal interagency process to determine if a military response was warranted or wise.

The demands by the NSC came and went, and throughout senior US military officials didn't know if it was the president who was demanding military options or his then national security advisor, John Bolton. Some Pentagon officials suspected the latter. More broadly, the fact was that the United States' seniormost military leaders did not know what the president wanted.

"Every feedback we got from the NSC was the president wanted to take strong military action against Iranian aggression," said Mick Mulroy, who was serving under Secretary of Defense Jim Mattis at the time. "And we resisted, thinking that, 'Okay, then he needs to tell us.' But we never really knew whether that was accurate or not."[2]

The aftermath of those wayward mortars in September 2018 began a months-long policy-making seesaw with Trump and Iran, alternating between urgency and inaction, threat and retreat. On which side would Trump emerge? And did he have a strategy?

A month later, I was at the anchor desk preparing to go live on the air when I learned startling new information from a source inside the administration: President Trump had just called off a military strike on Iran. Twenty-four hours earlier, Iran had shot down a US drone in international airspace over the Strait of Hormuz. The RQ-4A Global Hawk is one of the US military's most advanced surveillance aircraft.

Far bigger and more capable than the Predator drones the military relies on for strikes on personnel targets on the ground, the Global Hawk has the wingspan of a Boeing 737 and a price tag in excess of $100 million. That was a significant loss for US forces in the region and a significant escalation by Iran.

Notably, I was told that the president's decision to call off military action had come after US warplanes were already in the air and just minutes away from firing their weapons. Trump balked, the official said, because he was uncomfortable with the intelligence community's estimate of potential Iranian losses on the ground. The target package included a number of radar installations and surface-to-air missile batteries.[3] Given that each was staffed with dozens of Iranian soldiers, the IC estimated an Iranian death toll as high as 150 killed—too high for the president.

I shared the information with my editors at CNN for approval to report it live during our show. The decision to recall US military action moments before a strike was newsworthy under any circumstances. It was particularly remarkable for a president who had relentlessly attacked his predecessor for calling off a retaliatory attack against Syria. The fact that it was the casualty estimate that had precipitated the president's reversal raised further questions. Such estimates are normally included at the front end, when military options are first presented to the president. I was told that the Pentagon had done so in this case as well. Was the casualty estimate really the reason?

CNN does not approve enterprise reporting without managers thoroughly vetting and reviewing the information and the sourcing. When I received their sign-off, I was preparing to report the news of the president's reversal when the president tweeted the explanation himself. "On Monday they shot down an unmanned drone flying in International Waters," he wrote. "We were cocked [sic] & loaded to retaliate last night on 3 different sights[sic] when I asked, how many will die. 150 people, sir, was the answer from a General. 10 minutes before the strike I stopped it, not . . . proportionate to shooting down an unmanned drone."

As so often in his presidency, Trump had made a gut decision in the moment. And we would learn who was in his ear at that moment. According to the *New York Times*, Fox News host Tucker Carlson had spoken with Trump prior to the planned strike and reminded him that he had run for president promising to end wars in the Middle East, not start them. If he sparked another one, Carlson warned, "he could kiss his chances of re-election goodbye."[4]

The president had already sent conflicting messages on the US response. Soon after the shoot-down, Trump had tweeted—ominously— "Iran made a very big mistake!" But speaking later in the Oval Office, he raised the possibility—without citing any US assessment—that the Iranian strike had been unintentional.

"Probably Iran made a mistake. I would imagine it was a general or somebody who made a mistake in shooting that drone down," he said in answer to a question from my CNN colleague Kaitlan Collins. "I find it hard to believe it was intentional. I think it could've been somebody that was loose and stupid. It was a very foolish move, that I can tell you."[5]

He then brought up the campaign promise Carlson would later remind him of. "I want to get out of these endless wars, I campaign on that," he said.[6]

Nowhere was the surprise greater than in the Pentagon, where officials worried the whiplash between threats of retaliation and last-minute retreats would embolden Iran.

"When we first went over there with the options after the drone shoot-down," recalled Mulroy, "the idea was that he was going to take pretty strong action, because of all the feedback we got. When he said 'No,' that was surprising."[7]

Three months later, Iran escalated once again. In an elaborate attack involving a swarm of drones and cruise missiles, Iran struck a collection of key oil facilities in Saudi Arabia. The attack—on oil-processing centers in Abqaiq and Khurais in eastern Saudi Arabia—disabled a full 50 percent of all Saudi oil production, approximately 5 percent of global supply. Oil prices skyrocketed.[8]

Tehran deliberately attempted to conceal responsibility for the attack, shifting blame to the Iranian-backed Houthi rebels in Yemen, who quickly claimed responsibility. Those drones and cruise missiles had borne no Iranian flags. And they had followed a convoluted path into Saudi Arabia, not directly southwest from Iran but due west through Iraq and then Kuwait before approaching the Abqaiq and Khurais facilities from the east.

Those were classic "shadow war" tactics, akin to those employed by Russia and China in their acts of military aggression and provocation against US and Western interests around the world. (I describe them in detail in my book *The Shadow War: Inside Russia's and China's Secret Operations to Defeat America*.) A close parallel was Russia's invasion of Crimea in 2014. Russian troops showed up there without flags or patches identifying their nationality or military unit—forces that would come to be known as "the little green men." Ukrainians and international observers had no doubt about where the forces had come from: their weapons and accents were distinctly Russian. But by injecting doubt or the illusion of doubt, the Kremlin had created plausible deniability, however implausible the proposition was. Now Iran was mimicking those tactics in Saudi Arabia.

The serpentine approach of the missiles and drones did not fool the US military. A senior US military official told me, "We knew it was Iranian as the attack was happening." An investigation by the United Nations first reported by Reuters would later corroborate the

US military's assessment, finding that the Houthi rebels had not been responsible.[9]

In the days after the refinery attack, the White House again demanded military options for the president. The Pentagon complied. Mick Mulroy, as deputy assistant secretary of defense for the Middle East, recalled his team presenting the administration a broad range of possibilities. "We always have plans ready for the president, options to respond to aggression by countries, particularly ones that have already shown a willingness to do so," he told me. "So we were ready with options. I can't go into the options. It's classified. But I can tell you, as you would expect, you have high-end stuff, medium, and then the lower-end stuff."

Among the high-end options was a cruise missile strike inside Iranian territory. Also on the table were a number of options involving unconventional warfare, that is, "shadow war" tactics similar to those Iran used in its attack on the Saudi oil facilities. Such an approach would have allowed the United States, like Iran, to deny involvement. For Mulroy, that was the preferred route with the least danger of further escalation.

"My inject into it, and probably because of my background, was to do more things on the irregular warfare side," he told me. "Because that's the arena that they're playing in. It's plausibly deniable, which is politically not escalating. So, I was pushing for an unconventional response, less of a conventional one, like TLAMs [Tomahawk Land Attack Missiles] into the territory of Iran."

Mulroy lost the debate. The Pentagon presented mostly conventional options to the president.

"We presented what, I think, was too heavily weighed on the conventional side, which would lead to escalation. And the president essentially elected none of the above," he said.

For Mulroy, the president's rejection of high-end military action in response to the drone strike had been understandable; 150 dead Iranians would have represented a significant escalation.

"[The drone] is an expensive aircraft, but it's a robot at the end of the day," he explained. "It didn't kill any Americans. But we still thought we were going to send some kind of message, even if it was completely equal, like shoot down a bunch of their drones or whatever. Essentially, we didn't do anything, which we thought was strange."

Refusing to respond to a devastating Iranian attack on Saudi oil facilities was harder to understand. When he and his colleagues asked the NSC why, they got a simple answer. "'Well, [the president] didn't want to do it, so we're done,'" Mulroy recalled. "The first time that happened, I think there was kind of a sigh of relief. The second time, I think there was shock. So it's like, 'What do you mean, we're not doing anything? I mean, we've got to do something.'"

US military leaders were again concerned that the president's repeated refusal to respond militarily would further embolden Iranian leaders. And they appeared to have been right. Iran—reeling under President Trump's "maximum-pressure" campaign—launched a maximum-pressure campaign of its own.

"They've decided this is their counter-'maximum-pressure' campaign, and they're doing it deliberately," Mulroy explained. "So they're challenging our presence in Iraq. They are hitting the oil infrastructure itself. And they're hitting the means to deliver the oil. And they're just going to keep doing that, because that's the only thing they have available to them."[10]

Three months later, like clockwork, Iran escalated yet again. And that time, the targets were Americans.

K1 Air Base in Kirkuk Province north of Baghdad is a former Iraqi air force base that today houses Iraqi forces and the US troops and US civilian contractors advising them. It is one of several joint military bases around the country, symbols of the continuing US military presence in Iraq nearly two decades after the invasion. Each is a frequent target of rocket attacks.

On the evening of December 27, 2019, two days after Christmas, Katyusha rockets rained down on the camp. The attack was one of a series in the weeks preceding, but this one was more damaging and deadly. Several US and Iraqi service members were wounded, and, in what would prove to be consequential, one US civilian contractor was killed.

The US military did not immediately assign responsibility for the rocket attack, but a US official told CNN that night that its suspicions centered on Iran: "There are a lot of similarities to some of the other 10 rocket attacks in the last two months which we have linked to Iranian-backed militias. We are looking into a possible link to Kataib Hezbollah in particular."[11]

Kataib Hezbollah and other so-called popular mobilization forces (PMUs) are Iran's unofficial armies inside Iraq—funded, armed, and directed by Iran's own paramilitary force, the Quds Force. In a sign of Iran's influence, Abu Mahdi al-Muhandis, the leader of Kataib Hezbollah, had citizenship in both Iraq and Iran.

The United States soon assigned blame to the group definitively. And less than forty-eight hours after the rocket attack, the United States retaliated, striking five Kataib Hezbollah bases across Iraq and Syria. The attacks, launched from F-15E Strike Eagle fighter jets, were devastating, killing some twenty-five militia fighters and wounding dozens more, according to Iranian-backed militias.

US officials described the attack as "defensive" but immediately warned of the possibility of further strikes. "I would note also that we will take additional actions as necessary to ensure that we act in our own self-defense and we deter further bad behavior from militia groups or from Iran," Secretary of Defense Mark Esper said.[12]

Iran condemned the attack. And Iraq, increasingly sensitive to unilateral US military action on its soil, protested as well. "The Iraqi Prime Minister expressed his strong objection to this unilateral decision and his concern that it would lead to further escalation and demanded that he (Esper) stop it (airstrikes) immediately," said a spokesman for the commander of Iraq's Armed Forces, adding with a rhetorical flourish, "These strikes represent a treacherous stab in the back."[13]

Prime Minister Adel Abdul-Mahdi himself said on Iraqi state television that the Iraqi government staunchly opposed "unilateral action" by coalition forces inside his country: "We have already confirmed our rejection of any unilateral action by coalition forces or any other forces inside Iraq. We consider it a violation of Iraq's sovereignty and a dangerous escalation that threatens the security of Iraq and the region."[14]

The United States was unmoved. President Trump had apparently set his own red line for Iran: the death of an American. But Iran had its own red lines.

★ ★ ★

IN THE YEARS SINCE THE US INVASION OF IRAQ, THE US EMBASSY in Baghdad has grown into a fortress. Set inside the Green Zone encompassing Iraqi government buildings, the Iraqi Parliament Building, and international embassies, the US Embassy is an island unto itself, surrounded by high walls and protected by an expansive security contingent. Though US officials are reluctant to confirm the exact number of security forces stationed there, the embassy was protected by an estimated fifty to one hundred US Marines and two hundred civilian security contractors.

The embassy's first line of defense, however, is Iraqi, with security checkpoints leading to the compound manned by Iraqi security forces. On the morning of December 31, those checkpoints went empty.

Soon, thousands of fighters from Kataib Hezbollah and the militia's supporters surrounded the embassy. It was an enormous show of force by Iran on Iraqi soil. And unlike with its recent attack on oil facilities in Saudi Arabia, Iranian leaders were making no effort to hide Iran's involvement.

At the Pentagon, Mick Mulroy believed that by mobilizing Kataib Hezbollah to threaten the US Embassy, Tehran was making clear it didn't care about attribution anymore. "One, they wanted to be successful, because they actually train their paramilitary officers, like the Quds Force guys do," he said. "And two, they didn't care about Iran getting attributed with it, because you can't get any closer to Iran than Kataib Hezbollah.

"I mean, they swear allegiance to the ayatollah. It's the thinnest veil they could have used. So it's like they wanted to send a message that 'Yep. We're going to use a proxy, but we're going to use a competent proxy. And they're going to actually hit the target.'"[15]

Their target this time was the very center of US influence in Iraq. Unfolding live on international television, including on my and my coanchor Poppy Harlow's own broadcast, protesters laid siege to the embassy compound. In a scene reminiscent of the assault on the US Embassy in Tehran in 1979, militiamen broke into a reception area, looting it and setting it on fire. From the rooftop, US Marines and other security personnel fired tear gas canisters at the protesters. There were genuine fears that the pro-Iranian forces intended to take over the embassy.

President Trump ordered a further hundred US Marines to Baghdad to reinforce the hundreds of security forces already guarding the embassy. He also ordered the 82nd Airborne Division's Immediate Response Force—a brigade-sized unit comprising some three thousand troops—to stand by for possible deployment in case of a deadly threat to US personnel. Memories of Benghazi ran deep. Since May 2019,

Trump had already added more than fourteen thousand forces to the region in a show of force to Iran. As the standoff with Iran worsened, he was gradually but steadily violating one of his principal campaign promises of bringing home the troops from the Middle East.

The additional forces were tasked with a variety of missions. Some were deployed to provide further force protection for US soldiers already deployed there, others to protect shipping. More broadly, the Trump administration was signaling support to nervous Gulf allies, including Saudi Arabia, Kuwait, and the United Arab Emirates, and attempting to deter further acts of aggression by Iran. However, there were deep doubts in the Pentagon that it was a workable strategy.

"We had 150,000 troops in 2008," said Mick Mulroy, "and [the Iranians] were killing us left and right with proxies. I said, 'Look, I get it because we need to defend our folks. We need to defend the facilities. We need to give the president options, but let's not act like this is a real deterrent, because it hasn't been. I mean, it's just a fact.'"

In fact, as the US military presence in the region grew over the course of 2019, Iran seemed to be emboldened, not deterred. "They say, 'Okay, okay. We'll send our Maritime Special Operations Units and blast holes in ships and we'll use our proxies to kill Americans in Iraq,'" said Mulroy. "I mean, if anything, [attacks] have increased, which is the challenge to the whole Iran strategy."[16]

THE KILLING OF SOLEIMANI

The United States was about to send an even more striking message. On Thursday evening, January 2, CNN began to hear reports of an explosion near Baghdad's International Airport. In Iraq, explosions near the airport are routine. Like US military bases in Iraq, the airport is a favorite target for pro-Iranian militias. Early reports described the explosion as one more rocket attack. But when I started asking questions of US officials, one of them advised me to pay close attention. That had not been a rocket attack, the source told me; it had been a US military strike.

My eyes widened when the official informed me that the target of the strike was Iranian, in fact, arguably the second most powerful man in all of Iran. I was told that the United States had targeted Qasem Soleimani, the feared leader of Iran's Quds Force, the wing of Iran's Islamic Revolutionary Guard Corps responsible for military, terror, and intelligence operations around the world. And US intelligence believed that Soleimani was dead.

Soleimani held an almost mythical status in Iran. He was the face of Iranian military power beyond its borders—the architect of Iranian intervention in Syria and the driving force behind the pro-Iranian PMUs in Iraq, including Kataib Hezbollah.

For US military veterans of Iraq and their families, Soleimani was nothing short of a mass murderer. The Pentagon blamed the deaths of more than six hundred US service members on powerful IEDs provided by the Quds Force. Those IEDs had left thousands of other US service members with life-altering injuries.

Iraqi state television was the first to publicly confirm Soleimani's death, saying he had been killed by multiple rockets striking a convoy of vehicles just outside the airport where he had landed shortly before. Soon after, the Pentagon confirmed what my source had told me earlier: Soleimani had been the target, and he was dead.

"At the direction of the President," the Pentagon statement read, "the U.S. military has taken decisive defensive action to protect U.S. personnel abroad by killing Qasem Soleimani, the head of the Islamic Revolutionary Guard Corps-Quds Force, a U.S.-designated Foreign Terrorist Organization."[17]

The deadly strike was a remarkable success for the US military and a remarkable decision by a president who had repeatedly balked at less aggressive military action against Iran. Trump, speaking from his Mar-a-Lago resort the next day, took caution to note that he was not looking for a further escalation with Iran. "We took action last night to stop a war. We did not take action to start a war," he claimed in a statement.[18]

The risks were enormous. Soleimani was a senior Iranian official who had amassed significant political and military influence inside Iran and around the region. Though the United States had recently designated the Quds Force a terror organization and therefore Soleimani himself, as the group's leader, a terrorist, Iran might very well consider the strike an act of war.

Two days after the strike, Majid Takht Ravanchi, Iran's ambassador to the United Nations, told my colleague Erin Burnett exactly that, describing the strike as "tantamount to opening a war," and threatening revenge. "The response for a military action is a military action. By whom? When? Where? That is for the future to witness," he said.[19]

So what had changed? What had led a president who had deliberately balked at less aggressive military action against Iran to order perhaps the boldest military strike of his presidency?

THE "INTELLIGENCE": WAS SOLEIMANI ABOUT TO ATTACK?

In the aftermath of the attack, the Trump administration argued it was all about the intelligence, specifically information indicating that Iran had been planning "imminent" attacks on Americans. My colleagues Dana Bash and Pamela Brown and I were told that the United States had gathered intelligence that Soleimani had visited multiple countries in the region to prepare and plan attacks on US interests in the region, including US personnel.[20] A source familiar with the information described the intelligence as being "beyond the normal chatter" among Iranian operatives.

The president and his advisors would repeat the word "imminent" numerous times in the days that followed. But as time passed, they could not provide any detail as to whom exactly those "imminent" attacks were targeting and when. At CNN, we learned that no new warnings had gone out to diplomatic facilities in the region in advance, which was routine in the event of credible threats against US citizens abroad.

As the questions grew, President Trump only upped the ante. In an interview on Fox News, he claimed that Iran had been planning attacks on multiple US embassies in the region. "I can reveal that I believe it probably would've been four embassies," he said.[21]

When Secretary of Defense Mark Esper was asked two days later on CBS News to confirm the president's comments, he demurred. "I didn't see one, with regard to four embassies," he said. "What I'm saying is that I shared the president's view that probably—my expectation was they were going to go after our embassies."[22]

Those are not words and phrases normally used to describe credible and specific threats. In a second interview on CNN soon after his comments on CBS, Esper refused to discuss the intelligence at all.

That same day, Trump's national security advisor, Robert O'Brien, refused to provide new details. "All I can tell you is we've been clear from the start that there were very significant threats to American facilities in the region and American military officials—officers and men and women and also the U.S. diplomats. And I think that's consistent with what the president's saying now," he told Fox News.

Pressed further by anchor Chris Wallace on the inconsistencies among the president and his most senior advisors in their descriptions of the intelligence, O'Brien seemed to concede: "We knew there were threats to American facilities. Now whether they were bases, embassies—you know, it's always hard until the attack happens."[23]

The back-and-forth was not just a case of imprecise language from the president. The conflicting descriptions of the intelligence raised a crucial question: Did the president order the strike to stop an imminent attack or for another reason? There were certainly other reasons to want Soleimani dead. As a correspondent on assignment in Iraq in the years after the invasion, I had covered numerous attacks using IEDs supplied by Soleimani's Quds Force and witnessed their deadly aftermaths. And I knew that his killing would bring some comfort to the families of his more than six hundred American victims.

But had his past actions been the spark, or were there new "imminent" threats? And did the benefits outweigh the risks? It was impossible to know if the administration would provide no details about the intelligence. These questions and the imprecise answers brought back sobering memories of the run-up to the Iraq invasion, as many accepted the Bush administration's description of the intelligence on Saddam Hussein's weapons programs.

President Trump himself had repeatedly questioned or dismissed US intelligence—on threats ranging from Russian interference in the 2016 election to Iran's compliance with the 2015 nuclear deal to the continued expansion of North Korea's nuclear program. If he had not been confident in US intelligence then, why was he so confident now?

THE VOICES IN TRUMP'S EAR

If Tucker Carlson had been the voice in his ear before Trump canceled US retaliation for Iran's shootdown of a drone, Secretary of State Mike Pompeo was the one who pushed him toward the most aggressive military strike of his presidency. Killing Soleimani had been a goal of Pompeo's for more than a decade. A source from the secretary's inner circle told my colleague Jamie Gangel that the strike was Pompeo's idea and that he had brought it to Trump. Pompeo "was the one who made the case to take out Soleimani, it was him absolutely," the source said.[24]

Days later, Iran launched a retaliatory strike, firing a series of missiles on the al-Asad Air Base in Iraq, where dozens of US forces were deployed. The barrage caused serious damage to facilities but no apparent US casualties. In the immediate aftermath of the attack, all US service members were safe and accounted for.

In his first public comments on the Soleimani assassination on January 8, President Trump pointed to the lack of casualties in the Iranian attack as evidence that Tehran was ready to move on. "Iran appears to be standing down, which is a good thing for all parties concerned and a very good thing for the world," he said in a televised address from the Grand Foyer of the White House. He then went on to raise the surprising prospect of peace with Tehran: "We must all work together toward making a deal with Iran that makes the world a safer and more peaceful place. We must also make a deal that allows Iran to thrive and prosper, and take advantage of its enormous untapped potential. Iran can be a great country."[25]

His comments to Iran echoed his outreach to North Korea after his "fire and fury" threats. And as I listened to him live on CNN, I recalled another moment when another sitting US president had offered an olive branch to Iran: President Barack Obama in his 2009 address in Cairo. He had made what was at the time a groundbreaking entreaty to Iranian leaders: "Rather than remain trapped in the past, I have made it clear to Iran's leaders and people that my country is prepared to move forward. The question now is not what Iran is against, but rather what future it wants to build."[26]

I had been in Cairo for Obama's speech and still remember the hope it engendered there and the heat it sparked from Republicans at home. Now, more than a decade later and in the midst of an escalating military confrontation with Iran, Trump's words sounded reminiscent. "Finally, to the people and leaders of Iran: We want you to have a future and a great future—one that you deserve, one of prosperity at home, and harmony with the nations of the world," he said. "The United States is ready to embrace peace with all who seek it."[27]

Was Trump attempting another 180-degree turn from "fire and fury" to peacemaker? His call for negotiations was a risk. He was reaching out to a regime he had relentlessly attacked as both hostile and untrustworthy. But disrupters like Trump give themselves leeway other leaders do not. If he could disrupt US policy away from an international nuclear agreement and toward military action, he could disrupt the policy back again to diplomacy.

Trump was basing his change of heart, in part at least, on a lie. In the days that followed, it became clear that Iran had caused casualties in the attack on al-Asad, as US service members began to show symptoms of traumatic brain injury (TBI) from the missile strikes. The first reports showed just a handful of such injuries.

"While no U.S. service members were killed in the Jan. 8 Iranian attack on Al Asad Air Base," read an early statement from the US-led coalition in Iraq, "several were treated for concussion symptoms from the blast and are still being assessed.

"Out of an abundance of caution, service members were transported from Al Asad Air Base, Iraq to Landstuhl Regional Medical Center in Germany for follow-on screening. When deemed fit for duty, the service members are expected to return to Iraq following screening."[28]

In the days that followed, however, the toll of the injured steadily rose. In February, my CNN colleague Barbara Starr would report that more than a hundred US service members had been diagnosed with TBI.[29] TBI is a serious injury and one that has become a distressing hallmark of the US wars in Iraq and Afghanistan. Better body armor, up-armored vehicles, and shelters such as those on the al-Asad base can protect victims from shrapnel but not the concussive force of the blasts.

Iran's retaliatory strike had indeed caused US casualties. But this was inconvenient information for a president who had repeatedly insisted there was no significant Iranian retaliation. So Trump ignored the facts and downplayed the injuries. When reporters asked him to explain the discrepancy between his initial claim of there having been no casualties and news of multiple victims of TBI, the president played the injuries down: "No, I heard that they had headaches, and a couple of other things, but I would say, and I can report, it's not very serious."[30]

Trump's dismissal elicited scathing reactions from veterans and veterans' groups. "TBI is known to cause depression, memory loss, severe headaches, dizziness and fatigue—all injuries that come with both short- and long-term effects," said the national commander of Veterans of Foreign Wars William Schmitz in a statement. "The VFW expects an apology from the president to our service men and women for his misguided remarks. And, we ask that he and the White House join with us in our efforts to educate Americans of the dangers TBI has on these heroes as they protect our great nation in these trying times. Our warriors require our full support more than ever in this challenging environment."[31]

The apology never came. The injuries—a fact—did not gel with Trump's desire to claim victory and move on.

Two months later, Iran struck again, and this time, even the president could not deny the casualties. In March 2020, Iranian-backed militias fired rockets at Camp Taji north of Baghdad, killing two US service members and one British service member.

Secretary of Defense Mark Esper quickly assigned blame to Iran. "Yesterday's attack by Iranian backed Shia militia groups consisted of

multiple indirect fires ... and was clearly targeting coalition and partner forces on Camp Taji," he told reporters at the Pentagon. "... We've
got to hold the perpetrators accountable. You don't get to shoot at our
bases and kill and wound Americans and get away with it."[32]

THE IRAN STRATEGY BOARD

Inside the Pentagon, there were broader questions about whether the
president's entire approach to Iran was working. Skepticism had been
brewing for months, leading Secretary of Defense Esper to launch a
strategic review.

"The secretary, to his credit, said, 'I need a full-on assessment of:
Is the strategy working? And if it's not'—because he knew it wasn't—
'what do we need to do?'" Mick Mulroy told me.

At the core of the discussions was an awareness that harsh economic sanctions were clearly punishing the Iranian government. "One
of the main things we did is try to be an honest broker," Mulroy said.
"The economic pressure campaign is working, because their economy's
the worst it's been since the height of the Iran-Iraq War. But that's not
the goal. The goal was to reduce malign activities and prevent them
from getting anywhere near a nuclear weapon. But the consequences
have been [that] we probably increased the tensions in the Middle
East."

The strategic review, which came to be known as the Iran Strategy
Board, found that although the administration's approach was working at the tactical level, it was not delivering on the president's own
strategic goals, of reducing Iranian aggression in the region and preventing its progress toward a nuclear weapon.

"So part of the assessment was, 'Well, this is causing economic hard-
ships, so check the box on that,'" Mulroy said. "Secretary Esper's specific requirement was, I needed to do an actual assessment of whether

this is working. And if it's not working, he was going to take it to Secretary Pompeo and say, 'Hey, Mike. I get Iran's terrible, but we're not getting closer to JCPOA 2.0.'"[33]

That was the disturbing bottom line on President Trump's approach to Iran: he had campaigned on the deficiencies in the 2015 Iranian nuclear deal (known by its initials, JCPOA, for Joint Comprehensive Plan of Action), calling it a "horrible" agreement that had made the United States less safe.

"This was a horrible, one-sided deal that should have never, ever been made," the grim-faced Mr. Trump said after he had officially withdrawn the United States from the deal in May 2018. "It didn't bring calm, it didn't bring peace, and it never will."[34]

That was not the view of the US intelligence community, which repeatedly assessed that Iran had in fact been complying with the agreement and that the agreement was achieving its stated goal of lengthening Iran's so-called breakout period to building a nuclear weapon.

"It was an agreement that did restrict their ability to acquire a nuclear weapon," said Mick Mulroy. "I understand it didn't address the underlying activities, but our point was, 'Okay, stay in the JCPOA, just sanction them for malign activities.'"

Now, as Trump was expressing his openness to renewing negotiations with Iran, some of his advisors cautioned that he had made such negotiations next to impossible. "Once you bust the agreement that the United States signed on to, how do you expect to get to another agreement?" Mulroy said. "And they're just going to say, 'Well, you didn't stick in the last one.'"

Beyond the president's aspirational talk of peace were the alarming facts on the ground. "Empirically speaking, they've increased malign activities," said Mulroy. "And now they're breaking the limits on their enrichment, storage, hard water."[35]

By the president's own standards of success, his strategy was failing.

THE ANSWER

President Trump had set a new red line for Iran and enforced it: the United States would not tolerate the death of Americans. And he had fulfilled his campaign promise to withdraw from the Iran nuclear deal. But four years into that new, more aggressive Iran policy, Iran had become more, not less, aggressive, carrying out increasingly bold attacks across the region. And it had followed through on its threats to gradually break the terms of the nuclear agreement, enriching more uranium to a higher level and in doing so moving itself closer to a nuclear weapon.

By the estimation of his own Department of Defense, Trump's strategy was failing to deliver on its two most important goals: reducing Iran's aggression in the region and preventing Iran from attaining a nuclear weapon.

Trump World

The outbreak of coronavirus presented the country with a crisis that put Trump's worldview and his very way of leading to an unprecedented test. Trump's foreign policy had done real damage before—in Syria, Ukraine, and Russia—and failed to deliver on all or most of its objectives—in North Korea, Iran, and China—but the consequences of those foreign policy challenges were distant for most Americans. The plight of the Kurds was far away. Ukraine's desperate push for aid involved a war that was far away. North Korea's advancing nuclear program had yet to land a missile on the US homeland. The coronavirus, however, brought a life-and-death threat to Americans' doorsteps.

That did not change President Trump's response to the crisis. In fact, his "madman" was more apparent than ever. As the pandemic grew worse, I received calls from numerous former administration officials commenting on how, in their view, his handling of the coronavirus outbreak perfectly crystallized his approach to the world and to the office of the presidency: minimize, politicize, personalize, demonize the experts, and rarely strategize.

First, *minimize.* As one former senior administration official put it, "He does not want a crisis—whether it be Russian election interference or a pandemic—and so he minimizes the threat." And with the coronavirus outbreak, Trump would minimize even in the face of hard facts showing the threat was getting worse, not better.

Notably, the president would often falsely claim that covid-19 was no more dangerous than the seasonal flu. On March 9, one of several times Trump would make the claim, he tweeted, "So last year 37,000 Americans died from the common Flu. It averages between 27,000 and 70,000 per year. Nothing is shut down, life & the economy go on. At this moment there are 546 confirmed cases of CoronaVirus, with 22 deaths. Think about that!"

The fact was, at that point, the data from China, Italy, and elsewhere showed the death rate from covid-19 to be at least ten times as high as that of seasonal flu. Other estimates showed it to be twenty or thirty times as high. That is a point Dr. Anthony Fauci, the director of the National Institute of Allergy and Infectious Diseases at the National Institutes of Health, made repeatedly, sometimes moments before and after the president claimed otherwise.

That wasn't the only time he minimized the threat. As a fact check by CNN's Daniel Dale documented, the president "claimed to have the virus under 'control,' that the number of US cases would go 'down, not up,' that the virus might 'disappear' through a 'miracle' or something of the sort, that the virus might well vanish by April with the warmer weather, that the media and Democrats were overhyping the situation."[1]

Trump and his supporters continued to minimize the risk for weeks, taking a turn only when even he could not deny the growing death toll.

Next, *politicize*. In the real world, nothing is less political than health. Pathogens do not distinguish between Republicans and Democrats. And the facts and data are clear: means of transmission, infection rates, and rates of death. In the case of the coronavirus, the United States had the advantage of not being first to suffer its onslaught. US policy makers could look at the data from China, South Korea, Italy, and Spain to learn lessons about the pace and scope of the outbreak.

But in Trump world, the data itself became political. The president, his allies, and friendly news outlets attacked the data as skewed to inflame panic and, crucially, to damage Trump.

That allegation did not remain on the fringes. It came right from the president's mouth. At a rally in South Carolina on February 28, he compared the reaction to the outbreak to the Ukraine investigation and other investigations of his administration. "They tried the impeachment hoax. That was on a perfect conversation," he said. "They tried anything. They tried it over and over. They'd been doing it since you got in. It's all turning. They lost. It's all turning. Think of it. Think of it. And this is their new hoax."[2]

He would later explain that by using the word *hoax*, he had been speaking only about criticism of his response to the outbreak and not about the outbreak itself. And then on March 17, less than three weeks after his declaration in South Carolina and with all his public comments on the record for the world to see, the president attempted to rewrite history.

"I've always known this is a real—this is a real—this is a pandemic," he said in the White House briefing room. "I've felt it was a pandemic long before it was called a pandemic. All you had to do is look at other countries. . . . No, I've always viewed it as very serious. There was no difference yesterday from days before. I feel the tone is similar, but some people said it wasn't."[3]

His attempt to reverse the record was reminiscent of another appearance at the White House nearly two years before when he claimed the transcript of his comments next to Vladimir Putin in Helsinki had incorrectly captured what he said about Russia and its interference in the 2016 election. Both claims were easily disproved by his own prior public comments, but he persisted in selling the lie.

Fiona Hill, his former senior director for European and Russian affairs, saw clear parallels between Trump's response to the coronavirus and Russian election interference: "We needed a broader governmental and societal approach and strategy, at all levels, to tackle both Russian influence operations and the coronavirus pandemic, but in each case, there was an immediate rush to politicization, hyperpersonalization and an excessive focus on President Trump."[4]

This is the next element of the pattern: *personalize*. President Trump, even in the face of a pandemic threatening millions of people in the United States and around the world, could not help but see the crisis as all about him and his personal interests. And as he personalizes a crisis, as one former senior administration official described it to me, he has a tendency to portray himself as both the casualty and the cure. "When the problem won't go away, he has to be somehow the victim and the savior," the official said.

If anyone is surprised by his hyperpersonalization, they shouldn't be. Like so many elements of his worldview, this tendency was in his public comments from a very early stage. See his speech at the Republican convention in 2016, when he emphasized the words "I alone" in the notable line "Nobody knows the system better than me, which is why I alone can fix it."[5]

"The president fixated on what each crisis would mean for him and his political position and he perceived press and public reactions as solely directed at him," said Hill. "He also saw his own government's efforts to combat the issue and push forward with mitigation efforts

as an affront and even a threat given the fact that the press and commentators were consumed with what he, the president, was doing and
not doing and not addressing the context and the bigger picture of the
problem."[6]

Throughout, the president will often *demonize the experts.* The president's self-focus, according to former advisors, drives his need to be
in front—to be the face of the response—which then causes another
problem: confusion and contradiction resulting from his limited expertise and incomplete grasp of the facts.

"He wants to *do* things even before thinking them through," said
one former senior administration official.

Even when the facts don't back him up. In mid-March 2020, as entire states were beginning to issue shelter-in-place orders to reduce the
spread, the president and Dr. Fauci again differed in public, engaging
in a subtle but outrageous battle over the potential effectiveness of a
malaria drug against the coronavirus.

Asked directly if hydroxychloroquine could prove effective as a cure
for covid-19, Dr. Fauci was definitive. "No," he said. "The answer . . . is
no. The information that you're referring to specifically is anecdotal," he
continued. "It was not done in a controlled clinical trial, so you really
can't make any definitive statement about it."[7]

But Trump, citing no evidence, expressed his confidence that the
drug was still a possible cure. "Maybe and maybe not," he said. "Maybe
there is, maybe there isn't. We have to see.

"I think without seeing too much, I'm probably more of a fan of
that."[8]

Trump's championing of unproven treatments over the skepticism
of the actual medical experts would extend all the way to his trade
advisor, Peter Navarro. After Navarro got into a debate in the White
House with Dr. Fauci over those same antimalarial treatments in early
April, as first reported by Axios,[9] my colleague John Berman asked

him on CNN's *New Day* on what basis he was attempting to over-rule Fauci, who is a physician, immunologist, and veteran of the fights against HIV and Ebola, among other qualifications.

Navarro explained, "My qualifications in terms of looking at the science is that I'm a social scientist. I have a Ph.D. And I understand how to read statistical studies, whether it's in medicine, the law, economics or whatever."[10]

This sidelining, even contradiction, of the government's top experts is one more element of leadership in Trump world. With coronavirus, as with Russia, Ukraine, Syria, North Korea, and beyond, Trump and his lieutenants often believed they knew better. At times, they would express their confidence by dismissing the experts, at others, by attacking them.

As the pandemic spread across the United States, the country witnessed the debilitating effects of those attacks. In short, his attacks on the experts were working. Early on, views of the seriousness of the outbreak differed widely based on political affiliation. Taking their cues from the president, self-described Republicans were far less likely to take the pandemic seriously than were self-described Democrats. In mid-March, a Gallup poll found that 73 percent of Democrats worried that they or someone in their family would be exposed, compared with only 42 percent of Republicans.[11]

The skepticism about the seriousness of the outbreak had a real effect on the public's response to it. In a poll, also by Gallup, later in March, 65 percent of Democrats said they were avoiding public places as recommended by health authorities and even by the president at that point, compared with fewer than half—only 43 percent—of Republicans.[12] It was a bitter irony: Trump's attacks on government had undermined his own ability to mobilize the public to act at precisely the moment he wanted and needed them to.

As the facts and the reality caught up with him, Trump would attempt to make a turn—similar to the course corrections we saw him make in Syria, North Korea, and elsewhere. For a time, he would describe the threat in more serious terms and order his administration to take increasingly aggressive steps to confront both the outbreak and its economic consequences.

"In the case of Russian influence, government experts were sidelined and intelligence analysts demonized. It was simply impossible to depoliticize the issue," said Fiona Hill. "Fortunately, with the clear life-or-death stakes of the coronavirus pandemic, the need for expertise was finally recognized. This is also because states and local governments and institutions were able to exert their own authority in declaring a public health emergency and taking measures."[13]

There were other confusing tendencies Trump had difficulty escaping, even at the height of the deadly pandemic. In the span of a few days in early April, the president accepted an aid delivery from a US adversary, Russia, granting it an enormous propaganda victory, while attempting to block the shipment of some medical supplies to a US ally, Canada.

Prime Minister Justin Trudeau warned of the consequences to both the United States and Canada of the Trump administration's move. "It would be a mistake to create blockages or reduce the amount of back-and-forth trade of essential goods and services, including medical goods, across our border. That is the point we are making very clearly to the American administration right now," he said.[14]

Trump, meanwhile, was praising his old friend Putin. "It was a very nice gesture on behalf of President Putin and I could have said 'no, thank you' or I could have said, 'thank you.' And it was a large plane of very high-quality medical supplies. And I said, 'I'll take it,'" he said of the Russian aid delivery.[15]

Finally, *rarely strategize*. Trump's Republican and Democratic predecessors, George W. Bush and Barack Obama, had emphasized the need to prepare for deadly pandemics. President Trump's administration on the other hand attempted to cut the budget of institutions responsible for responding to them and ignored warnings from health officials as the coronavirus was spreading. On other national security priorities—from North Korea to Russia to China to Syria to Iran—senior advisors developed strategies, published them for the world to see in National Defense Strategy documents, and included them in the president's speeches and briefings, but Trump in practice often dismissed, undermined, or even contradicted them. In fact, many advisors wondered if he ever read the strategy documents. More important, there were times when it appeared that the president was making up the strategy as he went along, sometimes changing in midstream. Even senior members of his own administration didn't know what was coming next.

There was a much broader, more indelible lesson to Trump's response to the coronavirus. For a leader who sees the United States' interests as clearly separated from the interests of the rest of the world, a pandemic is a challenge that belies his views. A pandemic is, by definition, a global problem requiring a global response.

"He is not a global thinker," one of his former senior advisors told me, and with a pandemic, "It might be okay to focus on the US, but not *only* the US."

In this sense, coronavirus may be the crisis that finally exposed the emptiness at the core of "America First."

THE TRUMP RECORD: POSITIVE

President Trump committed maddening mistakes. President Trump managed remarkable victories. Both these statements are true of Trump's "madman" approach to US foreign policy.

As a reporter and anchor, I witnessed moments of both promise and incompetence in his trade war and trade negotiations with China, his three face-to-face summits with North Korea's Kim Jong Un, the fight against ISIS in Syria and Iraq, the escalating shadow war with Iran, and beyond.

Judging success or failure in each is made difficult because often even his most senior advisors couldn't explain to me what the president was up to or what he hoped to accomplish. And sometimes, his decisions and statements contradicted not only his administration's own national security strategy but also his own prior decisions and statements. President Trump took the country and the world through the looking glass, and we have yet to come out the other side.

Let's begin on the positive side. As president, Trump—finally— ended the United States' deference to China. For decades and under presidents of both parties, the United States had excused Chinese misbehavior, particularly in the economic sphere. US leaders knew that China was breaking the rules and doing so at the expense of the United States but hesitated to cry foul for fear of igniting worse behavior and of losing the opportunity to coax Beijing into more responsible behavior over time. That approach failed. Trump reversed it.

With NATO, Trump—finally—ended the United States' patience with European allies' failure to contribute a larger and fairer share of the alliance's budget and force requirements. For decades and under presidents of both parties, the United States had excused European nations' reluctance to pony up. US leaders knew that Europe could do more and that, in the absence of their doing so, US taxpayers and soldiers were bearing more of the burden. They had cajoled European leaders to change their ways, mostly in private. That approach had failed. Trump reversed it.

With ISIS, Trump accelerated the defeat of the terror group's claimed caliphate by providing increased military resources and deployments and granting more freedom for those forces to conduct military strikes independent of Washington.

With North Korea, Trump—at least for a time—opened the door to a diplomatic solution to America's most immediate national security threat.

Foreign policy is the least predictable realm of any president's legacy. And President Trump addressed—or attempted to address—several of the United States' most difficult international challenges in new and, yes, unpredictable ways.

THE TRUMP RECORD: NEGATIVE

Let's turn to the negative. With Russia, President Trump refused to confront repeated and growing Russian aggression against the United States and its allies or even to acknowledge Russia as a national security threat at all. He did this despite contrary advice from his own most senior advisors, the assessments of every national security and intelligence agency of the US government, and deep opposition from lawmakers of his own party. The best guess of officials who worked closely with him as to what's behind his deference to Russia is that he has an incurable admiration for Russia's despotic leader. That is better than Russia having undue influence over him, but it is not a comforting motivation for the elected leader of the United States.

With Ukraine, President Trump sold out an ally fighting for its sovereignty—against Russia no less—to extract a political favor. And he extorted Ukraine with military assistance needed desperately to repel Russian advances and improve its position for any future negotiations with Moscow. As Ukrainian officials told me, Ukrainians may have lost their lives as a result.

With Iran, Trump abandoned a nuclear agreement, negotiated

alongside the United States' European allies as well as Russia and China. US intelligence agencies and the IAEA repeatedly assessed that Iran was complying with the deal, despite Trump's claims to the contrary. His intention, he said, was to get a better deal that would restrict Iranian nuclear activity for longer, and to address Iran's missile program and other aggression in the region. But at the end of four years, Iran had expanded its nuclear activities, its missile tests, and its military aggression, including deadly attacks on US forces. The Pentagon's own Iran strategy review found that the administration's Iran strategy was failing to meet the president's objectives.

With Syria, President Trump abandoned another ally, in this case the ally that did the most to destroy ISIS, the Syrian Kurds. In doing so, he ceded their territory to Russia, Iran, and Turkey—three countries whose interests in the region directly contradict those of the United States. Here the evidence is clear: Syrian Kurds lost their lives as a result. Is there any more damning mistake for a commander in chief than causing the loss of lives in wartime?

By 2020, Trump's term was absent of a major foreign policy disaster some had warned of after his election but, at the same time, equally absent of a major and lasting accomplishment. For any president, some of this is luck and some the result of actions taken or avoided. But what Trump may be remembered for most is his lack of follow-through or, indeed, any demonstrated interest in follow-through. His advisors recount his consistent lack of a plan or strategy and his focus on short-term "wins" over lasting progress.

He finally confronted China but retreated from the confrontation by agreeing to a trade deal some of his own advisors described as a capitulation. He successfully pressured NATO allies to contribute more to the alliance but undermined the alliance's unity, as evidenced by its willingness to buck the president on China and 5G. He brought North Korea to the bargaining table but got nothing in the bargain. In fact, one year of "fire and fury" and three years of diplomacy left North Korea's nuclear and missile programs stronger, not weaker.

With Russia, Trump had a noble ambition to reduce the threat of nuclear war. But by the end of four years in office, his hope of delivering an agreement to reduce nuclear weapons stockpiles remained just that: a hope with no concrete results or follow-through.

He is not the first president to have a mixed foreign policy legacy. However, Trump is uniquely willing to lie about it. Trump would order the withdrawal of US forces from Syria by tweet for all the world to see, reverse that decision, and claim otherwise even as those same US forces fought and died on the battlefield. Trump would agree to a trade deal with China that fell short of his promises and tout China's commitment to purchase $200 billion in US goods but ignore doubts about whether Beijing would make good on its commitments.

He and his supporters create and accept their own reality.

History eventually overwrites even the best propaganda. Until then, his supporters, who make up a large portion of the country, may continue to see successes where there are only partisan mirages.

TRUMP WORLD: BEFORE AND AFTER

So let's test those mirages. President Trump has often said that the United States is more respected now than ever before, or at least more than it was under his predecessor, Barack Obama. Is that true? When it comes to public opinion, according to the Pew Research Center, which conducts global opinion surveys, the answer is no. "Across 24 countries that have been surveyed consistently since 2015 and 2016, a median of 53% of adults have a favorable view of the U.S., slightly below the 64% who had a positive view at the end of the Obama administration," it wrote in January 2020. As for the presidents themselves, the drop has been more pronounced: 74 percent of respondents expressed confidence in Barack Obama in 2016, while only 31 percent expressed confidence in Donald Trump in 2019, though that figure had edged up from 23 percent in 2017 and included exceptions in the Philippines and Israel, where Trump rated above 70 percent.[16]

Still, the best measure of Donald Trump's foreign policy is whether it improved or worsened America's position in relation to its most pressing national security threats, or left the status quo intact. Country by country, what did Trump inherit and what did he leave behind?

Russia Before

When Trump entered office in January 2017, Russia was an increasingly aggressive and hostile challenger to the United States and the West.

In Ukraine, it had annexed Crimea and occupied large swaths of the country's east.

In Syria, it had expanded and modernized its military presence, giving it its largest naval presence in the Mediterranean since the fall of the Soviet Union and land bases on Syrian territory.

In the United States and the West, Russia used cyber/social tools as well as more traditional disinformation tactics it had refined against countries like Ukraine to interfere in elections, influence political discourse, and stoke deep-seated social tensions. US intelligence has assessed that Russia's objective was to sow chaos and discord within the United States' democratic system while also undermining the rule of law.

Russian military aircraft had repeatedly entered and tested US airspace and the airspace of US allies in Europe and made hostile approaches to US ships from Asia to the Atlantic.

Moscow was developing new weapons systems and technologies to challenge American superiority at sea and in the air.

Russia After

By the end of Trump's first term in 2020, Russia was maintaining or expanding its acts of aggression abroad.

In Ukraine, it maintained control of territory in Crimea and the east. By 2018, according to UN estimates, the war in Ukraine had claimed some 13,000 Ukrainian lives, including soldiers and civilians.

In Syria, Russia continued to expand its naval and ground bases and had extended its territorial control right up to the Turkish border, taking over areas previously controlled by US forces and US allies, the Syrian Kurds. Russian airpower continued to provide cover for Syrian regime forces as they have advanced north. Russia's support for Iran had enabled Iranian proxies to continue to operate in Syria and across the region.

With the 2020 US presidential election approaching, US intelligence assessed that the Kremlin was continuing to interfere in politics in the United States and throughout the West, evolving its strategy and capabilities to do so. It assessed that Russian influence campaigns were driven by a desire to "watch us tear ourselves apart," according to the FBI.[17]

Russian military aircraft continued to enter and test US airspace and the airspace of US allies in Europe. Russian ships and aircraft also continued to aggressively challenge US military assets deployed around the world. When it came to new weapons systems, Moscow declared it is developing new hypersonic weapons capable of threatening the US homeland.

Russia also expanded its aggression in new and alarming ways. In March 2018, Russia attempted a bold murder on UK soil with the most powerful nerve agent in the world. The attempted assassination of former KGB agent Sergei Skripal and his daughter, Yulia, with the poison Novichok failed in the end, but the brazen act shocked US and European diplomats.

And in a rare confluence of interests, Russia and China increased cooperation in activities intended to undermine the US abroad. In July 2019, Russian and Chinese aircraft conducted their first long-range joint air patrol, sending four bombers and two early-warning aircraft into South Korean airspace. South Korean military aircraft scrambled to intercept them, firing hundreds of warning shots in an extremely dangerous encounter with real risk of escalation.[18] The month before, a Russian destroyer had nearly collided with a US cruiser, USS *Chancellorsville*, in the Philippine Sea. The US Seventh Fleet had described the encounter, which had brought the ships within 160 feet of each other, as "unsafe and unprofessional." The dangerous maneuver had happened, not uncoincidentally, while Russian president Vladimir Putin and Chinese president Xi Jinping had been meeting in Moscow. As they met in the Kremlin, Xi described Putin as his "best friend."[19]

Ukraine Before

When Trump entered office, as noted above, Russia had annexed Crimea and controlled large portions of eastern Ukraine. The Kremlin was interfering in Ukrainian politics, seeking to undermine the newly independent government that had replaced the pro-Russian government that had preceded it.

Ukraine After

In 2020, Russia continued to control Crimea and was solidifying that control with a series of measures including opening a bridge connecting the peninsula to Russia. In eastern Ukraine, according to Ukrainian officials and international observers, the separation line between Russian and Ukrainian forces had remained unchanged since 2015.

The Trump administration continued Obama-era sanctions and, under bipartisan pressure from Congress, implemented modest new sanctions on Russia for its invasion and other malign activities. Under Trump, the United States also provided military assistance to Ukraine, including lethal weapons for the first time, but as the impeachment inquiry found, the president withheld that aid in 2019 in order to pressure the Ukrainian government to investigate Joe and Hunter Biden. The aid hold came during a sensitive time in the battle and in peace negotiations with Russia, weakening the alliance between Washington and Kiev and the Ukrainian military and diplomatic position.

Ukrainian civilians and soldiers continued to die on the battlefield and Russia deployed its own antitank weapons to counter the Javelin antitank missiles supplied to Ukraine by the United States.

China Before

When Trump entered office in January 2017, China was already a rising challenger to the United States around the world.

In trade, China stole intellectual property, demanded that foreign firms share their technology with Chinese partners in order to gain access to the Chinese market, and severely restricted market access for foreign firms. The high hopes that Beijing's entrance into the World Trade Organization would gradually liberalize and open up the Chinese market had long since faded and disappeared. China's membership in the WTO was increasingly seen as a one-sided proposition: good for China, bad for the rest of the world.

According to US intelligence, Beijing continued to utilize covert and overt methods of espionage to steal military and technological secrets as well as influence the American democratic process. China is playing the long game, US officials warned, using its economic strength as leverage and targeting US government officials down to the state and local levels.

In the South China Sea, China had flouted international law and ignored US opposition to manufacture territory, in waters claimed by half a dozen Southeast Asian nations, including a US treaty ally, the Philippines. The United States continued to recognize the area as international waters and flew US military aircraft and sailed US warships over and around China's manmade islands to demonstrate its position. But the islands—"Unsinkable aircraft carriers," as some in the US Navy referred to them—remained. Moreover, in defiance of US demands and reneging on Xi Jinping's promise to Barack Obama not to militarize the islands, China had steadily added military capabilities, including installing surface-to-air missile batteries and landing nuclear-capable bombers there.

On Taiwan, China was preparing and expanding its military capabilities for invasion. The Pentagon's annual report on China to Congress found that the "PLA [People's Liberation Army] continues to prepare for contingencies in the Taiwan Strait to deter and, if necessary, compel Taiwan to abandon moves toward independence, or to unify Taiwan with the mainland by force, while simultaneously deterring, delaying, or denying any third-party intervention on Taiwan's behalf."[20]

In terms of its global ambitions, China set its target date for achieving dominance at the year 2049, which not coincidentally would be the one hundredth anniversary of the founding of the People's Republic of China. President Xi Jinping has described China's goal as achieving "national greatness" and becoming a "fully developed, rich, and powerful" nation, surpassing the United States as the world's primary economic and global power.

China After

By 2020, China was facing headwinds of its own, including slowing economic growth and deep damage due to the spread of the coronavirus. However, its rivalry with the United States continued unabated.

In trade, Washington and Beijing had reached agreement on a limited trade deal, which included new protections against intellectual property theft and Chinese commitments to buy some $200 billion is US agricultural products. However, the deal did not address many of the most divisive issues, including massive Chinese government subsidies of state-owned enterprises. There was also no clear way to guarantee Beijing would follow through on its promised purchases, particularly as its economy slowed.

In the South China Sea, China retained control of its man-made islands. And in 2018, it expanded its military installations on the islands. The Defense Department's 2019 report to Congress on Chinese military capabilities stated, "In 2018, China continued militarization in the South China Sea by placing antiship cruise missiles and long-range surface-to-air missiles on outposts in the Spratly Islands, violating a 2015 pledge by Chinese President Xi Jinping that 'China does not intend to pursue militarization' of the Spratly Islands. China is also willing to employ coercive measures—both military and non-military—to advance its interests and mitigate opposition from other countries."[21] In June 2019, at an event at the Brookings Institution, the then chairman of the Joint Chiefs of Staff, Joseph Dunford, said, "What is at stake [there] and elsewhere where there are territorial claims, is the rule of law, international laws, norms, and standards," adding that countries that violate such laws "need to be held accountable so that future violations are deterred."[22] What was not clear was exactly how the United States was now holding Beijing accountable, when the Obama administration had already failed.

In addition, China had more aggressively threatened its competing claimants for South China Sea sovereignty. At the ASEAN summit in November 2019, National Security Advisor Robert O'Brien said, "Beijing has used intimidation to try to stop ASEAN nations from exploiting the off-shore resources, blocking access to 2.5 trillion dollars of oil and gas reserves alone."[23]

Regarding Taiwan, China had further expanded its military forces and capabilities for taking the island by force. According to the Defense Department's 2019 congressional report, "Although China advocates for peaceful unification with Taiwan, China has never renounced the use of military force, and continues to develop and deploy advanced military capabilities needed for a potential military campaign."[24]

Increasingly, Chinese commentators were moving up their target date for global dominance from 2049 to decades earlier, driven in part by events that had preceded Donald Trump, such as the 2008 financial crisis, but also some exacerbated or initiated by Trump himself, including the downgrading of the US commitment to alliances in Europe and Asia.

North Korea Before

When Donald Trump entered office in January 2017, North Korea was moving closer to achieving its decades-long ambition to become a nuclear power, with functioning nuclear warheads and the ability to deliver those warheads to targets around the world. It had conducted five nuclear tests and multiple short- and intermediate-range ballistic missile tests and was working toward a viable intercontinental ballistic missile (ICBM) capable of reaching the US mainland. It had not yet perfected submarine-launched ballistic missiles.

US intelligence agencies assessed that North Korea was committed to maintaining and expanding its nuclear weapons and missile programs. In its 2017 "Worldwide Threat Assessment of the US Intelligence Community," the intelligence community found that "Pyongyang is committed to developing a long-range, nuclear-armed missile that is capable of posing a direct threat to the United States; . . . We have long assessed that Pyongyang's nuclear capabilities are intended for deterrence, international prestige, and coercive diplomacy."[25]

The US alliance with South Korea was strong, punctuated by regular joint military exercises designed to prepare for and deter a North Korean invasion.

The estimated number of North Korean military warheads: ten to twenty.[26]

North Korea After

In September 2017, North Korea welcomed Trump to office with its sixth and largest nuclear test. Pyongyang claimed to have successfully detonated a thermonuclear weapon.

Trump imposed a "maximum-pressure" campaign of enhanced economic sanctions on North Korea and showered the North Korean leader, Kim Jong Un, with a series of threats. He then pivoted to an ambitious campaign of summit diplomacy without any preconditions for the North Koreans. Trump met Kim for three face-to-face summits: in Singapore, in Hanoi, and—most dramatically—at the DMZ between North and South Korea, even taking a handful of steps into North Korean territory.

During the diplomatic outreach, North Korea suspended nuclear tests and long-range ballistic missile tests. But by 2020, Trump's combination of maximum pressure and summit diplomacy had generated no comprehensive nuclear agreement and no commitments by the

North to limit its nuclear program despite his repeated insistence that Kim had committed to denuclearization. In fact, US intelligence would assess that North Korea had expanded both its nuclear weapons and ballistic missile programs during Trump's time in office with no indication that it plans to reverse course.

Beginning in May 2019, the North resumed shorter-range missile tests as well as tests of submarine-launchable missiles—a development that greatly expanded its ability to carry out nuclear strikes with little to no warning. In one particularly active period, North Korea conducted twelve separate missile tests between May and October 2019, before and after the third Trump-Kim summit at the DMZ between North and South Korea. That testing continued into 2020 as diplomatic talks continued to stall.

US intelligence agencies continued to asses that North Korea would never give up its nuclear weapons. In his Senate testimony after the release of the 2019 "Worldwide Threat Assessment of the US Intelligence Community," then director of national intelligence Daniel R. Coats stated, "We currently assess that North Korea will seek to retain its WMD capabilities and is unlikely to completely give up its nuclear weapons and production capabilities," adding that North Korean "leaders ultimately view nuclear weapons as critical to regime survival. Our assessment is bolstered by our observations of some activity that is inconsistent with full denuclearization."[27]

The US alliance with South Korea was strained over Trump's demand for a five-fold increase in Seoul's financial contribution to the costs of US force deployment on the peninsula. Trump canceled a series of joint military exercises with the South. Some Korea experts worried about South Korea's drift closer to China.

The estimated number of North Korean military warheads: twenty to thirty.[28]

Syria Before

When Trump entered office, the ISIS caliphate in Syria and Iraq was shrinking but still a viable fighting force.

US troops were closely allied with Kurdish forces in Syria against ISIS.

Russian and Iranian forces were largely confined to the south and west of the country. Turkey had not conducted significant operations across its border into Syria.

Syria After

After four years, the ISIS caliphate was destroyed, though the US military assessed that its fighters were regrouping as US forces were withdrawn.

The United States has greatly reduced joint operations with its Syrian Kurdish allies.

Russian and Iranian forces have expanded north toward the Turkish border.

Turkey invaded Syria and now controls a broad swath of territory it referred to as a "safe zone." Turkey, a NATO ally, and the Syrian regime were engaged in more direct conflict.

Iran Before

When Donald Trump entered office in January 2017, Iran was complying with the 2015 nuclear agreement negotiated between Iran and the United States, Europe, Russia, and China. As the deal called for, Iran was not enriching uranium above the limit of 3.67 percent uranium-235—far below the 90 percent level considered weapons grade—and was maintaining its stockpile of enriched uranium below a 300-kilogram limit.

As late as early 2019, US intelligence agencies assessed that Tehran remained in compliance with the 2015 agreement. The intelligence community's 2019 "Worldwide Threat Assessment of the US Intelligence Community" stated, "We continue to assess that Iran is not currently undertaking the key nuclear weapons-development activities we judge necessary to produce a nuclear device."[29] In January testimony before the Senate Intelligence Committee, then DNI Coats reiterated that finding in public: "We do not believe Iran is currently undertaking activities we judge necessary to produce a nuclear device."[30]

In March 2019, the International Atomic Energy Agency also declared Iran to be in compliance with the agreement. "Iran is implementing its nuclear commitments," said Yukiya Amano, the IAEA's director general, on March 4. The IAEA report noted that the agency had access to "all the sites and locations in Iran which it needed to visit."[31]

Iran was continuing to test multiple short- and medium-range missiles, as well as satellite launchers, which were not covered by the nuclear agreement.

It was supplying arms and fighters to Syrian president Bashar al-Assad, against US allies in Syria, and supporting militias in Iraq.

Iran After

In 2020, at the end of Trump's first term, Iran was again enriching uranium above the 3.67 percent limit and its stockpile of enriched uranium had grown beyond the 300-kilogram cap. By February, it had nearly tripled its stockpile of low-enriched uranium from just the previous November, according to the IAEA. In its March 3 report to member states, obtained by CNN, the IAEA verified that "Iran's total enriched uranium stockpile . . . was 1020.9 kilograms (+648.6 kilograms since the previous quarterly report)."[32]

In 2019, Tehran took another significant step away from the nuclear agreement: restarting uranium enrichment at its underground Fordow facility. Under the 2015 nuclear agreement, enrichment at Fordow had been banned for fifteen years. That commitment, as the *Wall Street Journal* noted, "was one of the central achievements of the deal."[33] Iranian officials said they were doing so because Europe had "fail(ed) to honor their commitments to the international deal," though President Hassan Rouhani noted that the step was "revocable if it sees other parties comply with the deal."[34]

Iran was continuing ballistic missile tests. In one stretch of 2019, it conducted nearly a dozen such tests including two satellite launch vehicles, which could form the basis of an ICBM, as well as short- and medium-range missiles. Several qualified as nuclear capable.[35]

Iran was also expanding its acts of aggression around the region, including shooting down a US drone in international airspace, attacking shipping, and attacking Saudi oil facilities.

In Iraq, Iran had expanded attacks against US forces, causing multiple deaths and injuries to US service members.

THE NEW AMERICA

As the shepherd of American values and the American image, President Trump engineered changes that may prove more lasting.

Four years of Trump have fundamentally redefined the United States' position in the world. Trump has reduced the importance of alliances. He has undermined confidence in his country's commitment to treaties it negotiated and signed and international organizations it helped found. He has diminished values and human rights as priorities of US foreign policy. He has made relationships with allies and adversaries transactional. And by utilizing a Trumpian version of "the madman theory," he has helped foster an image of the United States as unpredictable, for better or for worse.

A second term would solidify these changes, though some may prove lasting regardless of how long he is in office. Confidence and trust are difficult to build and easy to destroy.

At home, Trump has dismantled the policy-making process in national security, reorienting the entire system around the decisions and inclinations of one man—so much so that often the policy making follows his most capricious moves, as opposed to the other way around.

More broadly, Trump has deliberately undermined confidence in the very institutions of government. He has left senior national security and foreign policy posts unfilled or occupied by "acting" officials who lack Senate approval and the vaguest guarantee of tenure. He has ignored both the advice and data provided by key agencies tasked with providing the president with that advice and data. More disturbingly, he has attacked essential institutions and the men and women who work for them as "tyrants," "scum," "losers," "criminals," "Nazis," and more. Altogether, he has transformed what had been a mostly rhetorical American distaste for big government into a fundamental distrust of the system.

"If you don't believe you need government, you're wrong," said Susan Gordon, the former principal deputy director of national intelligence under Trump. "You need government. You need a system and stability and a framework. You may not need the overregulated government that we have become; you may not need the government that just continues to promulgate the past; but you do need government. And so what happens if you start believing you don't need government and you don't have a structure to support things?"

We, as a country, will find out the answer. The next president can fill the empty posts, accept data as credible, and heed the experts' advice, but the system has suffered a shock that many of his former advisors worry will be difficult to recover from.

"If you don't trust your system, the gap between the decision and the decision-maker and the system gets bigger," Gordon said. "It's one thing to say, 'Listen, you guys just aren't doing enough. I need more, I need better.' That's totally legitimate. If you say that the leaders of the military are ineffective and biased or corrupt or something, I don't know how you recover."[36]

President Trump went even further in some quarters, proving that he was loath to tolerate any dissent. The days following his acquittal in the Senate impeachment trial offered a revealing case study in cleaning house. Within days, virtually every official who had contradicted his version of events, either in sworn testimony or in email messages at the time of his Ukraine decisions, was gone. The long list included Ambassador to the European Union Gordon Sondland, a Trump appointee and million-dollar donor to his campaign, and Ukraine expert and Purple Heart recipient Lieutenant Colonel Alexander Vindman. Even Vindman's brother Yevgeny, an NSC lawyer who played no part in the impeachment, was forced out.

Others who differed with him on withholding Ukraine aid would leave or be forced from their posts just before and after the Senate trial, including the NSC's senior director for European and Russian affairs, Fiona Hill, aide to Vice President Pence Jennifer Williams, and Undersecretary of Defense for Policy John Rood, the author of the letter to Congress in May 2019 certifying Ukraine's compliance with anticorruption measures. In February 2020, the White House pulled its own nomination of acting Pentagon comptroller Elaine McCusker, who had raised legal concerns about withholding the aid, to serve in that role permanently. A loyalty purge was taking place in the broad light of day.

In a further effort to quiet dissent, Trump made other changes to the system. He moved the transcripts of calls with world leaders to a highly classified, password-protected system and later allowed fewer officials to monitor the calls. He was creating practices and a team that not only discouraged dissent but made it less possible. The man he later appointed as deputy National Security Council legal advisor was Michael Ellis, who as an NSC lawyer had ordered officials to move the Ukraine call transcript to that classified system. Trump appointed a loyalist, his ambassador to Germany, Richard Grenell, acting director of national intelligence, after which Grenell conducted his own purge of intelligence officials seen as insufficiently loyal to Trump.

"It's the suggestion that we aren't good people. I think that is just hard," Gordon said. "I think it does wear over time. We're talking about people that, by and large, are believers. You can question judgments till the cows come home. You can say you don't believe intelligence as much as you want. If you're questioning the integrity of the people that put that in front of you, I think that's very difficult because those people, in their own minds, would never lack integrity."[37]

Our allies and adversaries are already adjusting to the new America. As the leader of the most powerful nation in the world, the consequences of President Trump's foreign policy and his approach to deciding that policy extend far beyond the United States' borders.

President Trump's distaste for alliances—and his deliberate efforts to undermine them—have disrupted not only our allies' confidence in our adherence to those alliances but also the sanctity of alliances in general.

"So you're hedging your bets," Gordon explained. "It's not that you're unwilling to be an alliance, but if your interests differ, you now see people not sure of what the alliance is going to do. So you see them making more choices in their own self-interest."[38]

For better or worse, the world is learning from the United States under Donald Trump.

★ ★ ★

SOME OF TRUMP'S SUPPORTERS WILL UNDOUBTEDLY ACCUSE ME OF being biased against him. Some of his critics will accuse me of failing to criticize him enough. As a reporter and as an American, I have no incentive to do either. I have based this book on the accounts and insight only of people who worked for President Trump and *chose* to do so. This is just one first draft of the history of his foreign policy, one of many that will be written. We will only come to know the lasting consequences of Trump's "madman" theory over time.

In trying to crystallize his foreign policy, I keep coming back to one phrase used by former ambassador to Ukraine Marie Yovanovitch. In a speech at Georgetown University in February 2020, she described his approach as "an amoral, keep-'em-guessing foreign policy that substitutes threats, fear and confusion for trust."[39] For Ambassador Yovanovitch it was clearly a criticism, but, interestingly, it was not far off from the description some of his allies used to praise his approach.

As with so many things Trump, where some see folly, others see virtue. Americans will have to decide for themselves if they share that vision of their country.

Acknowledgments

I'm deeply grateful to Susan Gordon, Joseph Yun, Fiona Hill, H. R. McMaster, Mick Mulroy, Peter Navarro, Steve Bannon, Brett McGurk, and other current and former officials for sharing their experiences from inside the Trump administration with insight and candor.

Heartfelt thanks to my family—Gloria, Tristan, Caden, and Sinclair—for once again surrendering me to the schedule and pressures of writing a book, and now twice in two years!

Thank you to Eric Nelson of HarperCollins for envisioning this book—and to Gail Ross of Ross Yoon and David Larabell of CAA for helping bring it to life. Mitch Ivers helped me make the manuscript much more readable. Julie Tate kept me honest on fact checking. Austin Lowe helped keep me smart on all China sections. My producer, Shelby Vest, dived in as always whenever I needed a hand.

And many thanks to Jeff Zucker, Rick Davis, Allison Gollust, Neel Khairzada, and CNN for backing this project and, even more so, for giving me my dream job in news.

—*Jim Sciutto, Washington, DC, May 2020*

Notes

INTRODUCTION: THE MADMAN THEORY

1. Tim Naftali, "The Problem with Trump's Madman Theory," *The Atlantic*, October 4, 2017, https://www.theatlantic.com/international /archive/2017/10/madman-theory-trump-north-korea/542055/.
2. Author's interview with Tim Naftali, January 29, 2020.
3. Naftali, "The Problem with Trump's Madman Theory."
4. Author's interview with Mick Mulroy, January 19, 2020.
5. Author's interview with Joseph Yun, January 29, 2020.
6. Author's interview with Fiona Hill, February 21, 2020.
7. Author's interview with Susan Gordon, December 26, 2019.
8. Author's interview with Joseph Yun, January 29, 2020.
9. Author's interview with Peter Navarro, January 19, 2020.
10. Author's interview with Steve Bannon, February 14, 2020.
11. Ibid.
12. Author's interview with Fiona Hill, February 21, 2020.
13. Author's interview with Susan Gordon, December 26, 2019.
14. Author's interview with Fiona Hill, February 21, 2020.
15. Author's interview with Mick Mulroy, January 2, 2020.
16. Jim Sciutto, Barbara Starr, and Zachary Cohen, "Trump Promises North Korea 'Fire and Fury' over Nuke Threat," CNN, August 9, 2017, https://www.cnn.com/2017/08/08/politics/north-korea -missile-ready-nuclear-weapons/index.html.
17. Kevin Liptak and Jeremy Diamond, "Trump to UN: 'Rocket Man Is on a Suicide Mission,'" CNN, September 19, 2017, https://www.cnn .com/2017/09/18/politics/donald-trump-un-speech-iran-north -korea/index.html.
18. Jeff Mason and David Lawder, "Trump's China Trade Rhetoric Turns

Harsh at U.N., Says Won't Take 'Bad Deal,'" Reuters, September 24, 2019, https://www.reuters.com/article/us-un-assembly-trump-china /trumps-china-trade-rhetoric-turns-harsh-at-u-n-says-wont-take -bad-deal-idUSKBN1W91ZC.

19. "Remarks by President Trump in Press Gaggle Aboard Air Force One," The White House, December 2, 2018, https://www.whitehouse.gov /briefings-statements/remarks-president-trump-press-gaggle-aboard -air-force-one-2/.

20. "Who Is Donald Trump's 'Brilliant Genius' Nuclear Uncle John?," BBC, June 13, 2018, https://www.bbc.com/news/world-us-canada -44457471.

21. Ibid.

22. Author's interview with Tim Naftali, January 29, 2020.

23. Ibid.

1: THE END OF AMERICAN EXCEPTIONALISM

1. Author's interview with Susan Gordon, December 26, 2019.

2. Author's interview with Joseph Yun, December 6, 2019.

3. Author's interview with Mick Mulroy, January 2, 2020.

4. Associated Press, "Nixon Timed Vietnam War to End After Re-election," *Deseret News*, August 8, 2004, https://www.deseret .com/2004/8/8/19844202/nixon-timed-vietnam-war-to-end-after -re-election.

5. Author's interview with Steve Bannon, February 14, 2020.

6. Author's interview with Peter Navarro, January 19, 2020.

7. Author's interview with Steve Bannon, February 14, 2020.

8. Author's interview with H. R. McMaster, January 11, 2020.

9. Christina Wilkie, "Trump Is Pushing NATO Allies to Spend More on Defense. But So Did Obama and Bush," CNBC, July 11, 2018, https://www.cnbc.com/2018/07/11/obama-and-bush-also-pressed -nato-allies-to-spend-more-on-defense.html.

10. Ibid.

11. Matt Clinch and David Reid, "Trump's Message Is Having an Impact on NATO, Secretary General Says," CNBC, February 16, 2019, https://www.cnbc.com/2019/02/16/trump-message-is-having-an -impact-on-nato-secretary-general-says.html.

12. Author's interview with Susan Gordon, December 26, 2019.

13. Brian Ellsworth, "Trump Says U.S. Military Intervention in Venezuela 'an Option'; Russia Objects," Reuters, February 3, 2019, https://www.reuters.com/article/us-venezuela-politics/trump-says

-u-s-military-intervention-in-venezuela-an-option-russia-objects
-idUSKCN1PS0DK.

14. Sophie Tatum, "Trump Defends Putin: 'You Think Our Country's So Innocent?,'" CNN, February 6, 2017.

15. Author's interview with Peter Navarro, January 19, 2020.

16. Author's interview with Susan Gordon, December 26, 2019.

17. Author's interview with Peter Navarro, January 19, 2020.

18. Ibid.

19. Author's interview with Steve Bannon, February 14, 2020.

20. Mike Allen, "'Don't Do Stupid Sh--' (Stuff)," Politico, June 1, 2014, https://www.politico.com/story/2014/06/dont-do-stupid-shit -president-obama-white-house-107293.

21. Thomas Friedman, "Obama's Foreign Policy Book," *New York Times*, May 31, 2014, https://www.nytimes.com/2014/06/01/opinion /sunday/friedman-obamas-foreign-policy-book.html.

22. David Rothkopf, "Obama's 'Don't Do Stupid Shit' Foreign Policy," *Foreign Affairs*, June 4, 2014, https://foreignpolicy.com/2014/06/04 /obamas-dont-do-stupid-shit-foreign-policy/.

23. Stephen Collinson, Nicole Gaouette, Elise Labott, and Laura Smith-Spark, "China Lodges Complaint over Trump-Taiwan Call," CNN, December 3, 2016, https://www.cnn.com/2016/12/02/politics /donald-trump-taiwan/index.html.

24. Teddy Ng and Lawrence Chung, "Chinese Foreign Minister Brushes Off Trump Call with Tsai as 'Petty Trick' by Taiwan," *South China Morning Post*, December 3, 2016, https://www.scmp.com/news /china/policies-politics/article/2051455/chinese-foreign-minister -brushes-trump-call-tsai-petty.

25. Anne Gearan, Philip Rucker, and Simon Denyer, "Trump's Taiwan Phone Call Was Long Planned, Say People Who Were Involved," *Washington Post*, December 4, 2016, https://www.washingtonpost .com/politics/trumps-taiwan-phone-call-was-weeks-in-the-planning -say-people-who-were-involved/2016/12/04/f8be4b0c-ba4e-11e6 -94ac-3d324840106c_story.html.

26. Transcript, "Anderson Cooper 360 Degrees," CNN, December 2, 2016, transcripts.cnn.com/TRANSCRIPTS/1612/02/acd.01.html.

27. "Assessing Russian Activities and Intentions in Recent US Elections," Office of the Director of National Intelligence, January 6, 2017, https://www.dni.gov/files/documents/ICA_2017_01.pdf.

28. Evan Perez and Daniella Diaz, "White House Announces Retaliation Against Russia: Sanctions, Ejecting Diplomats," CNN, January 2,

2017, https://www.cnn.com/2016/12/29/politics/russia-sanctions-announced-by-white-house/index.html.

29. Ned Price, "The Administration's Response to Russia: What You Need to Know," The White House, December 29, 2016, https://obamawhitehouse.archives.gov/blog/2016/12/29/presidents-response-russias-actions-during-2016-election-what-you-need-know.

30. Katelyn Polantz, "Mueller Releases Memo Summarizing FBI's Interview with Michael Flynn," CNN, December 18, 2018, https://www.cnn.com/2018/12/17/politics/mueller-memo-michael-flynn-interview/index.html.

31. Tom LoBianco and Stephen Collinson, "Sally Yates Says She Warned White House That Flynn Was a Blackmail Risk," CNN, May 9, 2017, https://www.cnn.com/2017/05/08/politics/sally-yates-senate-testimony/index.html.

32. Jim Acosta and Jeremy Diamond, "Obama Warned Trump About Hiring Flynn," CNN, May 9, 2017, https://www.cnn.com/2017/05/08/politics/obama-trump-michael-flynn/index.html.

33. Amy Davidson Sorkin, "Donald Trump's Crowd Cheers His Muslim Exclusion Ban," New Yorker, December 8, 2015, https://www.newyorker.com/news/amy-davidson/donald-trumps-crowd-cheers-his-muslim-exclusion-plan.

34. Ibid.

35. Jennifer Rubin, "Sotomayor's Searing Dissent Is Worth Savoring," Washington Post, June 27, 2018, https://www.washingtonpost.com/blogs/right-turn/wp/2018/06/27/sotomayors-searing-dissent-is-worth-savoring/.

36. Rebecca Savransky, "Giuliani: Trump Asked Me How to Do a Muslim Ban 'Legally,'" The Hill, January 29, 2017, https://thehill.com/homenews/administration/316726-giuliani-trump-asked-me-how-to-do-a-muslim-ban-legally.

37. Geneva Sands, "Trump Administration Expands Travel Ban to Include Six New Countries," CNN, January 31, 2020, https://www.cnn.com/2020/01/31/politics/trump-administration-travel-ban-six-new-countries/index.html.

38. Anthony Boadle, "U.S. Backs Brazil for OECD Membership Ahead of Argentina," Reuters, January 14, 2020, https://www.reuters.com/article/us-brazil-oecd-usa/u-s-backs-brazil-for-oecd-membership-ahead-of-argentina-idUSKBN1ZE01Z.

39. "Statement by President Trump on Jerusalem," The White House,

December 6, 2017, https://www.whitehouse.gov/briefings
-statements/statement-president-trump-jerusalem/.

40. Jeremy Diamond and Nicole Gaouette, "White House: Jerusalem
Embassy Move a 'Recognition of Reality,'" CNN, December 6, 2017,
https://www.cnn.com/2017/12/05/politics/trump-abbas-us
-embassy-jerusalem/index.html.

41. Author's interview with Susan Gordon, December 26, 2019.

2: COMMANDER IN CHIEF

1. Author's interview with Susan Gordon, December 26, 2019.
2. Ibid.
3. Demetri Sevastopulo and Gillian Tett, "Gary Cohn Urges Trump
Team to Do More to Condemn Neo-Nazis," *Financial Times*,
August 25, 2017, https://www.ft.com/content/b85beea2-8924
-11e7-bf50-e1c239b45787.
4. Jim Sciutto, "US Intelligence Director: 'We Have Been Clear' on
Russian Election Interference," CNN, July 16, 2018, https://edition
.cnn.com/politics/live-news/trump-putin-helsinki/h_42c8c8303938
232485b716cf1e0ceb7b.
5. David Shortell, "Barr Says Trump's Tweets About DOJ Cases Make
It 'Impossible to Do My Job,'" CNN, February 14, 2020, https://
www.cnn.com/2020/02/13/politics/barr-trump-twitter/index.html.
6. "Transcript: Fiona Hill and David Holmes Testimony in Front of
the House Intelligence Committee," *Washington Post*, November 21,
2019, https://www.washingtonpost.com/politics/2019/11/21
/transcript-fiona-hill-david-holmes-testimony-front-house
-intelligence-committee/.
7. Daniel Bush, "'Everyone Was in the Loop.' Sondland Confirms Quid
Pro Quo," *PBS NewsHour*, November 20, 2019.
8. Ashley Parker and Dan Lamothe, "Navy Secretary Forced Out by
Pentagon Chief over Handling of Navy SEAL's War Crimes Case,"
Washington Post, November 25, 2019, https://www.washingtonpost
.com/national-security/2019/11/24/pentagon-chief-asks-navy
-secretarys-resignation-over-private-proposal-navy-seals-case/.
9. Nikki Haley, *With All Due Respect* (New York: St. Martin's Press,
2019).
10. Author's interview with Susan Gordon, December 26, 2019.
11. Author's interview with Peter Navarro, January 19, 2020.
12. Author's interview with Susan Gordon, December 26, 2019.

13.　David Wright and Daniella Diaz, "Trump: Why Could the Civil War Not Have 'Been Worked Out?,'" CNN, May 1, 2017, https://www .cnn.com/2017/05/01/politics/donald-trump-civil-war-comments -sirius-interview/index.html.

14.　Author's interview with Susan Gordon, December 26, 2019.

15.　Ibid.

16.　Author's interview with Peter Navarro, January 19, 2020.

17.　Author's interview with Susan Gordon, December 26, 2019.

18.　Author's interview with Mick Mulroy, January 2, 2020.

19.　Fox News Video, March 30, 2020, https://video.foxnews.com /v/6145728961001#sp=show-clips.

20.　Peter Baker, "Viktor Orban, Hungary's Far-Right Leader, Gets Warm Welcome from Trump," *New York Times*, May 13, 2019, https:// www.nytimes.com/2019/05/13/us/politics/trump-viktor-orban -oval-office.html.

21.　Author's interview with H. R. McMaster, January 11, 2020.

22.　"Remarks by President Trump to the 72nd Session of the United Nations General Assembly," The White House, September 19, 2017, https://www.whitehouse.gov/briefings-statements/remarks -president-trump-72nd-session-united-nations-general-assembly/.

23.　Author's interview with H. R. McMaster, January 11, 2020.

24.　Author's interview with Mick Mulroy, January 2, 2020.

25.　Author's interview with Susan Gordon, December 26, 2019.

26.　Ibid.

3: STRONG MAN GOOD: RUSSIA

1.　"Assessing Russian Activities and Intentions in Recent US Elections," Office of the Director of National Intelligence, January 6, 2017, https://www.dni.gov/files/documents/ICA_2017_01.pdf.

2.　Makini Brice, "Trump Publicly Opposes Using CIA Informants Against North Korea's Kim," Reuters, June 11, 2019, https://www .reuters.com/article/us-usa-northkorea/trump-publicly-opposes -using-cia-informants-against-north-koreas-kim-idUSKCN1TC256.

3.　Nicole Gaouette and Kylie Atwood, "Democrats Mull Subpoenas for Interpreters amid Reports of Trump Secrecy About Putin," CNN, January 14, 2019, https://www.cnn.com/2019/01/14/politics /trump-secrecy-russia-interpreter/index.html.

4.　"Lawsuit over Administration's Unlawful Seizure of Trump-Putin Meeting Notes Moves Forward," American Oversight, December 11,

# #

2019, https://www.americanoversight.org/lawsuit-over
-administrations-unlawful-seizure-of-trump-putin-meeting-notes
-moves-forward.

5. Meg Wagner, Mike Hayes, and Veronica Rocha, "The Latest on the Trump Impeachment Inquiry," CNN, November 11, 2019, https://www.cnn.com/politics/live-news/impeachment-inquiry-11-11-2019/h_f8b359cc4f6f1785ba85365f56abd568.

6. Transcript, *CNN Newsroom with Poppy Harlow and Jim Sciutto*, CNN, October 11, 2019, http://www.cnn.com/TRANSCRIPTS/1910/11/cnr.04.html.

7. Wagner, Hayes, and Rocha, "The Latest on the Trump Impeachment Inquiry."

8. Gillian Brassil and Spencer Kimball, "'The United States Has Been Foolish': Read the Full Transcript of Trump's Press Conference with Putin," CNBC, July 16, 2018, https://www.cnbc.com/2018/07/16/i-hold-both-countries-responsible-here-is-the-full-transcript-of-tr.html.

9. Ibid.

10. Kevin Liptak, "Trump Says He Misspoke During Press Conference: 'I Said the Word "Would" Instead of "Wouldn't,"'" CNN, July 17, 2018, https://www.cnn.com/politics/live-news/trump-putin-helsinki/h_07bbf8f0efaecbe556cf2f1c04eedcd3.

11. Andrew Desiderio and Kyle Cheney, "'Alarm Bells': What Cooper, Croft and Anderson Told Impeachment Investigators," Politico, November 11, 2019, https://www.politico.com/news/2019/11/11/what-laura-cooper-told-impeachment-investigators-069364.

12. Ibid.

13. Author's interview with Susan Gordon, December 26, 2019.

14. Ibid.

15. Ibid.

16. Ibid.

17. "Press Conference by President Bush and Russian Federation President Putin," The White House, June 16, 2001, https://georgewbush-whitehouse.archives.gov/news/releases/2001/06/20010618.html.

18. "Clinton, Lavrov Push Wrong Reset Button on Ties," Reuters, March 6, 2009, https://www.reuters.com/article/idUSN06402140.

19. Author's interview with H. R. McMaster, January 11, 2020.

4: "L'ÉTAT, C'EST MOI": UKRAINE

1.   "Deputy Secretary of State George Kent Testifies at Impeachment
     Hearing—Read His Opening Statement," CBS News, November 13,
     2019, https://www.cbsnews.com/news/deputy-secretary-of-state
     -george-kent-testimony-read-full-opening-statement-impeachment
     -hearing-2019-11-13/.

2.   Congressional Research Service, "Ukraine: Background, Conflict with
     Russia, and U.S. Policy," September 19, 2019, https://fas.org/sgp/crs
     /row/R45008.pdf, 30.

3.   Ibid.

4.   Kevin Liptak, Kaitlan Collins, and Kylie Atwood, "White House
     Releases Rough Transcript of Trump's First Ukraine Call," CNN,
     November 15, 2019, https://www.cnn.com/2019/11/15/politics
     /donald-trump-volodymyr-zelensky-white-house-transcript-april
     -call/index.html.

5.   Glenn Kessler and Salvador Rizzo, "Fact-Checking the Opening
     Day of the Trump Impeachment Hearings," *Washington Post*,
     November 14, 2019, https://www.washingtonpost.com/politics
     /2019/11/14/fact-checking-opening-day-trump-impeachment
     -hearings/.

6.   Liptak, Collins, and Atwood, "White House Releases Rough
     Transcript of Trump's First Ukraine Call."

7.   Jack Fitzpatrick, "Readout of President Trump's Call with Ukrainian
     President-Elect Volodymyr Zelenskyy," April 21, 2019, FactCheck
     .org, https://cdn.factcheck.org/UploadedFiles/April-21_WH
     statement-Redacted.png.

8.   David Welna, "Pentagon Letter Undercuts Trump Assertion on
     Delaying Aid to Ukraine over Corruption," NPR, September 25, 2019,
     https://www.npr.org/2019/09/25/764453663/pentagon-letter
     -undercuts-trump-assertion-on-delaying-aid-to-ukraine-over-corrup.

9.   Zachary B. Wolf and Curt Merrill, "The Whistleblower Complaint,
     Annotated," CNN, September 26, 2019, https://www.cnn.com
     /interactive/2019/09/politics/whistleblower-complaint-annotated/.

10. Jeremy Herb, "White House Officials Testify Quid Pro Quo Effort
     Was Coordinated with Mulvaney," CNN, November 8, 2019,
     https://www.cnn.com/2019/11/08/politics/transcripts-released
     -fiona-hill-alexander-vindman/index.html.

11. Zachary B. Wolf and Sean O'Key, "The Ukraine Text Messages,
     Annotated," CNN, October 4, 2019, https://www.cnn.com
     /interactive/2019/10/politics/ukraine-text-messages-annotated/.

Notes

281

12. "Transcript: Sondland's Nov. 20 public testimony in front of the House Intelligence Committee," *Washington Post*, November 20, 2019, https://www.washingtonpost.com/politics/2019/11/20/transcript-sondlands-nov-public-testimony-front-house-intelligence-committee/.

13. Eric Lipton, "Emails Show Budget Office Working to Carry Out Ukraine Aid Freeze," *New York Times*, January 22, 2020, https://www.nytimes.com/2020/01/22/us/politics/ukraine-aid.html.

14. Ibid.

15. "Memorandum of Telephone Conversation: Telephone Conversation with President Zelenskyy of Ukraine," The White House Situation Room, July 25, 2019, https://www.whitehouse.gov/wp-content/uploads/2019/09/Unclassified09.2019.pdf.

16. "Read Trump's Phone Conversation with Volodymyr Zelensky," CNN, September 26, 2019, https://www.cnn.com/2019/09/25/politics/donald-trump-ukraine-transcript-call/index.html.

17. *The Impeachment Report: The House Intelligence Committee's Report on Its Investigation into Donald Trump and Ukraine* (New York: Broadway Books, 2019), 257–58.

18. Edward Wong, "Officials Discussed Hold on Ukraine Aid After Trump Spoke with Country's Leader," *New York Times*, January 16, 2020, https://www.nytimes.com/2019/12/21/us/politics/white-house-pentagon-ukraine-aid.html.

19. Kevin Liptak, "Laura Cooper Describes Three Inquiries on Ukraine Aid on July 25," CNN, November 20, 2019, https://www.cnn.com/politics/live-news/impeachment-hearing-11-20-19/h_7bf9f3b912d80572f5dffdcd2a9f69ed.

20. "Transcript: Fiona Hill and David Holmes Testimony in Front of the House Intelligence Committee," *Washington Post*, November 21, 2019, https://www.washingtonpost.com/politics/2019/11/21/transcript-fiona-hill-david-holmes-testimony-front-house-intelligence-committee/.

21. Wolf and O'Key, "The Ukraine Text Messages, Annotated."

22. Lipton, "Emails Show Budget Office Working to Carry Out Ukraine Aid Freeze."

23. Ibid.

24. Kylie Atwood, "Volker Admits He Was Wrong to View Biden and Burisma Separately," CNN, November 19, 2019, https://www.cnn.com/politics/live-news/impeachment-hearing-11-19-19/h_f30913e2622eb1fb31345ce33047f1fa.

25. Daniel Bush, "'Everyone Was in the Loop.' Sondland Confirms Quid Pro Quo," *PBS NewsHour*, November 20, 2019.

26. Ibid.

27. Manu Raju and Jeremy Herb, "'I Think This Is All Going to Blow Up': Witness Says EU Ambassador Was Running 'Domestic Political Errand,'" CNN, November 21, 2019, https://www.cnn.com/2019 /11/21/politics/fiona-hill-david-holmes-public-impeachment -hearing/index.html.

28. Veronica Rocha, Meg Wagner, and Amanda Wills, "Four Key Impeachment Witnesses Testify," CNN, November 19, 2019, https:// www.cnn.com/politics/live-news/impeachment-hearing-11-19-19 /h_a95a6c0731b8d6f53b9fa7588b35a743.

29. Ibid.

30. Ibid.

31. Ryan Browne and Kevin Liptak, "Republicans Are Questioning Why Vindman Appeared in Uniform, but US Army Points Out That This Is Normal," CNN, November 19, 2019, https://www.cnn.com /politics/live-news/impeachment-hearing-11-19-19/h_edce24980a 75bc4a2d21d3e98fa8e3fe.

32. Rocha, Wagner, and Wills, "Four Key Impeachment Witnesses Testify."

33. "Assessing Russian Activities and Intentions in Recent US Elections," Office of the Director of National Intelligence, January 6, 2017, https://www.dni.gov/files/documents/ICA_2017_01.pdf, 2.

34. "Report of the Select Committee on Intelligence, United States Senate, on Russian Active Measures Campaigns and Interference in the 2016 U.S. Election," vol. 2, July 2019, https://www.intelligence. senate.gov/sites/default/files/documents/Report_Volume2.pdf, 2.

35. Raju and Herb, "'I Think This Is All Going to Blow Up.'"

36. Tim Hains, "GOP Sen. Kennedy vs. Chuck Todd: 'Both Russia and Ukraine Meddled in the 2016 Election,'" RealClear Politics, December 1, 2019, https://www.realclearpolitics.com/video/2019 /12/01/gop_sen_kennedy_vs_chuck_todd_both_russia_and _ukraine_meddled_in_the_2016_election.html.

37. "Remarks by President Trump upon Arriving at the U.N. General Assembly," The White House, September 24, 2019, https://www .whitehouse.gov/briefings-statements/remarks-president-trump -upon-arriving-u-n-general-assembly-new-york-ny/.

38. "Impeachment Inquiry: Fiona Hill and David Holmes, Permanent Select Committee on Intelligence, House of Representatives,"

November 21, 2019, https://republicans-intelligence.house.gov /uploadedfiles/hill_and_holmes_hearing_transcript.pdf.

39. Ibid.
40. Natalia Zinets and Gleb Stolyarov, "Zelenskiy Wants Ukrainian Candidates to Run in Donbass Election," Reuters, October 3, 2019, https://www.reuters.com/article/us-ukraine-zelenskiy-russia-talks /zelenskiy-ukrainian-candidates-should-take-part-in-donbass -election-idUSKBN1WI1VB.
41. Ibid.

5: STRONG MAN BAD: CHINA
1. Peter Shadbolt, "Chinese Dissident Chen Guangcheng: NYU Is Forcing Me Out," CNN, June 17, 2013, https://www.cnn.com /2013/06/17/us/chen-nyu/index.html.
2. Ibid.
3. Author's interview with Steve Bannon, February 14, 2020.
4. Nick Corasaniti, Alexander Burns, and Binyamin Appelbaum, "Donald Trump Vows to Rip Up Trade Deals and Confront China," New York Times, June 28, 2016, https://www.nytimes.com/2016 /06/29/us/politics/donald-trump-trade-speech.html.
5. "Read Donald Trump's Speech on Trade," Time, June 28, 2016, https://time.com/4386335/donald-trump-trade-speech-transcript/.
6. Ibid.
7. Author's interview with Peter Navarro, January 19, 2020.
8. Author's interview with Steve Bannon, February 14, 2020.
9. Ibid.
10. Ibid.
11. Author's interview with Peter Navarro, January 19, 2020.
12. Robert E. Lighthizer, "Testimony Before the U.S.-China Economic and Security Review Commission: Evaluating China's Role in the World Trade Organization over the Past Decade," June 9, 2010, https://www.uscc.gov/sites/default/files/6.9.10Lighthizer.pdf.
13. Author's interview with Peter Navarro, January 19, 2020.
14. "Trade Works, Tariffs Don't," U.S. Chamber of Commerce, https:// www.uschamber.com/tariffs.
15. Ibid.
16. Author's interview with Peter Navarro, January 19, 2020.
17. Author's interview with Steve Bannon, February 14, 2020.
18. Ibid.
19. Author's interview with Peter Navarro, January 19, 2020.

20. Author's interview with Steve Bannon, February 14, 2020.

21. Koh Gui Qing, "China Halts Purchase of U.S. Farm Products,"
     Reuters, August 5, 2019, https://www.reuters.com/article/us-usa
     -trade-china-agriculture-purchase/china-halts-purchase-of-u-s-farm
     -products-idUSKCN1UV1WY.

22. Author's interview with Steve Bannon, February 14, 2020.

23. Author's interview with Peter Navarro, January 19, 2020.

24. Austin Lowe, "China Misses Its Chance to Clear Up Doubts About
     the Foreign Investment Law," *South China Morning Post*, January 16,
     2020, https://www.scmp.com/comment/opinion/article/3045898
     /china-misses-its-chance-clear-doubts-about-foreign-investment-law.

25. Author's interview with Peter Navarro, January 19, 2020.

26. Ibid.

27. Author's interview with Steve Bannon, February 14, 2020.

28. "Transcript: Chris Johnson Talks with Michael Morell on
     'Intelligence Matters,'" CBS News, November 6, 2019, https://www
     .cbsnews.com/news/transcript-chris-johnson-talks-with-michael
     -morell-on-intelligence-matters/.

29. Author's interview with Steve Bannon, February 14, 2020.

6: "FIRE AND FURY": NORTH KOREA, PART ONE

1.   Author's interview with Joseph Yun, December 6, 2019.

2.   Ibid.

3.   Jim Sciutto, Barbara Starr, and Zachary Cohen, "Trump Promises
     North Korea 'Fire and Fury' over Nuke Threat," August 9, 2017,
     https://www.cnn.com/2017/08/08/politics/north-korea-missile
     -ready-nuclear-weapons/index.html.

4.   Zachary Cohen and Euan McKirdy, "North Korea Threatens Strike
     on Guam," CNN, August 9, 2017, https://www.cnn.com/2017/08/08
     /politics/north-korea-considering-guam-strike-trump/index.html.

5.   Kevin Liptak and Jeremy Diamond, "Trump to UN: 'Rocket Man Is
     on a Suicide Mission,'" CNN, September 19, 2017, https://www.cnn
     .com/2017/09/18/politics/donald-trump-un-speech-iran-north
     -korea/index.html.

6.   Author's interview with Joseph Yun, December 6, 2019.

7.   Author's interview with Sue Mi Terry, December 18, 2019.

8.   Author's interview with Joseph Yun, December 6, 2019.

9.   Ibid.

10. Joshua Berlinger, "Kim Jong Nam: The Plot to Murder North Korea's

Exiled Son," CNN, September 26, 2017, https://www.cnn.com/2017 /07/26/asia/kim-jong-nam-killing/index.html.

11. Author's interview with Sue Mi Terry, December 18, 2019.
12. Ibid.
13. Author's interview with Joseph Yun, December 6, 2019.
14. Ibid.
15. Will Ripley, "First on CNN: U.S. Student Detained in North Korea Confesses to 'Hostile Act,'" CNN, February 29, 2016, https://www .cnn.com/2016/02/28/asia/north-korea-otto-warmbier/index.html.
16. Author's interview with Joseph Yun, December 6, 2019.
17. Ibid.
18. Ibid.
19. Joshua Berlinger, "North Korea's Missile Tests: What You Need to Know," CNN, December 3, 2017, https://www.cnn.com/2017 /05/29/asia/north-korea-missile-tests/index.html.
20. Author's interview with Joseph Yun, December 6, 2019.
21. Zachary Cohen, "Missile Threat Alert for Hawaii a False Alarm; Officials Blame Employee Who Pushed 'Wrong Button,'" CNN, January 14, 2018, https://www.cnn.com/2018/01/13/politics /hawaii-missile-threat-false-alarm/index.html.
22. Associated Press, "North Korea Readies Artillery Forces, Threatens Attack on Hawaii," Hawaii News Now, March 26, 2013, https:// www.hawaiinewsnow.com/story/21796982/north-korea-readies/.
23. Jason Silverstein, "North Korea Nuclear Attack: Hawaii Taking Major Steps to Prepare for Potential Strike from Kim," *Newsweek*, December 17, 2017, https://www.newsweek.com/hawaii-north -korea-nuclear-attack-prepare-750767.
24. Cohen, "Missile Threat Alert for Hawaii a False Alarm."
25. Author's interview with Joseph Yun, December 6, 2019.
26. Ibid.
27. "South Korean President Moon Jae-in Hopes Winter Olympics Brings 'Inter-Korean Peace,'" CNN, November 1, 2017, https://www .cnn.com/2017/09/20/sport/south-korea-north-korea-relations -pyeongchang-2018-winter-olympics/index.html.
28. Alanne Orjoux, "Kim Jong Un Offers Rare Olive Branch to South Korea," CNN, January 2, 2018, https://www.cnn.com/2017/12/31 /asia/kim-jong-un-new-year-address-nuclear/index.html.
29. Author's interview with Joseph Yun, December 6, 2019.
30. Author's interview with Sue Mi Terry, December 18, 2019.

7: "FALLING IN LOVE": NORTH KOREA, PART TWO

1. Ben Westcott, "What US and North Korea Mean When They Talk About Denuclearization," CNN, April 20, 2018, https://www.cnn .com/2018/04/20/asia/kim-trump-moon-denuclearization-intl /index.html.

2. "Joint Statement of President Donald J. Trump of the United States of America and Chairman Kim Jong Un of the Democratic People's Republic of Korea at the Singapore Summit," The White House, June 12, 2018, https://www.whitehouse.gov/briefings-statements /joint-statement-president-donald-j-trump-united-states-america -chairman-kim-jong-un-democratic-peoples-republic-korea -singapore-summit/.

3. "Remarks by President Trump to the 72nd Session of the United Nations General Assembly," The White House, September 19, 2017, https://www.whitehouse.gov/briefings-statements/remarks -president-trump-72nd-session-united-nations-general-assembly/.

4. Roberta Rampton, "'We Fell in Love': Trump Swoons over Letters from North Korea's Kim," Reuters, September 29, 2018.

5. Barbara Starr and Zachary Cohen, "US Intel Agency Believes Kim Won't Fully Denuclearize," CNN, July 2, 2018, https://www.cnn.com /2018/07/02/politics/north-korea-denuclearization/index.html.

6. Rebecca Morin, "Trump Hails $20 Billion in Boeing Orders by Vietnam," Politico, February 27, 2019, https://www.politico.com/story /2019/02/27/trump-boeing-vietnam-trade-agreement-1189984.

7. Jim Sciutto, Kylie Atwood, Jeremy Diamond, and Kevin Liptak, "A Snub and a Last Minute Hail Mary. Trump's Tough Lesson in North Korean Diplomacy," CNN, March 6, 2019.

8. James Griffiths, "Trump: 'Sometimes You Have to Walk,'" CNN, February 28, 2019, https://www.cnn.com/politics/live-news/trump -kim-jong-un-summit-vietnam-february-2019/h_d3f483b6a8a213c 7537f0786bc6e371f.

9. Author's interview with Joseph Yun, December 6, 2019.

10. Deirdre Shesgreen, "Exclusive: Pompeo on the Failed North Korea Talks, Otto Warmbier and His Own Trip to Iowa," USA Today, March 3, 2019, https://www.usatoday.com/story/news/world /2019/03/03/pompeo-north-korea-summit-stalemate-warmbier -military-exercises-trump-2020-caucuses/3028940002/.

11. Ian Schwartz, "Trump: I Take Kim Jong Un at His Word He Wasn't Involved with Otto Warmbier, 'He Felt Badly About It,'" RealClear Politics, February 28, 2019, https://www.realclearpolitics.com

/video/2019/02/28/trump_i_take_kim_jong_un_at_his_word_he
_wasnt_involved_with_otto_warmbier_he_felt_badly_about_it
.html.

12. Zeke Miller, Jonathan Lemire, and Catherine Lucey, "Trump
     Criticizes Rush to Condemn Saudi Arabia over Khashoggi," AP
     News, October 16, 2018, https://apnews.com/6ef4045b710b411086
     e93967eb8ffc4f.

13. Samuel Chamberlain, "Trump Says 'I Don't Want to Hear the Tape'
     of Purported Khashoggi Killing," Fox News, November 18, 2018,
     https://www.foxnews.com/politics/trump-says-i-dont-want-to-hear
     -the-tape-of-purported-khashoggi-killing.

14. Chris Cilizza, "Donald Trump's Shocking, Shameful About-Face on
     Otto Warmbier," CNN, March 1, 2019, https://www.cnn.com
     /2019/02/28/politics/donald-trump-otto-warmbier-kim-jong-un/.

15. Kevin Liptak and Allie Malloy, "Trump Tweets Kim an Invitation to
     'Shake His Hand' at DMZ," CNN, June 29, 2019, https://www.cnn
     .com/2019/06/28/politics/donald-trump-kim-jong-un-dmz/index
     .html.

16. Ibid.

17. Jordan Fabian and Saagar Enjeti, "Trump Offers to Meet North
     Korean Leader Kim Jong Un in DMZ," The Hill, June 28, 2019,
     https://thehill.com/policy/international/450816-trump-to-offers
     -to-visit-dmz-to-meet-kim.

18. Jordan Phelps, "President Trump Becomes 1st President to Step
     Inside North Korea Ahead of Meeting with Kim Jong Un," ABC
     News, June 30, 2019, https://abcnews.go.com/Politics/president
     -trump-travel-dmz-meet-kim-jong/story?id=64042883.

19. Ibid.

20. Author's interview with Sue Mi Terry, December 18, 2019.

21. "Press Conference by President Trump," The White House, June 12,
     2018, https://www.whitehouse.gov/briefings-statements/press
     -conference-president-trump/.

22. Eric Schmitt, "Pentagon and Seoul Surprised by Trump Pledge to
     Halt Military Exercises," New York Times, June 12, 2018, https://
     www.nytimes.com/2018/06/12/world/asia/trump-military-exercises
     -north-south-korea.html.

23. Ibid.

24. Phil Stewart and Arshad Mohammed, "U.S. Military Says No Plans
     to Suspend More Major Exercises on Korean Peninsula," Reuters,
     August 28, 2018, https://www.reuters.com/article/us-northkorea

-usa-exercises/u-s-military-says-no-plans-to-suspend-more-major
-exercises-on-korean-peninsula-idUSKCN1LD1UC.

25. Conor Friedersdorf, "Trump Defended Cuts to Public-Health Agencies, on Video," *The Atlantic*, March 17, 2020, https://www .theatlantic.com/ideas/archive/2020/03/trump-defended-cuts-public -health-agencies/608158/.

26. Dan Lamothe, "U.S. and South Korea End Military Exercises That Riled North Korea in Favor of Something Smaller," *Washington Post*, March 3, 2019, https://www.washingtonpost.com/national-security /2019/03/02/us-south-korea-end-military-exercises-that-riled -north-korea-favor-something-smaller/.

27. Ibid.

28. "READ: James Mattis' Resignation Letter," CNN, December 21, 2018, https://www.cnn.com/2018/12/20/politics/james-mattis -resignation-letter-doc/index.html.

29. Joe Gould and Leo Shane III, "Nominee to Lead US Forces Korea Says Pause in Exercises There Has Hurt Readiness," Defense News, September 25, 2018, https://www.defensenews.com/news/pentagon -congress/2018/09/25/nominee-to-lead-us-forces-korea-says-pause -in-exercises-there-hurt-readiness/.

30. Author's interview with Sue Mi Terry, December 18, 2019.

31. Ibid.

32. "Military Defense Budget, South Korea," GlobalSecurity.org, https:// www.globalsecurity.org/military/world/rok/budget.htm.

33. Author's interview with Sue Mi Terry, December 18, 2019.

34. "Pentagon Denies U.S. Is Considering Pulling Troops from South Korea," Reuters, November 21, 2019, https://www.reuters.com /article/us-southkorea-usa-military-pentagon/pentagon-denies -us-is-considering-pulling-troops-from-south-korea-idUSKBN 1XV0PY.

35. Author's interview with Sue Mi Terry, December 18, 2019.

36. Ibid.

37. Ibid.

38. Cornel Feruta, "Statement to Sixty-Third Regular Session of IAEA General Conference," International Atomic Energy Agency, September 16, 2019, https://www.iaea.org/newscenter/statements /statement-to-sixty-third-regular-session-of-iaea-general-conference.

39. Ibid.

40. Author's interview with Joseph Yun, December 6, 2019.

41. Ibid.
42. Author's interview with Sue Mi Terry, December 18, 2019.
43. Author's interview with Joseph Yun, December 6, 2019.

8: "RETREAT, REVERSE, REPEAT": SYRIA

1.   Jeremy Diamond and Elise Labott, "Trump Told Turkey's Erdogan in Dec. 14 Call About Syria, 'It's All Yours. We Are Done,'" CNN, December 24, 2018, https://www.cnn.com/2018/12/23/politics /donald-trump-erdogan-turkey/index.html.
2.   Ibid.
3.   Author's interview with Mick Mulroy, January 2, 2020.
4.   "READ: James Mattis' Resignation Letter," CNN, December 21, 2018, https://www.cnn.com/2018/12/20/politics/james-mattis -resignation-letter-doc/index.html.
5.   Author's interview with Mick Mulroy, January 2, 2020.
6.   Ibid.
7.   Ibid.
8.   Ibid.
9.   Barbara Starr, Ryan Browne, and Nicole Gaouette, "Trump Orders Rapid Withdrawal from Syria in Apparent Reversal," CNN, December 19, 2018, https://www.cnn.com/2018/12/19/politics/us -syria-withdrawal/index.html.
10. Julian Borger and Martin Chulov, "Trump Shocks Allies and Advisers with Plan to Pull US Troops Out of Syria," *Guardian*, December 19, 2018, https://www.theguardian.com/us-news/2018/dec/19/us -troops-syria-withdrawal-trump.
11. Tim Hains, "Rep. Adam Kinzinger: 'I Implore the President to Reconsider' Withdrawal from Syria," RealClear Politics, December 20, 2018, https://www.realclearpolitics.com/video/2018 /12/20/rep_adam_kinzinger_i_implore_the_president_to _reconsider_withdrawal_from_syria.html.
12. Author's interview with Mick Mulroy, January 2, 2020.
13. Ibid.
14. Ibid.
15. "Statement from the Press Secretary," The White House, October 6, 2019, https://www.whitehouse.gov/briefings-statements/statement -press-secretary-85/.
16. Helen Regan and Jeremy Diamond, "Turkey to Send Troops into Northern Syria as US Pulls Out of Area, White House Says," CNN,

October 7, 2019, https://www.cnn.com/2019/10/07/politics/white
-house-turkey-syria-intl-hnk/index.html.

17. Jennifer Hansler and Alex Rogers, "Trump Defends Syria Decision amid Republican Backlash," CNN, October 8, 2019, https://www .cnn.com/2019/10/07/politics/mitch-mcconnell-republican -response-syria-kurds/index.html.

18. Author's interview with Mick Mulroy, January 2, 2020.

19. Ibid.

20. Nicole Gaouette, "Republican Anger Grows as Trump Disavows Kurds by Saying They Didn't Help During WWII," CNN, October 10, 2019, https://www.cnn.com/2019/10/09/politics /turkey-syria-us-anger-ramifications/index.html.

21. Jacey Fortin, "Trump Says the Kurds 'Didn't Help' at Normandy. Here's the History," *New York Times*, October 10, 2019, https://www .nytimes.com/2019/10/10/world/middleeast/trump-kurds-normandy .html.

22. Kurt Schlichter, "Critics Aghast as Trump Keeps Word About No More Wars," Townhall, October 8, 2019, https://townhall.com /columnists/kurtschlichter/2019/10/08/critics-aghast-as-trump -keeps-word-about-no-more-wars-n2554328.

23. Author's interview with Mick Mulroy, January 2, 2020.

24. Ibid.

25. Ibid.

9: SHIFTING RED LINES: IRAN

1. Lauren Carroll, "Fact-Checking Trump's Changing Opinion on Syria and the 'Red Line,'" PolitiFact, April 5, 2017, https://www.politifact .com/factchecks/2017/apr/05/greta-van-susteren/fact-checking -trump/.

2. Author's interview with Mick Mulroy, January 2, 2020.

3. Jeremy Diamond, Barbara Starr, Jamie Gangel, and Kate Sullivan, "Trump Says US Was 'Cocked and Loaded' to Strike Iran Before He Pulled Back," CNN, June 21, 2019, https://www.cnn.com/2019 /06/21/politics/trump-military-strikes-iran/index.html.

4. Peter Baker, Maggie Haberman, and Thomas Gibbons-Neff, "Urged to Launch an Attack, Trump Listened to the Skeptics Who Said It Would Be a Costly Mistake," *New York Times*, June 21, 2019, https://www.nytimes.com/2019/06/21/us/politics/trump-iran -strike.html.

5. Kevin Liptak and Nicole Gaouette, "Trump Downplays Iran Tensions

After Drone Shot Down," CNN, June 20, 2019, https://www.cnn
.com/2019/06/20/politics/trump-iran-drone-downing/index.html.
6.   Ibid.
7.   Author's interview with Mick Mulroy, January 2, 2020.
8.   Julia Horowitz, "Oil Shock Hits a Global Economy That's Already on
      Shaky Ground," CNN, September 16, 2019, https://www.cnn.com
      /2019/09/16/economy/saudi-attack-world-economy/index.html.
9.   Michelle Nichols, "Exclusive: U.N. Investigators Find Yemen's
      Houthis Did Not Carry Out Saudi Oil Attack," Reuters, January 8,
      2020, https://www.reuters.com/article/us-saudi-aramco-attacks-un
      -exclusive/exclusive-u-n-investigators-find-yemens-houthis-did-not
      -carry-out-saudi-oil-attack-idUSKBN1Z72VX.
10.   Author's interview with Mick Mulroy, January 2, 2020.
11.   Barbara Starr, "US Civilian Contractor Killed in Rocket Attack in
      Iraq," CNN, December 27, 2019, https://www.cnn.com/2019/12/27
      /politics/iraq-rocket-attack-contractor-killed/index.html.
12.   Michael R. Gordon, Nancy A. Youssef, and Isabel Coles, "U.S.
      Strikes Shiite Militia Targets in Iraq and Syria," *Wall Street Journal*,
      December 29, 2019, https://www.wsj.com/articles/u-s-strikes
      -shiamilitia-targets-in-iraq-and-syria-11577642168.
13.   "US Strikes 5 Facilities in Iraq and Syria Linked to Iranian-Backed
      Militia," CNN, December 30, 2019, https://lite.cnn.com/en/article
      /h_21d7d8b9784232c0e347d28b6a60de35.
14.   Ibid.
15.   Author's interview with Mick Mulroy, January 2, 2020.
16.   Ibid.
17.   "Statement by the Department of Defense," U.S. Department of
      Defense, January 2, 2020, https://www.defense.gov/Newsroom
      /Releases/Release/Article/2049534/statement-by-the-department
      -of-defense/.
18.   Zachary Cohen, Hamdi Alkhshali, Kareem Khadder, and Angela
      Dewan, "US Drone Strike Ordered by Trump Kills Top Iranian
      Commander in Baghdad," CNN, January 4, 2020, https://www.cnn
      .com/2020/01/02/middleeast/baghdad-airport-rockets/index.html.
19.   Ibid.
20.   Dana Bash, Jim Sciutto, and Pamela Brown, "Soleimani Was Planning
      Specific Attacks from Multiple Countries, According to Source,"
      CNN, January 3, 2020, https://www.cnn.com/middleeast/live-news
      /baghdad-airport-strike-live-intl-hnk/h_f9d911972e147dcd0e8b9
      b6fc5fc6d11.

21. "Trump Tells Fox News' Laura Ingraham 'Four Embassies' Were Targeted in Imminent Threat from Iran," Fox News, January 10, 2020, https://www.fox5dc.com/news/trump-tells-fox-news-laura-ingraham -four-embassies-were-targeted-in-imminent-threat-from-iran.

22. Melissa Quinn, "Esper Says He 'Didn't See' Specific Evidence Showing Iranian Threat to 4 U.S. Embassies," CBS News, January 12, 2020, https://www.cbsnews.com/news/mark-esper-secretary-of -defense-iranian-threat-specific-evidence-didnt-see-face-the-nation -2020-01-13/.

23. "Sen. Chris Coons on Impeachment Developments, Efforts Curb Trump's Ability to Use Military Action Against Iran," Fox News, January 12, 2020, https://www.foxnews.com/transcript/sen-chris -coons-on-impeachment-developments-efforts-curb-trumps-ability -to-use-military-action-against-iran.

24. Nicole Gaouette and Jamie Gangel, "How Pompeo Convinced Trump to Kill Soleimani and Fulfilled a Decade-Long Goal," CNN, January 11, 2020, https://www.cnn.com/2020/01/09/politics /pompeo-trump-iran-soleimani/index.html.

25. "Remarks by President Trump on Iran," The White House, January 8, 2020, https://www.whitehouse.gov/briefings-statements/remarks -president-trump-iran/.

26. "Remarks by the President at Cairo University, 6-04-09," The White House, https://obamawhitehouse.archives.gov/the-press-office /remarks-president-cairo-university-6-04-09.

27. "Remarks by President Trump on Iran."

28. Jake Tapper, Ryan Browne, and Barbara Starr, "US Troops Were Injured in Iran Missile Attack Despite Pentagon Initially Saying There Were No Casualties," CNN, January 17, 2020, https://www .cnn.com/2020/01/16/politics/service-members-injured-iran-strike /index.html.

29. Barbara Starr, "Over 100 US Troops Have Been Diagnosed with Traumatic Brain Injuries Following Iran Strike," CNN, February 10, 2020, https://www.cnn.com/2020/02/10/politics/traumatic-brain -injuries-iran-strike/index.html.

30. Ibid.

31. "VFW Expects Apology from POTUS," Veterans of Foreign Wars, January 24, 2020, https://www.vfw.org/media-and-events/latest -releases/archives/2020/1/vfw-expects-apology-from-potus.

32. Ryan Browne, "Esper Blames Iranian-Backed Militias for Rocket

Attack That Killed American Troops," CNN, March 12, 2020, https://
www.cnn.com/2020/03/12/politics/esper-iraq-attack/index.html.

33.   Author's interview with Mick Mulroy, January 2, 2020.

34.   "Read the Full Transcript of Trump's Speech on the Iran Nuclear
Deal," *New York Times*, May 8, 2018, https://www.nytimes.com
/2018/05/08/us/politics/trump-speech-iran-deal.html.

35.   Author's interview with Mick Mulroy, January 2, 2020.

EPILOGUE: TRUMP WORLD

1.   Daniel Dale, "Fact Check: Trump Tries to Erase the Memory of Him
Downplaying the Coronavirus," CNN, March 17, 2020, https://
www.cnn.com/2020/03/17/politics/fact-check-trump-always-knew
-pandemic-coronavirus/index.html.

2.   Rem Reider, "Trump and the 'New Hoax,'" FactCheck.org, March 3,
2020, https://www.factcheck.org/2020/03/trump-and-the-new
-hoax/.

3.   "Remarks by President Trump, Vice President Pence, and Members
of the Coronavirus Task Force in Press Briefing," The White House,
March 17, 2020, https://www.whitehouse.gov/briefings-statements
/remarks-president-trump-vice-president-pence-members-coronavirus
-task-force-press-briefing-4/.

4.   Author's interview with Fiona Hill, March 15, 2020.

5.   "Donald Trump's Speech at the Republican Convention, as Prepared
for Delivery," CNN, July 22, 2016, https://www.cnn.com/2016/07
/22/politics/donald-trump-rnc-speech-text/index.html.

6.   Author's interview with Fiona Hill, March 15, 2020.

7.   Associated Press, "Trump vs Fauci: President and Doctor Spar over
Unproven Drug," KXAN, March 21, 2020, https://www.kxan.com
/news/coronavirus/trump-vs-fauci-president-and-doctor-spar-over
-unproven-drug/.

8.   Ibid.

9.   Jonathan Swan, "Scoop: Inside the Epic White House Fight over
Hydroxychloroquine," Axios, April 5, 2020, https://www.axios.com
/coronavirus-hydroxychloroquine-white-house-01306286-0bbc
-4042-9bfe-890413c6220d.html.

10.   Chandelis Duster, "Peter Navarro on His Qualifications to Disagree
with Dr. Anthony Fauci on Coronavirus Treatments: 'I'm a Social
Scientist,'" CNN, April 6, 2020, https://www.cnn.com/2020/04/06
/politics/peter-navarro-social-scientist-cnntv/index.html.

11. Justin McCarthy, "U.S. Coronavirus Concerns Surge, Government Trust Slides," Gallup, March 16, 2020, https://news.gallup.com/poll/295505/coronavirus-worries-surge.aspx.

12. Lydia Saad, "Americans Rapidly Answering the Call to Isolate, Prepare," Gallup, March 20, 2020, https://news.gallup.com/poll/297035/americans-rapidly-answering-call-isolate-prepare.aspx.

13. Author's interview with Fiona Hill, March 15, 2020.

14. James McCarten, "3M Says Trump Officials Have Told It to Stop Sending Face Masks to Canada. Trudeau Responds," *National Post* (Toronto), April 3, 2020, https://nationalpost.com/news/world/3m-says-trump-officials-have-told-it-to-stop-sending-face-masks-to-canada.

15. Jennifer Hansler and Kylie Atwood, "Russian Coronavirus Aid Delivery to US Prompts Confusion and Criticism," CNN, April 2, 2020, https://www.cnn.com/2020/04/02/politics/russia-medical-supplies-us-propaganda/index.html.

16. Jacob Poushter, "How People Around the World See the U.S. and Donald Trump in 10 Charts," Pew Research Center, January 8, 2020, https://www.pewresearch.org/fact-tank/2020/01/08/how-people-around-the-world-see-the-u-s-and-donald-trump-in-10-charts/.

17. Eric Tucker, "FBI Official: Russia Wants to See US 'Tear Ourselves Apart,'" AP News, February 24, 2020, https://apnews.com/a55930e0a02d2e21d8ed2be7bc496a6f.

18. Andrew Osborn and Joyce Lee, "First Russian-Chinese Air Patrol in Asia-Pacific Draws Shots from South Korea," Reuters, July 22, 2019, https://www.reuters.com/article/us-southkorea-russia-aircraft/first-russian-chinese-air-patrol-in-asia-pacific-draws-shots-from-south-korea-idUSKCN1UI072.

19. Scott Neuman, "As Relations with U.S. Sour, Xi Describes Putin as 'Best Friend' at Moscow Meeting," NPR, June 6, 2019, https://www.npr.org/2019/06/06/730200317/as-relations-with-u-s-sour-xi-describes-putin-as-best-friend-at-moscow-meeting.

20. Office of the Secretary of Defense, "Annual Report to Congress: Military and Security Developments Involving the People's Republic of China 2017," Department of Defense, May 15, 2017, https://dod.defense.gov/Portals/1/Documents/pubs/2017_China_Military_Power_Report.PDF.

21. Office of the Secretary of Defense, "Annual Report to Congress:

Military and Security Developments Involving the People's Republic of China 2019," Department of Defense, May 2, 2019, https://media .defense.gov/2019/May/02/2002127082/-1/-1/1/2019_CHINA _MILITARY_POWER_REPORT.pdf.

22. Adam Twardowski, "At Brookings, Gen. Joseph Dunford Comments on Threats from Russia, China, North Korea, and Beyond," Brookings, June 4, 2019, https://www.brookings.edu/blog/order -from-chaos/2019/06/04/at-brookings-gen-joseph-dunford -comments-on-threats-from-russia-china-north-korea-and-beyond/.

23. Patpicha Tanakasempipat and Liz Lee, "U.S. Envoy Decries Chinese 'Intimidation' in South China Sea," Reuters, November 3, 2019, https://www.reuters.com/article/us-asean-summit-usa-envoy/u-s -envoy-decries-chinese-intimidation-in-south-china-sea-idUSKBN 1XE0D1.

24. Office of the Secretary of Defense, "Annual Report to Congress: Military and Security Developments Involving the People's Republic of China 2019."

25. Daniel R. Coats, "Statement for the Record: Worldwide Threat Assessment of the US Intelligence Community," Office of the Director of National Intelligence, May 11, 2017, https://www.dni.gov/files /documents/Newsroom/Testimonies/SSCI%20Unclassified%20 SFR%20-%20Final.pdf.

26. Stockholm International Peace Research Institute, "Modernization of World Nuclear Forces Continues Despite Overall Decrease in Number of Warheads," June 17, 2019, https://www.sipri.org/media /press-release/2019/modernization-world-nuclear-forces-continues -despite-overall-decrease-number-warheads-new-sipri.

27. "North Korea Unlikely to Give Up Nuclear Weapons: U.S. Spy Chief Coats," Reuters, January 29, 2019, https://www.reuters.com/article /us-usa-northkorea-nuclear/north-korea-unlikely-to-give-up-nuclear -weapons-us-spy-chief-coats-idUSKCN1PN1Y7.

28. Stockholm International Peace Research Institute, "Modernization of World Nuclear Forces Continues Despite Overall Decrease in Number of Warheads."

29. Daniel R. Coats, "Statement for the Record: Worldwide Threat Assessment of the US Intelligence Community," Office of the Director of National Intelligence, January 29, 2019, https://www.dni .gov/files/ODNI/documents/2019-ATA-SFR---SSCI.pdf.

30. David E. Sanger and Julian E. Barnes, "On North Korea and Iran,

Intelligence Chiefs Contradict Trump," *New York Times*, January 29, 2019, https://www.nytimes.com/2019/01/29/us/politics/kim-jong -trump.html.

31. Kelsey Davenport, "IAEA Says Iran Abiding by Nuclear Deal," Arms Control Association, April 2019, https://www.armscontrol.org/act /2019-04/news/iaea-says-iran-abiding-nuclear-deal.

32. Nicole Gaouette, "UN Nuclear Watchdog Finds Iran Has Nearly Tripled Its Uranium Stockpile," CNN, March 4, 2020, https://www .cnn.com/2020/03/04/middleeast/un-nuclear-report-iran-intl-hnk /index.html.

33. Laurence Norman, "In Major Nuclear Step, Iran to Resume Enrichment at Underground Site," *Wall Street Journal*, November 5, 2019, https://www.wsj.com/articles/iran-plans-to-breach-nuclear -deal-again-11572955701.

34. Eliza Mackintosh, "Iran Makes Move on Centrifuges, Further Unraveling Nuclear Deal," CNN, November 5, 2019, https://www .cnn.com/2019/11/05/middleeast/iran-nuclear-deal-gas-injection -intl/index.html.

35. Behnam Ben Taleblu, "Iran's Defiance on Display in Recent Missile Tests," Axios, July 29, 2019, https://www.axios.com/irans-defiance -on-display-in-new-missile-tests-ea75e792-1b1e-4c86-9379-8c8a 62d9deea.html.

36. Author's interview with Susan Gordon, December 26, 2019.

37. Ibid.

38. Ibid.

39. Jennifer Hansler and Jamie Crawford, "Yovanovitch Swipes at Trump Administration as She's Honored for Her Diplomatic Work," CNN, February 12, 2020, https://www.cnn.com/2020/02/12/politics /yovanovitch-state-department-warning/index.html.

Index

About the Author

J im Sciutto is CNN's chief national security correspondent and
anchor of *CNN Newsroom*. After more than two decades as a foreign correspondent stationed in Asia, Europe, and the Middle East, he
returned to Washington to cover the Defense Department, the State
Department, and intelligence agencies for CNN. His work has earned
him Emmy Awards, the George Polk Award, the Edward R. Murrow
Award, and the Merriman Smith Memorial Award for excellence in
presidential coverage. A graduate of Yale University and a Fulbright
Fellow, he lives in Washington, DC, with his wife, Gloria Riviera, a
crisis communications professional and journalist for ABC News, and
their three children.